# THE
# MEDIEVAL
# ARCHER

# THE
# MEDIEVAL
# ARCHER

## Jim Bradbury

THE BOYDELL PRESS

First published 1985 by The Boydell Press, Woodbridge
Reprinted 1992, 1994
Reprinted in paperback 1996 and 1998


ISBN  0 85115 194 9  hardback
ISBN  0 85115 675 4  paperback



British Library Cataloguing in Publication Data
Bradbury, J.
    The medieval archer.
    1. Bow and arrow – History
    I. Title
    355.8'241     U877
    ISBN 0–85115–194–9

Library of Congress Catalog Card Number: 85–9718



The Boydell Press is an imprint of Boydell & Brewer Ltd
PO Box 9, Woodbridge, Suffolk IP12 3DF, UK
and of Boydell & Brewer Inc.
PO Box 41026, Rochester, NY 14604–4126, USA


This publication is printed on acid-free paper

Designed by Gillian Crossley-Holland
Printed in Great Britain by
St Edmundsbury Press Ltd, Bury St Edmunds, Suffolk

# Contents

To Ann

# List of Illustrations

Photo Giraudon). (ii) English 15th century harrow. (Victoria and Albert Museum). (iii) *Luttrell Psalter*. (British Library MS Add. 42130, f. 171).

Longbowmen flanking pikemen. From a French manuscript.

The Battle of Crécy. (Bibliothèque nationale, MS fr. 2643, f. 165v).

Plan of the Crécy campaign and of the Battle of Crécy.

The Battle of Crécy. (British Library, MS Cotton Nero E II, f. 152v).

Plan of the Battle of Poitiers. The Black Prince's route to Poitiers.

The Battle of Poitiers. (Bibliothèque national, Froissart *Chroniques*. MS fr. 2643 f. 207).

Longbowmen at Agincourt. (Lambeth Palace Library).

A pavise, c.1450. (The Armouries, HM Tower of London).

Pavises in action at the siege of Caen. The Beauchamp Pageant. (British Library, MS Cotton Julius E IV, art. vi, f. 19).

Archers in retinues. (British Library, MS Harley 782, f. 82b).

Henry V's route to Agincourt.

Plan of the dispositions for the Battle on the Somme.

Archers across the front of the army. (British Library, MS Royal 16 G VIII, f. 189).

Cannons and bows. Wavrin, *Chronique d'Angleterre*. Flemish, 15th century. (British Library, MS Royal 14 E IV, f. 59).

Plan of the Battle of Verneuil.

Plan of the Battle of Formigny.

12th century crossbows. Henry VI in Sicily, 1194. Petrus de Ebolo, *De Rebus Siculis Carmen*. (Bern, Burgerbibliothek, Codex Bernensis 120, f. 131).

Spanning a crossbow. Misericord carving. Formerly at the abbey of St Lucien. (Paris, Musée de Cluny).

Drawing a crossbow with one foot. Siege of Rhodes, 1480. *Descriptio Obsidionis Rhodiae Urbs* by Guillaume Caoursin, c.1490. (Bibliothèque national, MS lat. 6067, f. 55v).

Drawing a crossbow with two feet. *Luttrell Psalter*. (British Library, MS Add. 42130, f. 54).

Spanning a crossbow by bending the knee. *Luttrell Psalter*. (British Library, MS Add. 42130, f. 56).

A cranequin. 18th century. (The Armouries, HM Tower of London).

Longbows in a realistic art style. The Beauchamp Pageant. (British Library, MS Cotton Julius E IV, c.1485–90, art. vi).

The Battle of Barnet. French version of *The Arrivall of Edward IV*. (University of Ghent, MS 236).

The Battle of Tewkesbury. French version of *The Arrivall of Edward IV*. (University of Ghent, MS 236).

Tudor archers. Boulogne 1544. (Engraving by James Basire after S. H. Grimm. National Army Museum. From a painting at Cowdray destroyed by fire).

The Flodden window, Sir Richard Assheton and 16 archers. (St Leonard's, Middleton).

Arrows and spacers recovered from the 'Mary Rose'. (Mary Rose Trust).

Archers on the Moorfields map, 1559. (Museum of London).

A crossbow shooting competition. (Bodleian Library, MS Douce 93, f. 100v).

Target shooting with crossbows. (Hans Schaufelein, *Illustrations aus den Leben des Kaisers. Maximilian I*, 1520).

Woman shooting at a stag. (British Library, MS Royal 10 E IV, f. 159v).

Archers hunting. *Livre de Chasse* of Gaston de Foix, 15th century. (Bibliothèque nationale, MS fr. 616, f. 111v).

Hunting birds. (British Library, *Luttrell Psalter*. MS Add. 42130, f. 54).

John Gower with a bow, 15th century. (British Library, MS Cotton Tiberius A IV, f. 9v).

The martyrdom of St Sebastian. Boucicaut Master. (Musée Jacquemart-Andre, Paris, MS 2, f. 21v).

The martyrdom of St Edmund, 13th century version. (British Library).

# Preface

The origin of this book is threefold. Partly, it came out of my research thesis on twelfth century warfare, which provoked thoughts on warfare beyond the boundaries of that period. Secondly, it came from an interest in archery in the Hundred Years War. As a result of this, I gave a paper on longbows to one of the educational courses that are held in the Tower of London. Dr Richard Barber was also speaking on that course. Some casual remarks by him initiated the idea of a book, and I am grateful for the encouragement he has given me since that date. Thirdly, I am aware of the help and inspiration derived from books by many authors past and present, and in particular for the enjoyment derived from Sir Ralph Payne-Gallwey's *The Crossbow*, and Robert Hardy's *Longbow*. There is a book to be written on every aspect of the medieval archer, but this is not it. The wider plans with which I began have been slimmed down for reasons of time and practicality. This book pretends to do no more than survey the subject, and delve a little into some aspects that have interested me. The two main themes of the book are the development of the military role of the medieval archer, and his place in society. I should like to make public my gratitude to various people who have given me assistance, and beg the forgiveness of those whose names are not recorded. In particular, I should like to thank Professor R. Allen Brown for reviving my interest in medieval history, and awakening an interest in medieval warfare. I should like to thank my colleagues at West London for their tolerance in terms of the time I have been able to give to research. I am also grateful to the friends who have passed on titbits of information on archery that they have come upon during their own researches, not all of which I have been able to use, but all of which I have appreciated, for example, Chris Philpotts, Dr Alex Rumble, Jennie Kiff, Teresa Bonnick, Ruth Harvey, Dr Ann Williams and Ian Peirce. I should also like to acknowledge the help received in discussion on many a pleasant evening spent in the 'Marquess of Anglesey', and the U.L.U. bar, with Nick Hooper, Nicholas Kingwell, Matthew Bennett and others. None of these people are, of course, in any way responsible for the errors which are bound to exist in a work covering so much ground. Finally, I must offer more than thanks to the person who has suffered most for this book, my wife, without whose help, encouragement and tolerance the manuscript would never have been completed.

Selsey, 1985

# Chapter 1

# The Archer and His Weapons

*Attitudes to the Archer*

The medieval archer was not always given the respect he deserved in his own age. Only in the late middle ages did a practical recognition of his worth emerge; and only in the sixteenth century, when the bow as a weapon of war was yielding to firearms, did a nostalgic praise of its greatness enter literature. In the Tudor period, the gentry took to the bow as their national heritage, and 'never ceased piddling about with their bow and shafts'.[1] But through most of the medieval period the bow was scorned by the gentry as a war weapon for themselves. When its great effectiveness was demonstrated in the eleventh and twelfth centuries, it was immediately condemned by the church. In 1120 bows were prohibited in Flanders, in an effort to keep the peace. In 1139 the Second Lateran Council forbade the employment of bowmen and crossbowmen against other Christians.[2] The bow was seen as a weapon not proper to Christians and gentlemen. It was, however, too effective a weapon to be neglected, and the church prohibitions seem to have been largely ignored.

Early medieval chronicles and literature take little notice of archery. Only in the fourteenth century does the bow enter English literature as a weapon fit for heroes, and then only as the possession of Robin Hood and his men, outcasts from normal society. The reason for literary neglect was mainly social. The bow in war was the weapon of lesser men. Nobles might use it for hunting, but they scorned to arm themselves with it in battle. The knight's skills lay in sword, lance and horsemanship. The glory of chivalry belonged to the knight, and not to the mere foot soldier. Knights had their own code of war. In the earlier

[1] Roger Ascham, *Toxophilus*, p. 117: 'never ceasynge piddel-ynge about your bowe and shaftes'.

[2] On the prohibition in Flanders, see Galbert of Bruges, ed. Pirenne, p. 3. For the prohibition at the Second Lateran see Hefele and Leclercq, v, pt. 1, p. 733, no. 29: 'Deo odibilem ballis-tariorum et sagittariorum adversus Christianos et catholicos exerceri de caetero subanathemate prohibemus'.

*Archer from a fifteenth century manuscript.*

middle ages few knights were killed in battle. The object of combat was to capture and ransom rather than to kill. One notes the outcry when Henry V at Agincourt broke this code and slaughtered the prisoners who would otherwise have brought fat ransoms. Contrast the attitude of the knights to each other with their treatment of the common infantry. When Henry of Anjou captured Crowmarsh from Stephen, sixty archers of the garrison were beheaded. Knights fled in defeat, but were rarely punished as a result. Contrast that with the English archers who took to flight at Mauron in 1352, and were beheaded. The attitude of knight to archer was never more clearly demonstrated than by the French at Crécy. Their Genoese crossbowmen had failed, and in retreat were causing confusion. The French knights simply rode down their own archers, trampling them underfoot.[3]

There is, however, a significant change of attitude through the medieval centuries. There is a growing attention in the chronicles and in literature to the humble bowman. This may partly be because bows were more used and more successful, but that is not the whole explanation. When one reads between the lines, it becomes clear that bows were of great importance through these centuries. The attitude of writers such as Froissart, who does not respect the archer in the same way that he respects the knight, demonstrates at least a recognition of the military worth of the bow. The Robin Hood literature, beginning with the 'Lytell Geste of Robin Hode' in about 1400, reflects a movement in social attitudes. Despite the occasional veneer of noble background, Robin Hood and his men represented a repressed class, forced into outlawry. That literature should find them worthy of heroic status is significant, in the same way that it is of note that the twentieth century should take interest in the working classes. Literature was becoming more bourgeois and less aristocratic, more secular and less ecclesiastical. Where in the eleventh century could one find the parallel of the fifteenth century chronicler Jean de Venette, peasant become friar?[4]

[3] On scorn for archers: for the Henry of Anjou incident see Howlett, iv, pp. 173–4: 'exceptis lx sagittariis, quos decapitari fecerat'. For the Battle of Maldon, see Geoffrey le Baker, p. 120. For the riding down of the Genoese see, for example, Froissart, ed. Luce, iii, p. 177: the Count of Alençon says: 'This is what one gets for employing such rabble'; the King of France adds: 'Kill all this rabble, kill them. They are getting in our way, and they are serving no purpose.'

[4] On attitudes to archers, see *A Lytell Geste of Robin Hode*, and Jean de Venette.

To some extent we must be dominated by the literary tastes and attitudes of the day. What chroniclers and governments chose to ignore, we are often unable to recover. Nevertheless, we shall maintain that archery was important throughout the period from 1066 to 1485, and shall try to counter the bias and neglect of monastic chroniclers or secular clerks, generally writing to please their noble patrons. Our study opens with a battle which depended for its outcome largely on the efforts of the archers, and closes in the century which saw English archers win their most famed victory, at Agincourt. We intend to argue that throughout the period the bow was a major weapon, its central role only partially obscured by the neglect of chroniclers.

Although the nobility were not prepared to use the bow themselves in battle, they were aware of its worth as a weapon in war. One reason for hostility to the bow was precisely its effectiveness, especially from a distance. Nobles could be killed by low-class archers, without even an opportunity for retaliation. In literature, the bowman was sometimes portrayed as a coward: 'brave in waging war with beasts, in nought besides'; with his bow: 'that weapon of a dastard'.[5] There are many examples of nobles killed by arrows. Harold Godwinson is a prime illustration, but there are others. Geoffrey Martel, Count of Anjou, was killed at Candé on the Loire in 1106, by a crossbowman who was 'inspired by the devil'.[6] In England, Geoffrey de Mandeville was foolish enough to take off his helmet when making a reconnaissance of Burwell Castle in Cambridgeshire. The castle had been built by King Stephen in an effort to bring the rebel baron to heel. Geoffrey was hit in the head by an arrow from the bow of a 'very low-class archer',[7] and died of the wound a week later. In 1199 came an even more famous death, when Richard the Lionheart was besieging Chalus. The defenders were running short of ammunition. One man stood for half a day on a tower with nothing better than a frying pan to protect himself. Then he noticed a bolt, shot by one of Richard's men, that had stuck in the wall of the tower. He wrenched it out, fitted it to his own bow, and shot at the king. Richard was hit in the left shoulder, and the bolt penetrated his side. He tried to pull it out, but only broke the shaft. The surgeon who attended him, with the skill of the day, worsened the wound and the king died.[8] In the Hundred Years' War countless French nobles were to die from arrow wounds. The nobility could not ignore the effects of the bow.

There was no military situation in which the bow could not prove useful. Its ideal use in battle is generally seen as being in a

[5] A. J. Hatto, 'Archery and Chivalry: a noble prejudice', *Modern Language Review*, xxxv, 1940, pp. 40–54. The quotations are from Girard de Viane.
[6] Orderic, vi, p. 76: Geoffrey was hit in the arm by a 'balistarius instructu diaboli', and died the following day.
[7] Robert of Torigny in Howlett, iv. p. 147: 'a quodam pedite vilissima solus sagitta percussus est'. Compare *Chronicon Abbatiae Rameseiensis*, p. 322: 'quidam vilissim-us sagittarius'; and *Brut Y Tywysogyon*, p. 119.
[8] Ralph of Coggeshall, pp. 94–6.

defensive formation. It became common to emphasise that defensive position by using hedges, ditches, pits or stakes. At Morlaix in 1342 the English archers built ditches around themselves, and at Poitiers made mounds and ditches. It is noteworthy that Charles of Blois sought to minimise the effect of the English archers in 1347 by clearing the countryside of hedges and other obstacles. The use of protective stakes at Agincourt and Verneuil is well known.[9]

Archery proved just as useful in offensives, and in sieges. Archers were frequently posted on battlements and walls, behind loops. They could also be sent forward in attack. At Lisbon,

*A thirteenth century drawing of an archer on crusade.*

[9] Defences. For Morlaix see Tout, *Collected Papers*, ii, p. 224, quoting Knighton: 'foderunt foveas et fossas circa eos'. At Poitiers hedges, pits and mounds were used; see Geoffrey le Baker, pp. 82–4. Robert of Avesbury describes the efforts of Charles of Blois, translated in *EHD*, iv, p. 86. For Agincourt see, for example, *Gesta Henrici Quinti*, p. 86: 'palorum affixio'. For Verneuil see Monstrelet, ed. Douët-D'Arcq, iv, p. 193: 'ung penchon devant eulx aguisé et fiché'.

[10] Archers attacking. At Lisbon, see *De Expugnatione Lyxbonensis*, p. 160: 'impetum sagittarum'. For Winchcomb see *Gesta Stephani*, p. 174: 'istis sagittis spissim emittendis insistere'.

[11] Archers giving cover. On Magnus, see Anderson, *Early Sources*, p. 130. On the First Crusade see *Gesta Francorum*, p. 15: a tower was mined at Nicaea under cover from 'arbalistae et sagittarii'. See Galbert of Bruges, ed. Ross, p. 178; and for the Oxford incident, *Gesta Stephani*, p. 140.

[12] *Gesta Stephani*, p. 30.

[13] *Chronicle of Battle Abbey*, p. 36.

[14] William of Malmesbury, *De Gestis Regum*, ii, p. 335: 'quod nemo ejus arcum tenderet, quem ipse admisso equo pedibus nervo extento sinuaret'. On Curthose see Orderic, ii, p. 357.

during the Second Crusade, when the English contingent had been diverted to the Iberian Peninsula, the enemy were driven from a tower by 'a charge of archers'. Or again, when Stephen besieged Winchcomb in 1144, he ordered the place to be stormed. Some men were to advance 'shooting clouds of arrows', while others crawled up the castle mound.[10] It was a commonplace of warfare to use archers for cover, in attack or defence, in siege or battle. When the viking Magnus attacked Wales in about 1103, archers were used as cover from a ditch while the vikings tried to regain their ships. On this occasion they were not altogether successful, and Magnus was wounded by a spear which passed through both his thighs. He snapped it in two so that he could escape, only to be felled by a blow on the neck from an axe. Another example of cover was an incident on the First Crusade, when archers shot so that their comrades could undermine a tower. The long range and accuracy of the bow were always valuable. Galbert of Bruges described in detail a siege at which he was present. He says that the defenders did not dare to show their faces at the windows because of the thousand arrows that would be shot. The range of the bow was again demonstrated when Stephen came to take Oxford and found that the river crossing was made perilous by the archers shooting from across the water.[11] At Falkirk, archers were to provide the solution to the Scottish squares of pikemen for Edward I. The bow was also an ideal weapon for ambushes. When King Stephen attacked Robert of Bampton in his castle, he posted archers to act as pickets at night, and detailed others to lie in wait during the daytime.[12]

Noble commanders also knew something of the weapon from their own favourite sport of hunting. The Norman kings, who reserved large areas of the countryside for their own pleasures in the hunt, were themselves archers. There is a story of William the Conqueror running out of arrows on one hunting expedition. He discovered a smith called William, who was not however familiar with the technique of making arrows. The smith took up his hammers, and directed by the king fashioned what the latter required.[13] It was said of the Conqueror that he was of such immense strength of arm that people were often surprised that nobody could draw his bow, which he himself could bend while his horse was at full gallop. His eldest son, Robert Curthose was also said to be a powerful and sure archer.[14] All the Norman kings enjoyed the chase. On one occasion the Conqueror's youngest son, Henry, broke the string of his bow when hunting, and had to go into a peasant's hut to obtain a spare.[15] But of course the best known of William I's sons, to students of archery history, is William Rufus. Rufus, like other members of the family, could use the bow. On the fatal hunt in the New Forest, we find him drawing his bow and letting fly an arrow. The tale of the death of Rufus is best told by Orderic Vitalis, the chronicler who had been born in England, but went as a boy to Normandy where he spent the rest of his life as a monk.[16]

According to Orderic, William the Conqueror lost two sons, Richard and Rufus, as well as his grandson Richard, through hunting accidents in the New Forest. The accident to Rufus happened in July of 1100. The royal fleet was being prepared, when evil rumours began to spread. A monk of St Peter's Abbey at Gloucester received a vision in the night that William Rufus was about to suffer for the plunderings and adulteries of which he was guilty. The story came to the abbot of St Peter's, who sent a warning letter to the king. Also at Gloucester, Fulchred, the visiting abbot of Shrewsbury, preached a sermon on the theme that 'the bow of divine anger is bent against the wicked, and the arrow swift to wound is taken from the quiver. It will strike suddenly; let every wise man avoid the blow by mending his ways.' The tale sounds a little unlikely, but Orderic's family did live near Shrewsbury.

The next morning the king dined, and made preparations to go hunting in the New Forest. He was in a cheerful mood, laughing and joking with those around him. As he pulled on his boots, a smith arrived with six arrows, which he offered to the king. Rufus was pleased with the workmanship, kept four for himself and gave the remaining two to Walter Tirel, the lord of Poix and castellan of Pontoise in the French Vexin. Walter also held an English manor at Langham in Essex. 'It is only right', said Rufus, 'that the sharpest arrows should go to the man who knows how to inflict the deadliest shots.' Orderic says that Walter was a powerful magnate, very skilled in the use of arms, and a close friend of the king's.

At this point, the warning letter arrived from the abbot of Gloucester. Rufus, when he had read it, treated it with his usual scepticism and burst out laughing, refusing to heed what he called 'the dreams of snoring monks'. He asked those around him if they thought he was the sort of man who acted like the English, and took notice of the dreams of little old women. Then he leaped on his horse and galloped into the forest. As the hunt proceeded, Rufus was placed near Walter Tirel. They waited with weapons ready, when a stag suddenly ran between them.

[15] Wace, p. 259, ll.10075–10090.
[16] Orderic Vitalis, v, pp. 284–94. See also Hollister, 'Death of William Rufus', pp. 637–653.

6

Walter loosed an arrow, which flew over the animal, grazing its back, but then struck the king. Orderic says the king 'fell to the ground and, dreadful to relate, died at once'. The king's younger brother, Henry, galloped off to Winchester to secure the treasury and the crown. Henry has been accused of complicity in the killing. Certainly he benefited. Robert Curthose, the king's elder brother, was still returning from the Crusade. It was an opportune moment for Henry to seize the throne. However, no one will ever know for certain whether William Rufus died by accident or design. Some of the king's lesser attendants covered the body with rags and carried him 'like a wild boar stuck with spears' to Winchester. Walter Tirel fled to France, and later died as a pilgrim on his way to Jerusalem.

Although chronicle versions of this death differ in detail, all are agreed that the fatal blow was delivered by an arrow. It is possible that Geoffrey of Monmouth had this incident in mind for a passage in his largely fictional *History of the Kings of Britain,* where Brutus kills his father Aeneas with an arrow when hunting.[17] Nor were hunting accidents confined to the royal family. Miles of Gloucester died on Christmas Eve pierced through the breast by an arrow shot by one of his own knights aiming at a stag.[18]

All this makes it clear that kings and nobles were well aware of the capabilities of the bow: they knew how to shoot, and they knew the damage it could do. Although they preferred horse, lance and sword for themselves in battle, they were not ignorant of the potential of their archers. But, hunting apart, the bow was seen as the weapon of the lowly, of peasants and mercenaries, of citizen militias. Mercenaries in particular were scorned by the chroniclers: they were the lowest of the low, men of the greatest cruelty, profane scoundrels.[19] Yet such men could be skilled. William FitzStephen describes the young men of London, who spent all summer practising at archery, and excelled in games with the bow. Gerald of Wales similarly speaks of Welsh peasants practising with bow and spear during peace time in order to be ready for war. Some individuals were noted for outstanding skill. Galbert of Bruges decribes a mercenary called Benkin, who was expert and swift in shooting arrows. In the siege of Bruges, he ran round the walls, shooting so quickly that the enemy thought he was several men. Orderic Vitalis describes the career of the notorious Robert Boet, a 'famous archer' in the service of Richer de l'Aigle. Robert led a band that terrorised the country, but finally the local people turned on him and he was hanged.[20]

[17] Geoffrey of Monmouth, p. 36: 'the young man killed his father by an unlucky shot with an arrow, when they were out hunting together'.

[18] *Gesta Stephani*, pp. 24, 148, 160.

[19] See, for example, *Gesta Stephani*, p. 230: 'viris scilicet summae crudelitatis'; and p. 232: 'sacrilegi'. Compare Orderic Vitalis, v, p. 316, and Howlett, i, p. 209, where mercenaries are called 'pestilentes homines'.

[20] For practice in London, see William FitzStephen, p. 11. For practice in Wales, see Gerald of Wales, *Opera*, vi, pp. 54, 181: 'et quasi sub pace praelia dum cogitant, nunc lanceando, nunc sagittando, bella praeludunt'. On Benkin, see Galbert of Bruges, ed. Pirenne, pp. 59, 120; and in the same work, on Lambert Archei, 'most expert with the bow', p. 78. On Robert Boet, see Orderic Vitalis, vi, pp. 458–60.

# The Archer's Weapons

So far we have not troubled to distinguish between the kinds of bow that our archers have used. Often this is the simplest way, since the chroniclers rarely make it clear whether the bow is a shortbow, a crossbow, or an ordinary wooden bow. It can be seen from illustrations that all three bows were known, but only occasionally in any particular incident or battle can we be certain what type of bow is concerned. In the case of the crossbow, there is an additional difficulty, since the words normally used, French *arbaleste*, or Latin *balista*, can mean either a cross-bow or a siege engine with a similar action. In a few instances the terms *arcubalista* or *manubalista* are used, to denote a handbow. At other times we must simply do our best with the context to judge which weapon is intended. Thus it is probable that the *balista* used at the siege of Paris by the Frankish defenders was an engine, since it shot a bolt that went through several vikings at once, so that a Frank with a macabre sense of humour was reminded of a kebab and ordered the whole skewerful to be taken off to the kitchens.[21] Where the *balistae* are used with considerable mobility in battles, it is most likely that crossbows are involved.

Crossbows were certainly common in our period; it is a weapon with a very long history. Actual weapons survive in China from as far back as the third century BC. They were also used by the Romans. There is still some debate as to whether or not crossbows were used at Hastings, but they probably were, as we shall see in the next chapter. The crossbow was especially associated with trained and skilled mercenary bands, such as the Genoese in the Hundred Years' War, or the Gascons employed by Edward I. English kings certainly employed crossbowmen, but as a weapon it was not much favoured by English foot soldiers.

The **crossbow** is a mechanical bow, operated by a release mechanism. It was to undergo considerable improvement during the course of the middle ages, to improve its trigger release, its loading method, and its strength. Nevertheless the basic concept was retained: a small bow attached to a stock which provided a groove for the bolt and handle, with a bowstring that was held in place ready for trigger release. One advantage of the crossbow was that it could be prepared in the shooting position and held there without any effort. The disadvantage was that this preparation took time, even for an expert, and placed restrictions on its use in rapid shooting. Whatever the case at Hastings, the

*Chinese crossbow. Detail from sixth century painting on silk.*

[21] The kebab incident is in Abbo, pp. 22–4. The editor comments on p. 23, n. 4: 'Il est difficile de ne pas croire qu'ici Abbon exagère'.

8

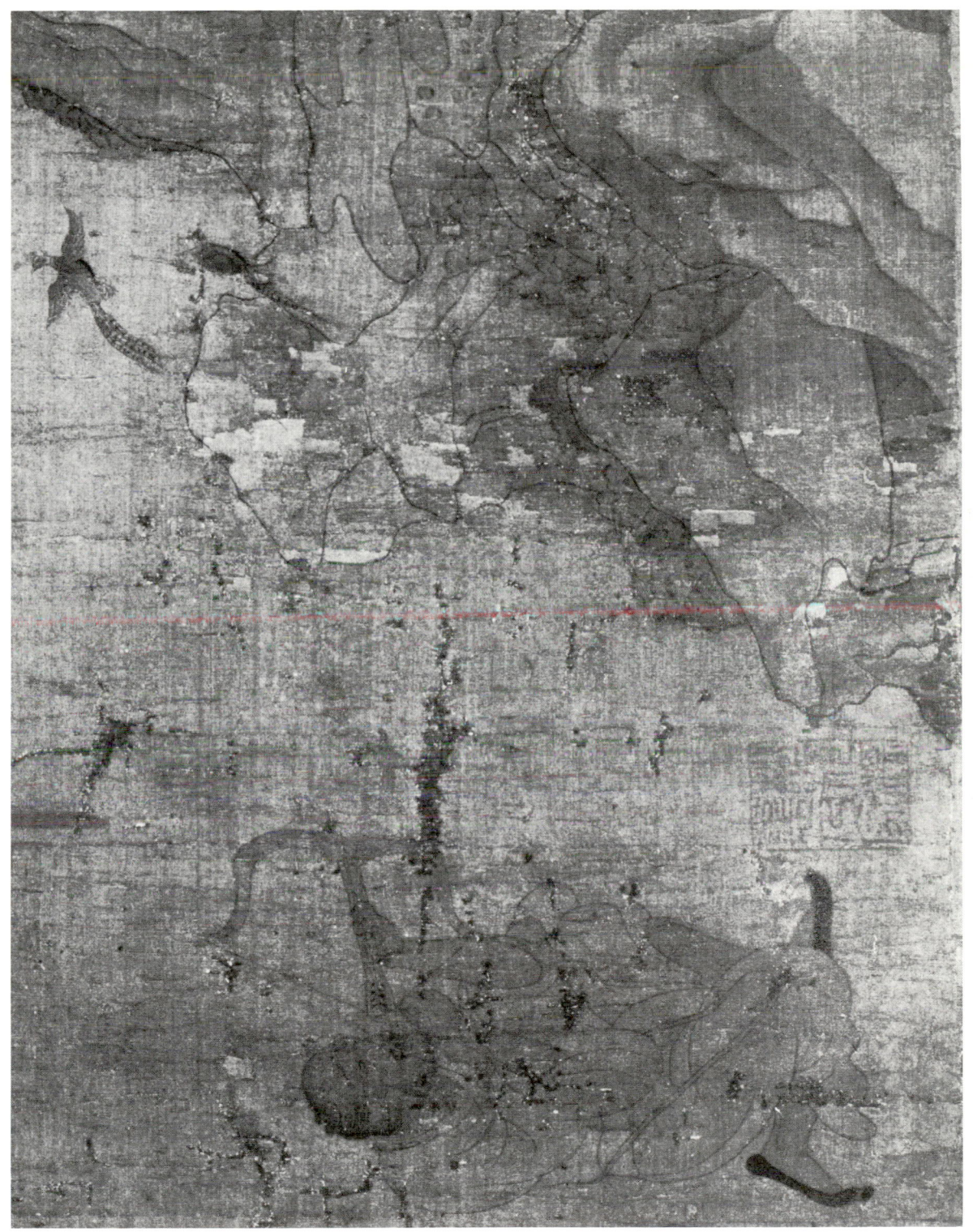

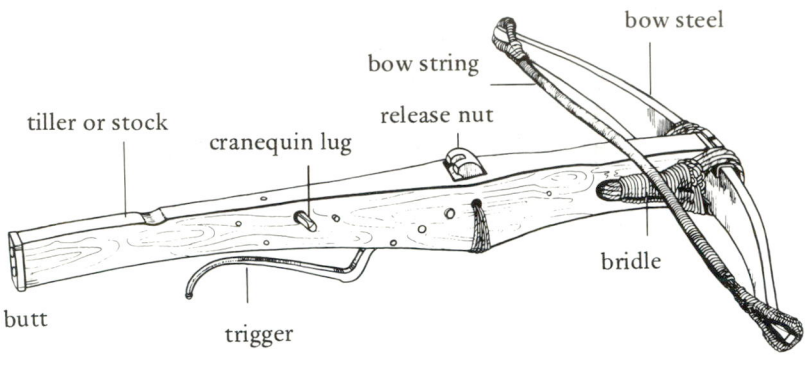

*A crossbow. Line drawing of crossbow with a steel bow.*

Franks certainly used crossbows on the First Crusade. Anna Comnena, the daughter of the Byzantine emperor, gives a rare and detailed description of this weapon in *The Alexiad*:

The crossbow is a weapon of the barbarians, absolutely unknown to the Greeks. In order to stretch it one does not pull the string with the right hand while pushing the bow with the left away from the body; this instrument of war, which shoots missiles to an enormous distance, has to be stretched by lying almost on one's back; each foot is pressed forcibly against the half-circles of the bow and the two hands tug at the bow, pulling it with all one's strength towards the body. At the mid-point of the string is a groove, shaped like a cylinder cut in half and fitted to the string itself; it is about the length of a fair-sized arrow, extending from the string to the centre of the bow. Along this groove, arrows of all kinds are shot. They are very short, but extremely thick with a heavy iron tip. In the shooting the string exerts tremendous violence and force, so that the missiles wherever they strike do not rebound; in fact they transfix a shield, cut through a heavy iron breastplate and resume their flight on the far side, so irresistible and violent is the discharge. An arrow of this type has been known to make its way right through a bronze statue, and when shot at the wall of a very great town its point either protruded from the inner side or buried itself in the wall and disappeared altogether. Such is the crossbow, a truly diabolical machine. The unfortunate man who is struck by it dies without feeling the blow; however strong the impact he knows nothing of it.[22]

[22] Anna Comnena, *Alexiad*, pp. 316–7. On the crossbow in general, see Payne-Gallwey, *The Crossbow*.

10

Sometimes a bow was used as a trap, and is referred to as a **spring-bow**.[23] No description is clear enough to tell if this was a crossbow or a special device, but it clearly comes into this mechanical category. The term for it, 'li ars qui ne fault', the bow which does not miss, or perhaps the bow which does not fail, the unerring bow, became a literary cliche. It first appears in the Anglo-Norman *L'Estoire des Engleis* by Gaimar. The author describes an *engin* devised by the traitor Eadric to kill Edmund Ironside. At night the king was shown into a newly-built privy in which the engine was concealed: 'A drawn bow, with the string attached to the seat, so that when the king sat on it, the arrow was released and entered his fundament, piercing his lung'. The arrow vanished inside the unfortunate king, who collapsed and died. Another reference to the unerring bow is found in Beroul's *Tristan*, in this case as a trap for hunting stags. The term became a literary commonplace. The fourteenth century bourgeois poet, Jean Bretel, claimed that he did not mind being kept waiting by his lady love, for he himself is 'li ars qui ne faut'. It became a figure of speech for any trap that could not fail. Probably the spring-bow should be seen as a type of crossbow. Chrétien de Troyes speaks of a crossbow when he means a kind of rat-trap.

[23] For the springbow, see M. D. Legge, 'The Unerring Bow', pp. 79–83.

*An eastern style short-bow with its distinctive curve, shown in a Western manuscript of the tenth century.*

There is another sort of difficulty over the **shortbow**. The problem would be diminished if modern writers avoided describing short ordinary bows as shortbows. The shortbow proper is a particular kind of bow, built with considerable craftsmanship. It is a composite bow, the stave made normally in three pieces: a centre part and two wings. The shape is formed over pieces of wood. To these is glued horn on one side, and sinew on the other. The whole stave is then bent over backward. The horn on the inside pushes, the sinew on the outside pulls. This gives the shortbow great power, despite its relatively small size. The only evidence for shortbows in the west comes from manuscript illustrations. They required great skill in manufacture and in use. The likelihood is that they were very rare in the west. They were common in the east, and the crusaders encountered them in the hands of their Saracen foes, who were noted horse archers. Nevertheless shortbows certainly do appear in western manuscripts, easily detected by their distinctive curly shape. They are to be seen, for example, on a series of Frankish manuscripts. Perhaps the explanation is not that shortbows were normal in the west at the time, but that the manuscript illustrations were based on Byzantine or eastern originals, for even dated manuscripts must not be taken as literal evidence of the form of arms and armour. The appearance of shortbows in Spanish manuscripts, however, is another matter. The influence of the east in Spain, through the Islamic conquest of the Iberian Peninsula, is a strong possibility.

One does meet with a few mounted archers in the west in the eleventh and twelfth centuries. It is likely that from a practical point of view they would have had to use either the shortbow like eastern archers, or the crossbow. The length of the stave of an ordinary wooden bow would make it too cumbersome to be useful on horseback. Yet the best known illustration of a western mounted archer in this period shows him with an ordinary wooden bow.[24] Probably the illustration is inaccurate, but how many pitfalls there are for the poor historian! The other reason for the lack of mounted archers in the west relates to horsemanship. The mounted archer had to be a very skilled rider, in order to shoot accurately while at the same time controlling his mount. In the east the mounted archer was a respected warrior. In the west military archers were always from the lower classes, and were not normally trained horsemen. The predilections of the western knights thus denied to western armies what could have been a very valuable addition to their ranks.

[24] *Bayeux Tapestry*, pl. 73.

*Two shortbows and a crossbow used at a siege in Sicily, from an early thirteenth century manuscript.*

13

The chronicler Fulcher of Chartres described the Saracen horse archers on the First Crusade. He says the Turks were very keen archers and bowmen, who had come originally from Persia, and that the enemy had 360,000 warriors, that is archers, whose custom was to use the bow, and that they were all cavalry. Such fighting, he says, was 'unknown to any of us'. He also describes the Saracen bows, which 'in those parts were fitted together with glue', making it quite clear that they were shortbows.[25]

Crossbows and shortbows are encountered in medieval English history, but neither plays as large a role as the **ordinary wooden bow**, which in a later age would be called the longbow. For this weapon, the stave is made from one single piece of wood, though sometimes horn was added for the nocks. There is a strong school of thought that dates the emergence of the longbow only to the time of Edward I, and sees its apogee in the Hundred Years' War. The point at issue is whether some new type of bow suddenly appeared at the time of Edward I. The evidence is in fact very tenuous. Later in this book we shall look at the arguments more fully: suffice to say for now that it is

*A Turkish mounted archer shooting over his shoulder in eastern fashion, fifteenth century.*

[25] Fulcher of Chartres, pp. 35, 80.
[26] On Nydam bows see J. G. D. Clark, 'Neolithic Bows', p. 87; H. C. Engelhardt, *Nydam Mosefund*; and Tucker, 'Nydam', p. 7.

14

unlikely a new weapon emerged in that age. It is far more likely that the longbow is simply the result of the evolution of the ordinary wooden bow over a long period of time. There is no fundamental difference between the Nydam bows from the Roman period, the Norman bows on the Bayeux Tapestry, and the longbows of the Hundred Years' War.[26] The bows portrayed on the Tapestry seem to match up exactly with the description of Welsh bows given by Gerald of Wales in the late twelfth century. Gerald had spent his boyhood in Manorbier Castle in South Wales, which he later recalled with affection. In 1188 he made a journey through Wales, his description of which survives. He makes several references to the skill in archery of the men of South Wales:

> It is worth mentioning, or so I think, that the men of Gwent, for that is what they are called, have much more experience of warfare, are more famous for their martial exploits and, in particular, are more skilled with the bow and arrow than those who come from other parts of Wales. I will give you a few examples to show just how true this is. In this capture by stratagem of Abergavenny Castle, which I have just described to you, two men-at-arms were rushing across a bridge to take refuge in the tower which had been built on a great mound of earth. The Welsh shot at them from behind, and with the

*The earliest illustrations of Welsh archers from a thirteenth century manuscript. They seem to be using ordinary wooden bows rather than longbows.*

15

arrows which sped from their bows they actually penetrated the oak doorway of the tower, which was almost as thick as a man's palm. As a permanent reminder of the strength of the impact, the arrows have been left sticking in the door just where their iron heads struck. William de Braose also testifies that, in the war against the Welsh, one of his men-at-arms was struck by an arrow shot at him by a Welshman. It went right through his thigh, high up, where it was protected outside and inside the leg by his iron thigh armour, and then through the skirt of his leather tunic; next it penetrated that part of the saddle which is called the alva or seat; and finally it lodged in his horse, driving in so deep that it killed the animal. An arrow pinned the thigh of another soldier to his saddle, although the skirt of his leather tunic was there to protect him outside and inside the leg. He tugged on the reins and pulled his horse round in a half circle, whereupon another arrow, shot by the same bowman, hit him in exactly the same place in the other thigh, so that he was skewered to his horse on both sides. It is difficult to see what more you could do, even if you had a crossbow. The bows they use are not made of horn, nor of sapwood, nor yet of yew. The Welsh carve their bows out of the dwarf elm trees in the forest. They are nothing much to look at, not even rubbed smooth, but left in a rough and unpolished state. Still, they are firm and strong. You could not shoot far with them; but they are powerful enough to inflict serious wounds in a close fight.[27]

The question of longbow length will be pursued in subsequent chapters. Probably the ordinary bow in England did have a longer stave in the later middle ages, but this should not be emphasised to the point of treating the weapon of the fifteenth century as something quite divorced from that used at Hastings. Between the eleventh and the fifteenth centuries bows were improved, but there were more drastic changes in the crossbow than in the ordinary bow.

We shall then in this book follow the fortunes of archers in war and peace through the medieval centuries: their role in battles and in sieges, their social status, their place in fact and in fiction. We shall stress that not only on a few noted occasions, but throughout these centuries, the bow was significant, and perhaps even that its great triumphs played some small part in improving the condition of its largely peasant owners.

[27] Gerald of Wales, *Opera*, pp. 123, 177, 179. The translation here is based on that in Gerald of Wales, ed. Thorpe, pp. 112–3, and is from the 'Itinerarium Cambriae'.

# Chapter 2

## Archers at Hastings

### *Archery in England before 1066*

To choose 1066 as the starting point for a study of the medieval archer might seem a deliberate neglect of the Anglo-Saxon achievement. The Anglo-Saxons did use the bow, but evidence concerning it is not extensive. There is even less knowledge of the Old English using the bow in war, though just enough to suggest that they did so. In England as in Normandy, the Scandinavians made an impact upon warfare, and included bows in the range of their weaponry. There is a tradition of Scandinavian archery skill, yet even this can be exaggerated. In Scandinavian mythology the spear plays a greater role than the bow. It is possible that the martyrdom of St Edmund, a popular subject in English art, and from the twelfth century onwards always portrayed as being perpetrated by bows and arrows, was originally caused by spears.

In the battle of Maldon in 991, according to a later poem, bows were used.[1] Anlaf and the Danes had come with 93 ships and ravaged the south-east. At Maldon they were met by Ealdorman Byrhtnoth and the English. The poem has several references to swords and spears, and three interesting references to either bows or arrows. In a famous line, we are told that 'bows were busy', but the context does not make it clear whether they are busy in the hands of English or Danes, or indeed both. In some ways, the passage about the hostage fighting on the English side is more informative:

[1] Alexander, *Earliest English Poems*, p. 117, l. 110; and p. 121, ll. 266–72.

17

The hostage lent them help willingly;
he was a Northumbrian of a hard-fighting clan,
the son of Edgeleave, Ashferth his name;
wavered not at the war-play, but, while he might,
shot steadily from his sheaf of arrows,
striking a shield there, or shearing into a man,
and every once in a while wounding wryly.

It cannot be put forward as more than a hesitant hypothesis, but it may be that archery was already a specialist skill in England, possessed by those in some regions and some kingdoms. England had not long been a unified nation, and the old kingdoms had kept many of their traditions and customs. Later it will be noted how often archers come from certain areas, for example, Cheshire. It could also be noted that Gerald of Wales repeated the point that the men of Gwent were famed for their archery, whereas in other parts they preferred the spear.[2]

The Anglo-Saxons certainly used the bow, and there are a few illustrations of it employed for the hunt. The Exeter Book contains some references which are almost certainly to bows.[3] Riddle 17 is probably about a siege engine, a *balista*, but could possibly be a crossbow: 'I am the protector of my flock, fast strengthened with wires ... I often spit forth deadly spears ... missiles of war fly from my belly'. Riddle 23 seems to be the ordinary bow:

Wob's my name, if you work it out;
I'm a fair creature fashioned for battle.
When I bend, and shoot a deadly shaft
from my stomach, I desire only to send
that poison as far away as possible.
When my lord, who devised this torment for me,

[2] Gerald of Wales, *Opera*, vi, pp.123, 177.
[3] *Exeter Book*, ii, p.106 for no. 17; and p.112 for no. 23, which begins 'Agof is min noma'; and Henry of Huntingdon, p.211, where William says the English are 'A people not even in possession of arrows'.

*The lid of the eighth century Franks' casket, made of whalebone in Northumbria. Aegil is shown defending his house with a bow.*

*A seventh century Northumbrian carving of an archer on the Ruthwell Cross.*

[4] Aldhelm, ed. Lapidge and Herren, p. 163 for the quotation in the text; the Latin is in Aldhelm ed. Ehwald, p. 230. I am indebted for the information on Aldhelm to Dr Ann Williams who passed on the reference, and for familiarity with the works in general to Jennie Kiff.

[5] Snorri Sturlusson, p. 152.

[6] Henry of Huntingdon, p. 200. Compare William of Malmesbury, *De Gestis Regum*, ii, p. 13; and Florence of Worcester, ed. Thorpe, i, p. 226.

releases my limbs I become longer
and, bent upon slaughter, spit out
that deadly poison I swallowed before.
No man's parted easily from the object
I describe; if he's struck by what flies
from my stomach, he pays for its poison
with his strength — speedy atonement for his life.
I'll serve no master when unstrung, only when
I'm cunningly notched. Now guess my name.

There are references to archery in the works of Aldhelm. In the letter to Heahfrith Aldhelm uses an archery simile: 'just as the warlike bowman in the midst of battle is hemmed in by a dense formation of enemy legions, then, when his bow is tensed by his powerful hands and arms and arrows are drawn from the quiver, ... the throng, swollen with the arrogance of pride, their shield-wall having been shattered, turn their backs and flee headlong to the dark recesses of their caves'. This is probably derived from classical sources rather than contemporary experience, and what is translated as 'shield-wall' in only the Latin *testudo*. Aldhelm also uses the bow as an example in his *Tract on Virginity*. The sources may be classical but Aldhelm seems to anticipate that his contemporaries will recognise the archery terms, and it certainly suggests that the Anglo-Saxons were familiar with the bow.[4]

According to one source, the Anglo-Saxons used archery at Stamford Bridge in 1066.[5] In that year a Scandinavian invasion preceded that by William of Normandy. Harald Hardrada, King of Norway, arrived in the north accompanied by Harold Godwinson's disgruntled brother Tostig. Harald Hardrada was a doughty warrior, who had once served in the Byzantine emperor's Varangian Guard, and who was to become a legend in Icelandic literature. The Norwegian king established himself in England, and fought off the first attempt to dislodge him, made by the northern earls at Gate Fulford. Harold Godwinson, King of England, made a rapid march north, and surprised Hardrada at Stamford Bridge.

Henry of Huntingdon tells a story of a Scandinavian hero who stood on a bridge to block the English advance, like another Horatius.[6] He was brought down by a somewhat dirty trick: 'Here a single Norwegian, whose name ought to have been preserved, took post on a bridge, and hewing down more than forty of the English with a battle-axe, his country's weapon stayed the advance of the whole English army till the ninth hour. At last someone came under the bridge in a boat, and thrust a spear into him through the chinks in the planking. The English having gained a passage, King Harald and Tostig were slain; and their whole army were either slaughtered, or, being taken prisoner, were burnt'.

This is a twelfth century chronicle, and already shows signs of legend-building, but like all the early accounts, it has no mention of archery on either side. There is, however, a source which has been unwisely used by some recent historians: the *Heimskringla* by Snorri Sturluson. It is a marvellous literary work, in the tradition of the sagas. Snorri was an Icelander, who lived from 1179 until 1241, when his farmhouse was attacked at night. Five men found him in his cellar, unarmed, and murdered him. Harald Hardrada figures as one of the great heroes in the *Heimskringla*. Snorri's account of Stamford Bridge has been given so much attention, that we need to examine it.

He describes the viking preparations: 'The weather was exceptionally fine, with warm sunshine; so the troops left their armour behind and went ashore with only their shields, helmets, and spears, and girt with swords. A number of them also had bows and arrows. They were all feeling very carefree'. The armies faced each other, and Harald Hardrada drew up his force for battle. He 'formed a long and rather thin line; the wings were bent back until they met, thus forming a wide circle of even depth all the way round, with shields overlapping in front and above. The king himself was inside the circle with his standard and his own retinue of hand-picked men ... The army was formed up in this way because King Harald knew that cavalry always attacked in small detachments and then wheeled away at once ... "Our archers are also to stay here with us. Those in the front rank are to set their spear-shafts into the ground and turn the points towards the riders' breasts when they charge us".' The battle begins. 'The English made a cavalry charge on the Norwegians, who met it without flinching. It was no easy matter for the English to ride against the Norwegians because of their arrows ... The English cavalry kept charging them and falling back at once when they could make no headway. The Norwegians observed this, and thought the enemy assaults rather half-hearted; so they launched an attack themselves on the retreating cavalry. But as soon as they had broken their shield-wall, the English rode down on them from all sides, showering spears and arrows on them.' Harald Hardrada fought bravely, but 'now King Harald Sigurdsson was struck in the throat by an arrow, and this was the death-wound. He fell, and with him fell all those who had advanced with him'.

This account has been accepted at its face value by Richard Glover, and as a result he has argued that the Anglo-Saxons used both archers and cavalry in their battles.[7] It is however not the kind of source that can be accepted without question, especially when it is contradicted by earlier and sounder evidence. There is no early source which describes the Anglo-Saxons using cavalry in battle. Warriors did have horses, and they did use them to ride to battle, and for pursuits, but never in battle. An exception is the skirmish in 1055 between Earl Ralph the Timid and the Welsh, but it is very much the exception that proves the rule. Earl Ralph himself was a Norman favourite of Edward the Confessor, indeed his nephew. The Worcester Chronicle tells us quite clearly that: 'he ordered the English to fight on horseback, against their custom'.[8] If the English normally fought as cavalry, why did they not do so at Hastings? Several chroniclers make the point that the English did not fight on horseback.

This should make us wary of the *Heimskringla* as an historical source. It was after all a literary work in the saga tradition, based on historical events but much embroidered. Some historians believe that the saga accounts of the voyages to Vinland, or America, are historical accounts. Do they accept as historical record the stories of people rising from the dead?[9] The sagas do contain historical material, but so used that it becomes untrustworthy if not confirmed. Snorri's work was written in the thirteenth century, nearly two hundred years after the battle of Stamford Bridge. The battle saw the death of his hero, Harald Hardrada, who had to figure importantly in his story. Clearly what Snorri did was to embroider the few available details of the battle. What did he embroider them with? The shield wall, the cavalry, the archers, the king hit by an arrow. No one will ever be able to prove it, and the details are not exactly the same, but many historians have fancied an echo of that more famous battle at Hastings: the Normans at Hastings with cavalry and archers transfigured into the English at Stamford Bridge. If this is so, it still remains interesting that Snorri, unlike his models, has archers on both sides. Stamford Bridge remains an enigma, but it cannot be taken to prove that the Anglo-Saxons had archers in their armies. Snorri's evidence is too late, distant and confused to be accepted. It does not help us to show there were Anglo-Saxon archers at Hastings. No literary account mentions them. Henry of Huntingdon, putting words into the mouth of William of Normandy in the battle speech, says the English are 'a people not even in possession of arrows'.[10] There is, however, one solitary English archer on the Bayeux Tapestry, and this must caution us

[7] Glover, 'English Warfare', pp. 1–18. Compare Wace, ii, p. 206, ll. 8603–4: 'Engleis ne saveient joster/ ne a cheval armes porter'; and *Carmen*, p. 25: 'the English scorn the solace of horses and trusting in their strength they stand fast on foot'; and *Chronicle of Battle Abbey*, p. 39: 'the English were defenceless and on foot'.

[8] Florence of Worcester, i, p. 213: Ralph instructed the English 'contra morem in equis pugnare'.

[9] Vinland Sagas, ed. Magnusson and Palsson.

[10] Henry of Huntingdon, p. 202: 'gentem nec etiam sagittas habentem'.

*The only English archer in the Bayeux tapestry — his costume indicates low social rank.*

against stating categorically that the Anglo-Saxons had no archers at Hastings.[11] It is more likely that the English did have archers, and that some appeared at Hastings. Pursuing our earlier conjecture, it may be that the local levies used at Hastings, from the south, were not soldiers skilled in archery.

## Archery in Normandy before 1066

The evidence for the use of the bow in Normandy before 1066 is as slight as that for England, though our knowledge of the Battle of Hastings itself clearly suggests a strong likelihood that military archery in Normandy was by that time well developed.

The Normans like the English had strong links with Scandinavia. Normandy had been settled by the vikings, and since 911 had been ruled by a Scandinavian dynasty. The vikings had a great military reputation. They were great spearmen, and

[11] *Bayeux Tapestry,* pl. 63.

22

had played an important role in the development of methods for forging swords. They also employed archery. Some early bow-staves have been discovered in Scandinavia, and in viking settlement areas. Saxo Grammaticus describes the Norwegians as famous archers. Abbo describes vikings at the siege of Paris using bows and arrows, and the sagas contain many tales of archery skill. Einar Thambarskelfir was called a famous bowman. He stood in the 'Long Serpent', alongside Olaf Trygvasson, in opposition to Erik Jarl. Erik called up an archer, whose shot hit Einar's bow and shattered it, but Einar took his lord's bow and continued the fight. Another hero in the sagas was Palnatoki, who brought up Sweyn Forkbeard, and was said to be the first chief of the fortress of Jomsborg. One story tells of Palnatoki's role in the fight between his lord, Svend, and King Harald Bluetooth. As the king bent over a fire to warm himself, Palnatoki's well-aimed arrow hit him in the rear and pierced his back passage. But the viking use of archery has been much exaggerated. In fact one knows little more about it than about Saxon or Norman archery before 1066. Most of the sources quoted in support of viking archery are from the twelfth century and even later, and the sagas in particular are not to be trusted as historical evidence. The most that can be said is that the vikings did use the bow, and there was a later medieval tradition of archer-heroes. [12]

References to the Normans themselves using bows before 1066 are few. The brief accounts of William's earlier battles in early sources have no mention of archery. The only relevant reference is to be found in the late and unreliable work of the Channel Islander, Master Wace. He wrote during the time of Henry II, composing verse works in the fashion of his day, in Anglo-Norman French. They are lively works and full of detail. Unfortunately the detail often seems to be inaccurate, and Wace is suspected of embroidering upon his theme, if not of downright invention. It is Wace, in his *Roman de Rou*, who mentions that William of Normandy had archers in his army at Varaville in 1057. [13] That is the only pre-Conquest reference to William's use of archery, but as has been said before, the evidence of Hastings itself is enough to postulate the previous possession and use of archery in battle.

Apart from viking influence upon Norman warfare, one must consider the influence of the Franks. Normandy before the tenth century had been part of the Frankish empire. It is still uncertain how many vikings settled in Normandy, but it seems clear they were absorbed into the Frankish population, and that by the

[12] Anstee and Biek, 'Pattern-welding', pp. 71–93; Bartlett Wells: 'Swordsmith'; and the same author, 'Heat Treatment'. Finds have been made, for example, at Hedeby, Vibbymyren, Sikan, Birka, Staraja Ladoga. For the siege of Paris, see Abbo, p. 72: 'fortis et arcus erat, fortisque sagitta'; and for Norwegian archers, Saxo Grammaticus, i, p. 24 on Enarus, whose 'wonderful bow' could transfix the mast of a ship; and ii, p. 484, on the Norwegians placing most reliance on their archers.

[13] Wace, ii, p. 80, l. 5206: 'e od les ars traient archiers'. Compare *Chroniques des Comtes d'Anjou*, ed. Marchegay and Salmon, p. 103, on Robert the Magnificent; and William of Apulia, p. 266, l. 4, on a 'grando sagittarum' by the Normans in Italy.

eleventh century Normandy was more Frankish in its customs and culture than it was viking. Indeed, the basic foundation of Norman warfare was Norman feudal society, and that derived from Francia. As with the Saxons, the Normans and the Vikings, there are only a few references to the use of bows by the Franks, for example by the defenders during the siege of Paris. In the capitularies again the bow appears as a Frankish weapon: on one occasion there is a warning to bring a proper bow, and not a stick as a substitute.[14] Frankish manuscripts also have representations of bows, but unexpectedly they are usually shortbows. Lacking much in the way of literary detail on the type of bows, it might seem foolish to refuse this evidence, yet it does pose a serious problem. In the later medieval period, when evidence of all kinds is better, the shortbow does not figure in France or England. There is no evidence of the west possessing the necessary skill for producing such bows. The solution may be in the manuscript tradition. The figures represented in manuscripts of different dates are often very similar; costumes and poses are often derivative. The shortbows in the Frankish manuscripts probably have an ancient and eastern manuscript origin.[15]

Archaeological evidence should be more convincing, but it is in short supply. Few bows survive from the early period. Bows are less likely to survive than weapons such as the sword, which was not only made of metal, but also treated as a more valuable personal possession. The bow was not treated as the personal

[14] For Paris, see Abbo, p. 36. For the capitulary, see Munz, *Charlemagne*, p. 73.
[15] For example, the *Gospel Book of Epernay*, and the whole series of manuscripts stemming from the *Utrecht Psalter*.

*A Frankish manuscript (the Epernay Gospels) showing an archer with a shortbow, ninth century.*

*Yew bow from Hedeby of the Viking period.*

weapon of the noble, and so does not appear in the more careful burials. Nevertheless, some bows do survive, and all the bowstaves found in Western Europe before 1066 are either of longbow length, or are frangments of ordinary wooden staves.[16] None are shortbows. This may simply be an accident of survival, but it must be taken into account. Our conclusion must be that the most common bow was probably the ordinary wooden bow, and its length probably approached that of the later longbow.

Thus it would seem that Hastings was the first battle in medieval European history in which bows not only played a significant role, but can be shown to have done so. And yet we know little enough about the men who used the bows at Hastings.[17] William of Poitiers, the Conqueror's chaplain, tells us that William drew his army from Maine, Aquitaine, France — that is from the territories of the French king around the Isle de France, Brittany and Normandy.[18] The evidence of the *Carmen de Hastingae Proelio* (*Song of the Battle of Hastings*) that there were Normans from Italy can no longer be trusted.[19] We do know that the Normans in the south used archery, but the presence of southern Normans at Hastings is unlikely. The Norman army came chiefly from Northern and Western France.

One thing is certain, that the archers in the army were not knights. In the Norman army the knights formed the cavalry, and fought with lance and sword. One can, however, distinguish between different categories of foot soldiers. William of Poitiers describes the way in which the Conqueror ordered his army: 'In front he placed the foot soldiers, armed with bows and crossbows. Then, in the second line, he put the stronger, mailed infantry; last were the squadrons of cavalry, with himself in the middle of them'.[20] The distinction between light and heavy infantry is commonly made. The archers were usually treated as light infantry, not well armoured. The heavy infantry could be expected to engage in hand to hand fighting, whereas the archers were expected to be mobile, and effective at a distance. Armour was not deemed necessary for the bowmen, but this does not necessarily mean that they were the least-regarded troops. On the contrary, in the Anglo-Norman period they are often mentioned as being a specialist group. Wace may be unreliable

[16] See n. 12 above, and Chapter Five n. 4.
[17] See n. 20 below.
[18] William of Poitiers, p. 192.
[19] R. H. C. Davis, Carmen, *EHR*, pp. 241–61; also R. H. C. Davis, 'Discussion', pp. 1–20. The *Carmen* was first thought to be the work by Guy of Amiens, mentioned in Orderic Vitalis, ii, p. 214: Guy, 'who had already celebrated the battle between Harold and William in verse'. Davis is probably right that the work is later, but it may well be based on the lost work of Guy.
[20] William of Poitiers, p. 184: 'pedites in fronte locavit, sagittis armatos et balistis, item pedites in ordine secundo firmiores et loricatos; ultimo turmas equitum, quorum ipse fuit in medio'.

for details of Hastings, but we can at least believe that much of what he wrote applied by the twelfth century. At Varaville in 1057 he said that the Norman army consisted of knights with lances, archers with bows, and villeins with pikes: the implication is that the archers had a greater military worth than the spearmen.[21] We know that some of William's army at Hastings was paid to follow him, and it is possible that this included archers. In the battle they are treated as a coherent group, sent forward to open the battle, brought forward again at the climax. They also seem to be used across the line, and not attached only to one section. The poet Wace does offer a verse on the origins of the Norman archers. He seems to represent an oral tradition otherwise lost, but when his comments are not confirmed, as in this case, he must be treated with caution. He says they came from Vaudreuil and Breteuil, and hit the English in the eye with their steel arrows. His versification alone makes the names suspicious, but for what it is worth, according to Wace the Norman archers came from the west of the duchy, near the border with France.

What bows did the Norman archers use? At this point it is crucial to evaluate the sources. The *Carmen* again becomes important. It, more than any other source, gives clear details of the use of crossbows, mentioning not only the bows but also the four-sided bolts.[22] Professor R. H. C. Davis is probably right to argue that the *Carmen* is late. It is difficult, for example, to accept the Taillefer incident, or the killing of Harold by four Norman knights, one of whom was William of Normandy himself. Had this happened, it seems incredible that the duke's own chaplain would have omitted it from his account. The *Carmen* does seem to include elements of legend that would support a later date. The question remains as to how late. The handwriting suggests a date no later than 1100. In any case the poem is very likely based upon that poem about the Battle of Hastings which we know Guy of Amiens wrote. Legendary and later elements have been introduced, but the value of the work is not altogether destroyed. As to the crossbows, there is every reason to accept that they were used at Hastings. One of the earliest, and perhaps the best of the sources for Hastings, is *The Deeds of William*, written by William of Poitiers. He was formerly a knight, who had become chaplain to the Conqueror. In his account he refers to crossbows. He uses the word *balistae*. The men using them are sent forward with the archers, and are moved to make way for the cavalry. Their mobility makes it clear that they are crossbowmen.[23]

[21] Wace, ii, p. 80, ll. 5205–7: 'de lances fierent chevaliers/ e od les ars traient archiers,/ e od les pels vilain lor donent'. The same work, ii, p. 202, ll. 8505–7, comments on the Norman archers: 'Le archier de Val de Rooil,/ qui esteient de grant orgoil,/ ensemble od els ci de Bretoil'.
[22] *Carmen*, p. 24, l. 3821: 'quadratis iaculis'; and see p. 22, l. 338; p. 26, l. 411; App. C, pp. 112–5.
[23] William of Poitiers, pp. 184, 188.

The existence of crossbowmen at this time is well attested.[24] Within a few years, we even find a woman using the weapon, when Judith attacked Henry I, her own father. There is a Norman charter, dated 4th August 1060 which is issued by William I, confirming a donation by Richard de Redvers the castellan of Thimert to the Abbey of St Père de Chartres. One of the witnesses is Fulcher the crossbowman. The term used in the charter is *arcibalister*, which leaves no doubt about the type of weapon. Within a few years of the conquest the crossbow makes its entrance into the chronicles of both the Welsh and the English. In each case, the term *arbaleste* is used, a new French term for a new weapon. This shows that the English and the Welsh had previously not used the crossbow, but also that the Normans had.

## The Tactical Role of the Archers at Hastings

And so to battle, and indeed to Battle: the most famous military site in England, and one of the best documented of medieval conflicts.[25] This is the first time in a medieval battle that the role of the archers can be examined in depth.

Harold Godwinson had seized the English throne, vacated by the childless Edward the Confessor. In 1066 he faced two invasions. The first was made by Harald Hardrada in conjunction with Harold Godwinson's brother, Tostig. The latter's interest in regaining his northern earldom of Northumbria, led him to throw in his lot with the Norwegian king. As we have seen, Harold Godwinson marched north with great speed and defeated his enemies at Stamford Bridge. Harald Hardrada and Tostig were killed. No sooner had Harold Godwinson triumphed at Stamford Bridge, than his other great rival, William of Normandy, appeared on the south coast, ravaging the Godwin family lands in Sussex. Harold moved with speed to deal with the new, though long-expected, threat from Normandy.

This time he failed to take his enemy by surprise. William had been warned by his own scouts, and made his preparations on the night of Friday 13th October. He marched northwards in the early hours of Saturday 14th, to confront the English some seven miles from the coast on the road from London. The Normans breasted the rise of Telham Hill, and the two armies faced each other over a distance of two miles apart. Harold Godwinson immediately formed his forces upon the eminently suitable ridge

[24] *Carmen*, pp. 112–5. On Henry I's daughter see Orderic Vitalis, vi, pp. 212–4. For Fulcher, see Fauroux, *Recueil*, p. 329, no. 147: a charter of William the Conqueror dated 1060 is witnessed by 'Fulcherius arcibalister'. Compare Gruffydd ap Cynan, p. 62 on a Norman crossbowman in 1081; and *Anglo-Saxon Chronicle*, ed. Plummer, ii, p. 215: archers specifically described as 'Frenchmen' created a disturbance at Canterbury in 1083, shooting arrows from the gallery into the cross over the altar, and killing three monks.
[25] Brown, 'Battle of Hastings', pp. 1–21, is the best modern account of the battle. The main sources include William of Poitiers, pp. 183–205; the Bayeux Tapestry; and William of Jumièges, pp. 134–5; 196–7.

of the hill on which Battle Abbey now stands. He took the centre with his standard, his men ranged about 400 yards on either side of him. The English army formed the traditional shield wall, with housecarls protecting the lighter-armed levies. Wace says they made a palisade, building 'a fence before them with their shields, and ash and other wood, and had well joined and wattled in the whole work, so as not to leave a crevice, and thus they had a barricade in their front, through which any Norman who would attack them must first pass.'[26] It is a good example of the kind of problem that Wace presents. No other source mentions such a barricade. It seems likely that he had read an account of the shield wall, something which no longer figured in warfare in his own day, and then embroidered upon the shield wall the idea of a wall made with shields. Freeman in the 19th century accepted Wace's account, but both his view and the palisade were well demolished by Round. 'Mr Freeman', wrote the latter, 'like the Bourbons, never learnt, and never forgot.'[27] Even without such defences, the English army, reinforced by Danes, in its tight infantry formation, proved difficult to break.

The Norman army approached: archers first, then heavier infantry, and finally cavalry. William opened the battle by exploiting in turn his two main advantages, archery and cavalry. The bowmen were ordered to attack, provoking the English, wounding and killing them. The English line held. William's intentions were clear. Archers were being used, as they often would be again, to soften up the enemy in preparation for a decisive cavalry attack. At Hastings, the cavalry attack was made, but it was not decisive. Those who have climbed the slopes of the hill at Battle, will appreciate the reason for failure. An ideal cavalry field is flat and open. Hastings was anything but that. There was wooded country all about, ditches and obstacles, some possibly prepared by the English, though they cannot have had time for anything elaborate. Several chroniclers, while not going to the lengths of Wace, do mention either natural or ancient ramparts in the vicinity. William of Poitiers speaks of a deep gully and ditches encountered during the flight.[28] Such obstacles have never been certainly identified. At the foot of the hill there was also marshy land. All in all the land was not suited to cavalry fighting. Riding up the hill it would be impossible to maintain speed, and the impact of a charge would be much reduced.

In 1066 it is not clear that cavalry charged in a concerted fashion.[29] Cavalry tactics were still developing. On the Bayeux Tapestry more Norman knights are shown using the lance for an

[26] Wace, ii, p. 175, ll. 7795–800; translation in Taylor, Master Wace, p. 176.
[27] Freeman, Norman Conquest, iii, p. 445: for the palisade; and opp. p. 443 for the map. For the most famous response, see Round, 'Mr Freeman', in Feudal England, p. 375.
[28] William of Poitiers, p. 202: 'praerupti valli et frequentium fossarum'.
[29] Ross, 'Turoldus', pp.8127–138.

overhead thrust than couching it firmly under the arm. It is probable that the couched lance charge was in its infancy at this time. In any case, it would have been difficult to employ such a charge up the steep slope of Battle hill. The position, together with the determination of the Anglo-Saxon shield wall, foiled the Norman cavalry.

Two developments in the battle are generally said to have given the Normans victory: the use of feigned flights, and the death of Harold Godwinson. It is important to consider their relative importance. The use of feigned flights has been questioned by some historians, who believe that eleventh century cavalry could not succeed in such a manoeuvre. They are flying in the face of the evidence. Every major source for the battle describes the use of feigned flights.[30] There are also numerous other contemporary cases of this manoeuvre being employed, both before and after Hastings, by the Normans and by other knights. They were prepared for such tactics by practice in horsemanship from boyhood.[31] There is no need for us to enter into the argument over whether the first retreat was deliberate or not, or over how many feigned flights were used: the chroniclers vary in their details. It can be said that at one point the Normans were sorely pressed, since William the Bastard himself was thought to have been killed, and he had to reveal his face to rally his men. 'Look at me,' he called, 'I am alive and I shall conquer through the grace of God.'[32] This episode probably relates to an English counter-attack, which was halted; but at any rate the ruse was then used deliberately, and with some success. The feigned flights were almost certainly executed not by the whole of the Norman cavalry in unison, so much as by relatively small units trained to work together. In that event, isolated pockets of English would have been trapped by the trick, and not the bulk of the English army. This would explain how although the chroniclers speak of the success of the feigned flights, the English line clearly remains in control of the hilltop. It may have been at this point in the battle that the *Malfosse* incident occurred.[33] Some chroniclers place it in the middle of the battle, some afterwards. At one point or the other, some Norman cavalry found itself in difficulties in a ditch defended by the English. Whatever the true details, blurred in the confusion of time, the battle was not concluded by the feigned flights. The ruse was a factor in the victory, but not the final one.

The second incident which is seen as decisive was the death of King Harold. This may well have been more significant in settling the issue, though it too has suffered from unclear and

[30] Bachrach, 'Feigned retreat', pp. 344–7; and Brown, 'Battle of Hastings', pp. 14–6. Burne, Lemmon, and Beeler are among those who have queried the reality of the feigned flight. Source references to a flight, include William of Poitiers: 'they withdrew deliberately pretending to turn in flight'; the *Carmen*: they 'pretended to fly'; Orderic Vitalis: they 'feigned flight'. There are other references to such flights before and after Hastings, for example, by the Normans at St Aubin-le-Cauf and at Messina; also at Montbayou 1025, and Cassel 1071. The pre-conquest historian of the Norman dukes, Dudo of St Quentin, also refers to a flight.

[31] Verbruggen, 'Tactique militaire', pp. 161–80.

[32] William of Poitiers, p. 190: 'Me, inquit, circumspicite. Vivo et vincam, opitulante Deo'.

[33] Brown, 'Battle of Hastings', p. 18.

varying accounts. That Harold was killed should not be doubted, though legends of a surviving Harold, like a second Arthur, were to dog the Norman conquerors for years.[34] The first question to decide is at what point in the battle Harold was killed. William of Jumièges says that Harold was killed in the first clash. This is an important early source, and is followed by Orderic Vitalis. It does not, however, fit with other accounts of the battle, nor does it fit with the account in which it is placed, coming near the conclusion. Baring's suggestion seems to offer the best explanation: that William of Jumièges' original words were wrongly copied, and what became 'in the first clash' was originally 'in the front rank'. This would certainly fit better with the general view of the battle.[35]

The question then remains, how was Harold killed, was it indeed by an arrow in the eye? Doubt has been thrown on this

*The Bayeux tapestry showing the two stages of Harold's death, left — the arrow in Harold's eye — right — Harold cut down by sword. Stitch marks show that the second figure also had an arrow in the eye, and this adds to the likelihood that both figures are Harold.*

[34] H. R. Loyn, in a lecture to the London Medieval Society, 1980.
[35] William of Jumièges, p. 135; followed by Orderic Vitalis, ii, p. 176; and see Baring, *Domesday Tables*, Appendix B, p. 220.
[36] The arrow in the eye and the hewing of the thigh, *Bayeux Tapestry*, pls 71, 72. Gibbs-Smith is convinced that Harold was not killed by an arrow, see *Bayeux Tapestry*, pp. 175–6; and in *JSAA*. Baudri de Bourgueil, p. 209, is the first work, apart from the Tapestry, to have the arrow. See also William of Malmesbury, *De Gestis Regum*, ii, p. 303; Henry of Huntingdon, p. 203; and Wace, ii, p. 189, ll. 8161–4.
[37] Dodwell, 'Bayeux Tapestry', p. 549, questions whether the obscenity and lewdness of the Tapestry was suitable for a cathedral.
[38] Brooks and Walker, 'Bayeux Tapestry', pp. 1–34, which is the best modern discussion on the Tapestry. Bernstein, 'Blinding of Harold', pp. 40–64, provides new evidence.
[39] William of Malmesbury, *De Gestis Regum*, ii, p. 303.

version.[36] It is argued that either the Bayeux Tapestry shows Harold throwing a spear, or that the warrior with the arrow is not Harold at all, and Harold is the following figure on the Tapestry, the warrior cut down by a sword. It is said that early sources do not mention the arrow. This negative evidence is less convincing than at first it sounds. The Bayeux Tapestry is itself early evidence, probably made for Odo of Bayeux' cathedral in 1077.[37] There is some argument over this, but a general agreement that the Tapestry is of eleventh century date. The object in the eye, or at least in the head, is surely an arrow, confirmed by the arrows sticking in the shield. Equally certainly the figure is meant to represent Harold. The designer of the Tapestry is always at pains to make clear who the figures are, in this case by clearly placing the name right above the man. Whether the following figure is also Harold is less material to us, it being accepted that Harold has received an arrow in the eye. Nicholas Brooks has argued convincingly that both figures are meant to represent Harold, in cartoon strip style.[38] There are several chronicles which present the death in two stages, the most telling of these being William of Malmesbury, who writes of Harold 'receiving the fatal arrow from a distance, then yielding to death. One of the soldiers with a sword gashed his thigh, as he lay prostrate; for which shameful and cowardly action, he was branded with ignominy by William, and lost his knighthood.'[39] It may be that these later chronicles, which present the death in two stages, were based upon the Tapestry. This would still be important, since it would show that a twelfth century interpretation of the Tapestry, before any repairs were made, was of the death of Harold by an arrow. William of Malmesbury's story of the punishment of the soldier for then using the sword is also important, for it clearly suggests it was the arrow which delivered the blow that counted. In a paper given to the Anglo-Norman Studies conference at Battle in 1982, the American art historian, David Bernstein, demonstrated that the second, falling figure had also originally had an arrow in the eye. He had noticed a line of needle holes, which remain although the embroidery for this second arrow has gone. The conclusion from this discovery is firstly that both figures clearly do represent Harold, and secondly that Harold, according to the Tapestry definitely was hit by an arrow. We may then firmly conclude that it was an arrow which struck the fatal blow, and that archery was significant in the incident which decided the battle. Although William of Poitiers does not say how Harold died, his description of the climax of the battle includes the use of

arrows: 'the Normans shot arrows, battered and pierced the enemy.' That this early source makes it clear the archers were called on again is important.[40]

It remains to be discussed how this final archery blow was delivered. In short, did the Normans shoot their arrows into the air? Twelfth century sources do say this. Henry of Huntingdon writes that William 'commanded his men not to aim their arrows directly at the enemy, but to shoot the arrows in the air over them, to split up the enemy mass with arrows.'[41] It is often repeated that arrows were shot high into the air to fall on the heads of the English. From a practical point of view this is extremely unlikely, since it would mean spent arrows falling on the enemy. If Harold's death was caused by a spent arrow, it was indeed a lucky shot. The story seems to be supported by looking closely at the archers in the lower margin of the Tapestry. As the main strip reaches the climax of the battle, the lower margin archers begin to raise their bows.[42] The explanation is surely a simple one. Consider the ground at Hastings. The archers were operating from the foot of a hill. In any case, to shoot at a distance, one allows for a certain rise and fall in the flight arc of the arrow. In other words the archers at Hastings are simply acting in the way that all archers in battle would. There is no need to dress it up as a special and unrealistic ploy. We know that this late use of archery was effective in the battle: some telling hits were made, not least the wounding of the English commander. This was the blow that settled the battle. As the monastic chronicler of the abbey soon to be built on this very spot would write: 'when their king was laid low by a chance blow, the army broke up and fled in different directions.'[43]

In the Bayeux Tapestry, there is one Norman archer on horseback.[44] This raises the question of whether or not the Normans had mounted archers. It must be stressed that this is not strictly a battle scene, but one of pursuit. Another possibility raised by the picture is that archers, at least sometimes, owned horses. Later this would certainly be the case, and it should not be dismissed out of hand for the eleventh century, though it can be no more than conjecture.

*The Bayeux tapestry: archers raising their bows as the battle reaches its climax. Note the size of the bow on the left in particular. It could be a longbow.*

40  William of Poitiers, p. 194: 'sagittant, feriunt, perfodiunt Normanni'.
41  Henry of Huntingdon, p. 203: 'Docuit etiam dux Willelmus viros sagittarios ut non in hostem directe, sed in aera sursum sagittas emitterent, cuneum hostilem sagittas secarent'. Also in Baudri and Wace. The use of a high trajectory is also met with Stephen at Bedford, and at Agincourt, where, according to Monstrelet, iv, p. 177; the archers shot 'as high as possible so as not to lose their effect'.
42  *Bayeux Tapestry*, pls 71, 72.
43  *Chronicle of Battle Abbey*, p. 80.
44  *Bayeux Tapestry*, pl. 73.

*The only mounted archer on the Bayeux tapestry. Note that this occurs in the pursuit and not in the battle.*

[45] 'Tuck', 'Norman Doodle', p. 175.
[46] *Bayeux Tapestry*, pl. 61, and colour pl. X, has the group of four; pl. 63, has the English archer; pl. 73, the mounted archer; pls 68, 69, 70, 71, the archers in the lower margin.

## The Archers Portrayed on the Bayeux Tapestry

We cannot leave Hastings without examining more closely the pictorial evidence of the Bayeux Tapestry. Illustrations of archers in this period are very rare. One of the few that survive was scratched on the stone of Colchester castle.[45] On the Tapestry there are 29 archers, and this is a wealth without compare.[46] There are six archers on the main strip of the narrative, and 23 in the lower margin. The archers on the main strip are rather more carefully depicted, and rather better dressed.

33

*This interesting figure is scratched on the wall of Colchester Castle, and is thought to be Norman. The bow seems to be of longbow length.*

Twenty-eight of the twenty-nine archers are Normans. The sole English bowman is presented as a small figure overshadowed by the mail-clad warriors. In eleventh century artistic conventions, this does not signify a diminutive individual, but one of insignificant rank. He wears a tunic rather than mail, has no helmet to protect his head, and does not even have a quiver.

Four standing Norman archers are placed in a group together. This might well be intended to suggest that the archers acted in unison as a cohesive body. One of the four is the only archer on the Tapestry wearing mail, with a cloth garment showing underneath. He also has a helmet with a nasal, apparently of the type with a metal brow band and quarter plates. Possibly his helmet has a neck cover, such as those shown in the picture of the Norman preparations. He wears a quiver belted at the waist, and is holding four arrows in a manner that would be unlikely in practice. This figure suggests that at least some archers were armoured in the same way as the heavy infantry and the knights. Of the other three in this group, two seem to be wearing cloth garments, while the third is either in cloth or leather. This latter figure has quilted breeches, and a quiver slung round his neck. The two at the front are similar to each other, wearing Phrygian caps, breeches, and belted quivers.

The sixth archer on the main strip is the lone mounted archer, a Norman participating in the pursuit of the defeated English. It is not clear if he is wearing breeches or a tunic. He has no helmet or cap. His bow is the same as all the others on the Tapestry, an ordinary wooden bow, though one would have expected a horse archer to have shortbow or crossbow. There is no need to believe that every single detail on the Tapestry must be accurate. The narrative was probably the work of a monastic writer, the design probably by a monastic artist influenced by the Canterbury school if not a member of it.[47] We do not know who was responsible for the embroidery itself: ladies in the royal household, or in that of a noble lady are usually suggested. Certainly those concerned were not likely to have been warriors.

[47] Brooks and Walker, 'Bayeux Tapestry'.

The group of four Norman archers on the Bayeux tapestry. The grouping suggests they fought as a massed body.

Some of the military details are not exact. Many of the hauberks look trousered, but it is unlikely that mounted warriors wore anything but skirted mail. Some of the Tapestry hauberks certainly are skirted, those in the lower margin being pulled over the heads of dead warriors.[48] With the archers we find a recurring error. The majority of the bowmen appear to have the arrow ready to shoot placed on the wrong side of the bowstave, on the right-hand rather than the left-hand side. Of those which can be determined, only three are holding the arrow correctly, nineteen have placed it wrongly. Probably the embroiderer sewed in the more significant shape of the bow first, and then placed the arrow across it, without consideration of military accuracy. We know there were crossbows at Hastings, but none are shown, so we ought not to take too literally the horse archer with his wooden bow. Of the archers on the Tapestry in general it may be said that they were not well protected with armour: the great majority are bare-headed and in cloth garments.

As has been said, the weapons on the Tapestry seem to be all ordinary wooden bows, roughly shaped. The suggestion that one is intended to be a crossbowman cannot be taken seriously, since his weapon is so clearly not a crossbow.[49] It can only be assumed that the makers of the Tapestry were not familiar with crossbows, and this reinforces the idea that they were English. One notes that in both an Old English and a Welsh source written soon after the Conquest, the word for crossbow is the French *arbalest*.[50] It would seem likely that the English were not familiar with the crossbow until after 1066, and even then it found no great favour. One problem relating to the bows on the Tapestry is to decide how long were the originals. The general impression is of a bow of no great length. Probably we should be correct in concluding that ordinary bows in the eleventh century

[48] *Bayeux Tapestry*, pls 71, 72.
[49] *Carmen*, p. 115.
[50] *Two of the Saxon Chronicles Parallel*, i, p. 214: under 1079, has a man 'mid anan arblaste'; compare the *Brut y Tywysogyon*, p. 197: 'saethydyon acarblas-twyr', that is, archers and crossbowmen; and p. 183: 'chwarel' for the bolt. Compare Gruffydd ap Cynan, p. 137–8: 'saytheu ac a chuareleu' (arrows and bolts). I am grateful to Chris Lewis for acquainting me with this last source.

*Two of the nineteen archers on the Bayeux tapestry with the arrow sewn on the wrong side of the bow.*

*These archers are shown with the arrows in the correct position; from an English manuscript of c.1480.*

were shorter than those in the late middle ages, but a certain amount of caution is necessary. The artistic conventions of the eleventh century are not those of the later medieval period. Realism in a photographic sense was less desirable for the eleventh century artist than for his counterpart in the fifteenth century. Proportions in the Tapestry are not intended to be as in life. The size of figures denotes social status rather than physical height. It could be a reason for making small not only the archers, but also their weapons. It is certainly odd that the only surviving early bow-staves are all long. On the main strip the bows do not seem very long. A longbow is about the height of its owner, and we should be looking for a stave something over five feet in length and nearer to six. If one examines the lower margin of the Tapestry, however, a good proportion of the bows do look as long as their owners, and could possibly be of longbow length. Lacking conclusive evidence, it would be rash to reach any definite decision over the length.

It is worth pointing out that to be effective in battle, an ordinary bow would need to have a certain strength. The impact of such a bow depends to a great extent upon the length of the stave. We do at least know that the bows at Hastings were effective. Our rather tentative conclusion is that the Hastings bows were not as long as later medieval longbows, but were probably not all that much shorter, perhaps about five feet.

# Chapter 3

# From Hastings to Lincoln on Foot

*Battle Tactics in the Twelfth Century*

This is a lost chapter in the history of English archery. Most histories, with scarcely a pause, skip from Hastings to the time of Edward I and then the Hundred Years' War. It is partly because of this omission that the idea has taken root that a novel and powerful weapon appeared at the end of the thirteenth century and was then instrumental in the English winning a series of victories against their enemies in Scotland and France. Although there is an element of truth in this view, it is grossly unfair to the contribution of the twelfth century to battle tactics.

The unusual tactics in the Anglo-Norman battles of the first half of the twelfth century have not gone entirely unnoticed, but something of their true significance has been missed.[1] It has been pointed out, for example, by Sir Charles Oman, that in the battles fought by the Anglo-Normans after Hastings up to and including the Battle of Lincoln in 1141, knights who had been trained to fight as cavalry dismounted and fought on foot. The modern historian who has discussed this most fully is the American scholar, Professor Warren Hollister. He suggested that in the development of these tactics one could discern the influence of the Anglo-Saxons upon Anglo-Norman warfare. It is known that the English before 1066 normally rode to battle, and then dismounted to fight as infantry. It cannot be denied that some who had been trained in Anglo-Saxon warfare fought for

[1] Hollister, *Military Organization*; Oman, *Art of War*, 1924, i.

the Anglo-Norman kings. As far as the English aristocracy is concerned, it is virtually impossible to show in what capacity they fought. It is therefore unclear whether they continued to fight as infantry, or were re-trained to become cavalry. It may be that some of the so-called 'knights' of the Anglo-Norman period were Anglo-Saxon warriors fighting in their normal manner. Lacking evidence on the point, the suggestion must remain supposition.[2] It is not supposition, however, that at times knights who had been trained as cavalry were asked to fight on foot. It is of course possible that the effectiveness of the Anglo-Saxon foot methods against the Normans at Hastings had some influence upon later methods, but it was certainly not the only influence. It must be made clear from the beginning, that the tactics developed by the Anglo-Normans were very different from those of the Anglo-Saxons.

Those who dismounted can be more easily shown to be Norman than Anglo-Saxon. Even when chroniclers speak of Norman and English knights, they may simply mean Normans who were based either in Normandy or England. From those knights who can be identified, the contribution of Normandy was clearly very much greater. What has sometimes been overlooked is that the Anglo-Norman tactics involved more than simply knights dismounting. There are two other equally important elements, both of which are more obviously of Norman than English origin.

Some knights did indeed dismount in the five battles which Oman and Hollister discussed, but some also remained on horseback and fought as cavalry. The significance of this in the individual battles we shall shortly consider. Cavalry in this period may not have been as dominant as Oman at one point suggested, but it was always in evidence, and always important.[3] In addition to cavalry, the Anglo-Normans made considerable use of archery. Again in the chronicles we meet the 'infantry syndrome', a relative lack of interest in the lower class foot soldiers and their exploits. Nevertheless, in three of the battles shortly to be discussed, archers played a prominent role. Neither cavalry nor archery was significant in Anglo-Saxon warfare, and both were signally lacking on the English side at Hastings. That they are important to Anglo-Norman warfare suggests what should have been clear from the start, that although there may have been some Anglo-Saxon influence upon the Normans, the more dominant influence was that of the Normans' own experience in war, and the methods that had already brought them success.

[2] William of Malmesbury, *De Gestis Regum*, ii, p. 471.
[3] Oman, *Art of War*, 1953, p. 57: in which the time between the eleventh and fourteenth centuries is seen as 'the period of the supremacy of the mail-clad feudal horseman'.

# Warfare Under the Sons of the Conqueror

It is time to examine the battles of the period, and to see how the various sections of the army acted. We shall only consider the battles for which the chroniclers give sufficient detail for an analysis of the tactics: that is, the five battles discussed by Oman and Hollister, together with a sixth which should have been examined with them. It must, however, be noted that there were other battles, several of which involved at least as many men as fought at Bourgthéroulde.[4] It should also be recognised that in battles other than the six we shall examine, there is no evidence of men dismounting. In at least one of those other battles which is described as a 'cavalry battle', the knights almost certainly stayed on horseback.[5]

The first major Anglo-Norman battle was not fought until exactly forty years after the Battle of Hastings, by which time the Conqueror had been dead for nineteen years, and William Rufus, the son who inherited the English throne, had also departed this life. It was in 1106 that the younger son of the Conqueror, now Henry I the King of England, staked his claim to the Duchy of Normandy, and met his brother Robert Curthose in pitched battle under the walls of Tinchebrai.[6] The castle of William, Count of Mortain, can no longer be seen, apart from a few traces among the houses of the old hilltop town; but the fields and slopes over which the battle was fought are still green.

The brothers were very different in character. Robert, the Conqueror's eldest son, had inherited Normandy on the death of his father, but had not made a great deal of his inheritance. William Rufus, the second son, had inherited the English throne, and sought to re-unite it with the Norman dukedom. Rufus had already established a base in Normandy, when Curthose abandoned the struggle in order to go on the First Crusade, the one genuine achievement of his career. Curthose returned to Normandy to find his brother William had been killed in the New Forest, and his younger brother Henry had taken possession of the English throne. Curthose made an abortive invasion of England, and then in 1106 faced a counter-attack into Normandy made by his younger brother.

Robert Curthose had few admirers, despite his pleasant, amiable ways. He was thought too lax. He was said often to sleep away his mornings after late carousings, and then frequently he did not dare to go to church because he had no clothes to wear, since harlots and scoundrels had stolen his

[4] For example, under Stephen: battles at the Gower with 516 men; near Cardigan with 3000; Baldwin Fitz-Gilbert took 500 knights to Brecon. There were battles at Dunster, 1139; Winchester, 1141; Wilton, 1143. At the Battle of Vaudreuil, Waleran had 500 knights.
[5] The Battle of Dunster, 1139, in *Gesta Stephani*, p. 82: 'in equestri . . . congressione'. 104 knights were taken prisoner.
[6] David, *Robert Curthose* has an appendix on the battle; and see Leroux, *Tinchebray*.

breeches and boots. William of Malmesbury spoke of his indulgence in sensual pleasure, believing him 'generous to worthless men'. His government of the duchy was widely agreed to be a disaster.[7]

Henry on the other hand, though hardly possessing a likeable personality, was agreed to bring good government. He was ruthless, vigorous and ambitious . He is said to have counted his inheritance of cash, while his father was still on his deathbed. One baron who had opposed him, was pushed to his death from a tower by Henry himself. He showed no sense of humour over the scurrilous verses made against him by Luke de la Barre. The poet, when taken prisoner, was treated so barbarously, that he chose to take his life by banging his head against the cell wall rather than face further tortures. Henry also blinded the Count of Mortain for opposing him, in an age when aristocrats did not expect such punishments. Nor was Henry's private life any more blameless than his brother's. He was 'perpetually enslaved by female temptresses', and seems to hold the record among English kings for mistresses and bastards.[8]

Henry in 1106 came to attack his older brother in Normandy. He laid siege to Tinchebrai, held by a supporter of Curthose. The latter came to try and relieve the castle, and the two armies faced each other in sight of the castle walls. Each brother commanded the rear section of his own army. According to one chronicler, both leaders ordered some of their knights to dismount.[9] A number of other sources show that Henry I followed this practice in the battle. In many ways the most interesting record of the battle is a letter written immediately afterwards by a priest of Fécamp.[10] This letter was printed in 1872, but with a vital line omitted. It was 're-discovered' by H. W. C. Davis in 1909, printed again, and with the same error, since Davis had not checked the original. The omission was finally noted by Malden, and re-printed, though still with one minor word incorrect. The background of this letter is important, and the accuracy of its content, because only when it was fully printed could one see the extent of the dismounting in Henry's army. The first line, men from the Bessin, the Avranchin, and the Cotentin were all on foot. The second line, including Henry and his barons was also dismounted. There were also 700 cavalry with each line. Robert Curthose was said to have learned his methods of fighting on crusade, but it is not clear what the lesson was.[11] From the context it would seem to refer to his method of making a cavalry charge rather than to the idea of dismounting knights: 'since the duke and his troops had

[7] William of Malmesbury, *De Gestis Regum*, ii, p. 462. Compare Orderic Vitalis, ii, p. 356; v, pp. 26, 300, 308.

[8] Henry I's character. On the cash, see Orderic Vitalis, iv, p. 96. The same work, iv, p .226, has the pushing of Conan from the tower in Rouen; and vi, pp. 352–4, the death of Luke de la Barre, 'pro derisoriis cantionibus', and 'indecentes . . . cant-ilenas'. Henry of Huntingdon, p. 255, has a discussion on Henry's character, and the kill-ing of the Count of Mortain; on p. 256, the enslavement of temp-tresses. On Henry's bastards see White: 'Henry's illegitimate children'. White com-ments that Charles II's record in this respect is easily beaten by Henry I. Henry had a minimum of twenty bastards, probably twenty two, by at least six mistresses.

[9] Henry of Hunting-don, p. 235: 'rex namque, et dux, et acies caeterae pedites erant, ut con-stantius pugnarent'. Etienne of Rouen, ii, p. 649, l. 1517, suggests that Curthose was captured because he was on foot: 'Dedignatur enim quis resilire retro'.

[10] H. W. C. Davis, 'Tinchebrai'; Poole, 'Tinchebrai'. The manu-script, Jesus College Oxford, li, f. 104, in fact

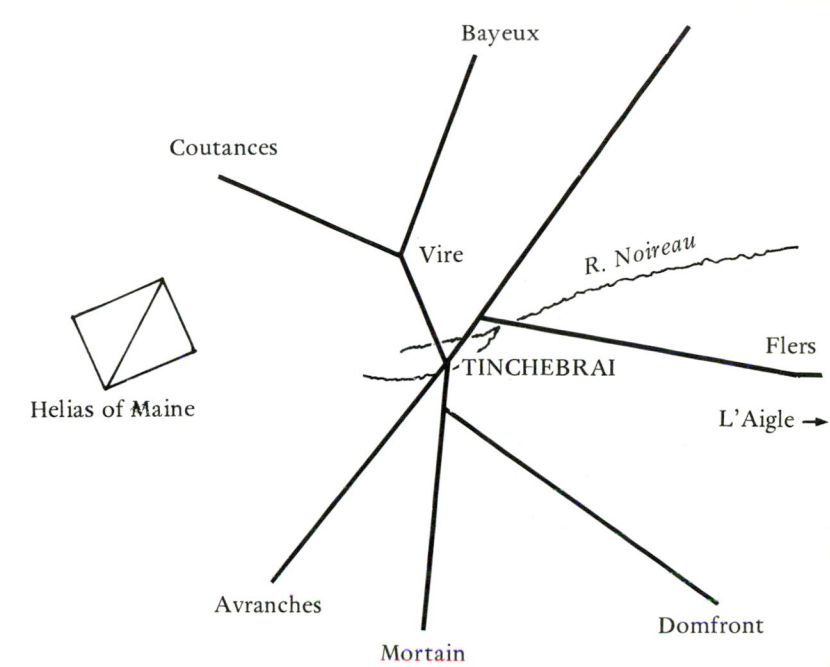

Robert de Bellême

CURTHOSE & Mortain

Men of Bessin, Avranchin & Cotentin

HENRY I

The neighbourhood of Tinchebrai.

*The disposition of the army. The evidence in medieval chronicles rarely allows one to plot army dispositions on maps with any precision. Therefore in this book ground plans and dispositions are ususaly shown separately. For example, in this plan it is not known on which flank Helias was placed.*

reads: 'in secunda rex cum innumeris baronibus suis, omnes similiter pedites'.
[11] Henry of Huntingdon, p. 235: 'assuetusque bellis Jerosolimitanis'.
[12] Henry's letter is also in Jesus College Oxford MS li, f. 104; and in Eadmer, *Historia Novorum*, p. 184.
[13] Symeon of Durham,

been well trained in the wars of Jerusalem, their onslaught upset the royal army'. Henry had sent a cavalry troop, under Helias of Maine, to a distance from the field, and out of sight of Curthose. Robert sent a cavalry charge under the Count of Mortain, which though causing trouble, was held. The battle was in the balance, when Helias of Maine made a cavalry charge by surprise with the hidden force from the flank. Robert of Bellême fled, Robert Curthose was captured. The fight had scarcely lasted an hour, but it had decided the fate of Normandy for a generation. Henry I himself wrote a letter after the battle to Archbishop Anselm, claiming that he had 'won the day without any great slaughter of our own men.'[12] Curthose was never to be released from an imprisonment spent in England and Wales. He died in 1134 at Cardiff. In the battle of Tinchebrai there is no reference to archers, or to the weapons of the foot soldiers. It should be noted, however, that when Curthose had been preparing his invasion of England in 1101, he had collected a multitude of cavalry, archers and foot.[13]

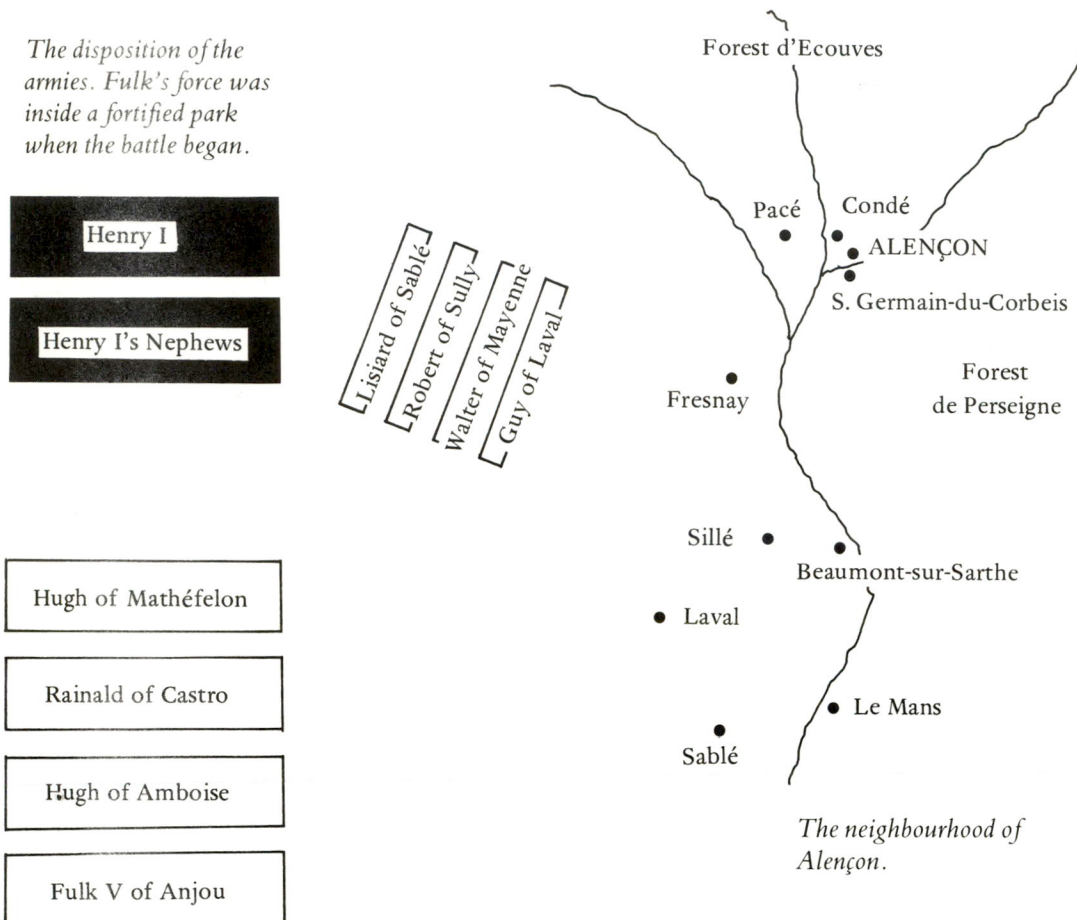

*The disposition of the armies. Fulk's force was inside a fortified park when the battle began.*

Henry I

Henry I's Nephews

Lisiard of Sablé · Robert of Sully · Walter of Mayenne · Guy of Laval

Hugh of Mathéfelon

Rainald of Castro

Hugh of Amboise

Fulk V of Anjou

Sées

Forest d'Ecouves

Pacé · Condé · ALENÇON

S. Germain-du-Corbeis

Forest de Perseigne

Fresnay

Sillé · Beaumont-sur-Sarthe

Laval

Le Mans

Sablé

*The neighbourhood of Alençon.*

The Battle of Alençon is 1118 is not included in the canon of either Oman or Hollister. Admittedly the chronicle account in the *Deeds of the Counts of Anjou* is not very clear, but it is a battle involving an Anglo–Norman army; in one version knights are said to dismount, and it gives sufficient detail for an analysis of tactics.[14] The reason for the neglect of this battle is probably that the only detailed source is not an Anglo–Norman chronicle but an Angevin one which has never been translated into English. The reason that Norman chronicles either ignore or barely mention the battle is that Henry I received a humiliating beating. For our purposes, it is a battle which very much deserves attention.

RS, ii, p. 233: 'equitum, sagittariorum, et peditum non parvam congregans'. Compare Florence of Worcester, RS, ii, p. 48.
[14] *Chroniques des Comtes d'Anjou*, 1913.

[15] *Chroniques des Comtes d'Anjou*, 1913, p. 148: 'qui cooperuerunt faciem terrae sicut locustae'.

[16] *Chroniques des Comtes d'Anjou*, 1856–71, p. 148: 'dissellatis equis et recenciatis, induti etiam thoracibus, loricis et galeis, ordinaverunt acies suas. In prima acie erat Lisiardus, Sabolii dominus, commilitibus, archeriis et peditibus suis.'

[17] Knights dismounted at the Dyle, see *Annals of Fulda*, p. 408 and Regino of Prüm, p. 138 and at Narbonne in 962, see Bachrach, 'Military Organization', p. 7; at the second Battle of Conquereux; at Damascus, see *Historiens Occidentaux*, i, pt. II, p. 764: 'Ubi tam ipse quam sui de equis descendentes, et facti pedites, sicut mos est Theutonicis in summis necessitatibus bellica tractare negotia.'

The battle of Alençon arose from the hostility between Normandy and Anjou. Henry collected an army of knights and foot, which 'covered the face of the earth like locusts'.[15] The Angevin Count, Fulk V, kept his main army within a defensible enclosure which the chronicle calls 'The Park'. Henry I's attack included bows and crossbows, and when Fulk sent out his men, division by division, archers were included. The first sortie was led by Hugh of Mathéfelon, with 100 knights and 200 sergeants or archers. The second group consisted of 100 knights and 200 archers. The sorties made no headway against Henry I's army. Fulk was saved by the appearance of a second army coming to join him under the command of Lisiard of Sablé. This force dismounted in the cover of a wood, mustered, dressed in breastplates, hauberks and helmets, and ordered their ranks.[16] Lisiard himself was in the first rank with his knights, archers and foot. When this relief army appeared on the battlefield, the effect was immediate. One of Henry's main allies, Theobald of Blois, was hit a glancing blow on the forehead by an arrow. The blood flowed into his eye so that he was unable to see. In conjunction with the surprise attack, Fulk himself emerged from The Park. The Angevin lances threw enemy warriors from their saddles. The Anglo-Norman army fled. The chronicle says that Henry lost many knights, archers and foot soldiers whereas the Count of Anjou lost only four archers and 25 infantry.

Tactically Alençon is a fascinating battle. Even if by accident, the Angevins used two converging armies. The main army fought from within an enclosure. The second army, acting as a reserve, seems to have attacked dismounted. On both sides, archers figured prominently, and Lisiard's bowmen were significant in the climax of the conflict. It is also useful to have evidence from this period of another region beyond England and Normandy which made use of dismounted knights. It should not be assumed that Anglo-Norman tactics developed in isolation from European tactics in general. Although the dismounting of knights became almost a commonplace in the first half of the twelfth century, it was not an entirely novel idea. As early as 891 one hears of Franks dismounting to fight the Battle of the Dyle, Arnulf setting the example: 'I first will dismount from my horse.' It is probable that the Bretons did the same at the second Battle of Conquereux in 992. On a later occasion, at Damascus during the Second Crusade, German knights dismounted. The chronicler William of Tyre, describing this incident, made the interesting observation that this was the custom of the Teutons in a crisis.[17]

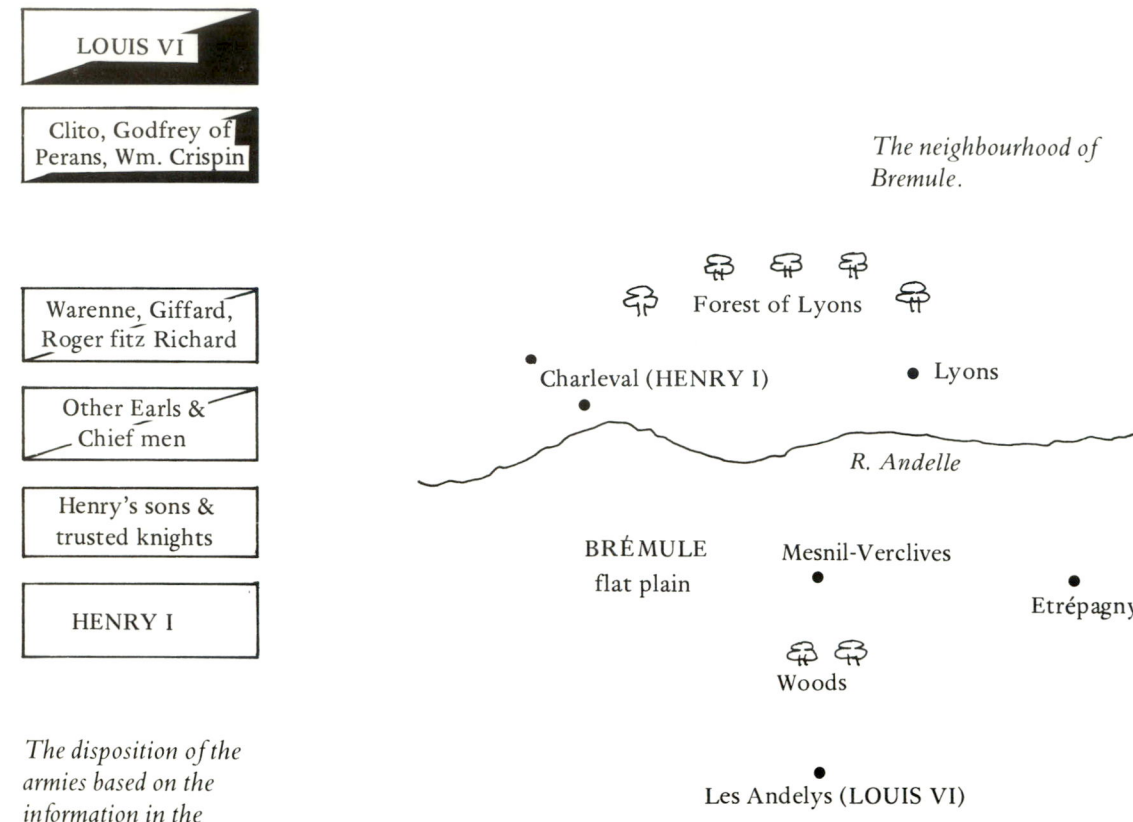

LOUIS VI

Clito, Godfrey of Perans, Wm. Crispin

*The neighbourhood of Bremule.*

Warenne, Giffard, Roger fitz Richard

Other Earls & Chief men

Henry's sons & trusted knights

HENRY I

Forest of Lyons

Charleval (HENRY I)          Lyons

*R. Andelle*

BRÉMULE          Mesnil-Verclives
flat plain                                          Etrépagny

Woods

Les Andelys (LOUIS VI)

*The disposition of the armies based on the information in the Book of Hyde.*

The Battle of Brémule was fought in the year following Alençon, and was part of the same political struggle. It is a battle much better known to students of English history, and the only one in this group of battles in which kings commanded both armies. It arose from the war between Henry I and the King of France, Louis VI. Louis, in alliance with Count Fulk of Anjou, invaded Normandy on behalf of Curthose's son William Clito. The allies aimed to win Noyon. Henry I employed four knights to watch the movements of the enemy. The knights stationed themselves on the hill of Verclives, the only high ground in the area. It is now built on so that houses obscure the view, but it is still possible to find a vantage point such as the four knights had. The plain stretches away below, and the distant line of woods is clearly visible. The knights saw Louis' army emerging from these woods, and reported back to Henry. Both kings were prepared to let battle decide the issue, and faced each other on the plain called Brémule. There is no settlement with this name, and the exact site of the battle is impossible to identify, but there is a broad, flat plain beneath Verclives, ideal for cavalry, on which the fight took place.

It is important first to discuss the sources of evidence for the battle. Most modern accounts of the battle have omitted the version in the *Hyde Chronicle*, though it has been in print for many years.[18] The chronicle seems to have been written by someone close to the Warenne family, which is often mentioned. William de Warenne played a role in the battle, and he figures more largely in the Hyde account than in other chronicles. This source breaks off abruptly in 1121, which may indicate the date of writing. It should probably be treated as an early and therefore an important account.

As is often the case, the main chronicles differ over details, and the Hyde version adds to the problems of interpretation by providing yet further variations, but this is no reason to neglect it. The other main accounts are by Orderic Vitalis, Henry of Huntingdon, and the great French ecclesiastic and administrator, Suger. They agree in their main outline of the battle. There are differences over the precise formation, though it seems clear that Henry I dismounted knights again. The *Hyde Chronicle* suggests there were four divisions in the Anglo-Norman army, rather than three. William de Warenne, Walter Giffard, and Roger Fitz Richard were in the first division; the other earls and chief men of Henry in the second. Henry instructed the third division to stand on foot, this line including his sons and his most trusted knights. He placed himself in the midst of the fourth division in order to strengthen it. Although other accounts vary in describing the divisions, the probability is that this comes simply from making less distinction either between the first two lines, or the last two. The only problem in the accounts which cannot easily be resolved is the role of the king's sons, who in some accounts appear to be among the dismounted men, but in Orderic, Richard at least is clearly stated to be on horseback. In the battle the French attacked, and lost 80 knights in the first charge. Dr Chibnall interprets this, as in other similar battles, to be the effect of Anglo-Norman archery.[19] Not one chronicle mentions archers in the battle, but in his account of Henry's previous campaign, Suger tells us that he made use of archers and crossbowmen in the incident at Malassis.[20] The opening of the battle bears close comparison with Bourgthéroulde, when we know the archers were responsible for unhorsing many knights

[18] The main sources for Brémule are *Liber Monasterii de Hyda*, pp. 316–8; Suger, pp. 196–8; Henry of Huntingdon, pp. 241–2; Orderic Vitalis, vi, pp. 234–42.

[19] Orderic Vitalis, vi, pp. xxi, 238.

[20] Suger, p. 189: 'balistariorum et sagittariorum repulsione'.

in the opening phase, and it is probable that archers played this role at Brémule. The second French attack had more success initially, and broke through the first part of the Anglo-Norman army only to be halted by the division of dismounted men. The rear division became involved in the battle, and Henry I himself was wounded by a blow on the helmet, which forced the metal into his head so that the blood rushed out, but he returned the blow bringing down horse and rider. According to Henry of Huntingdon, an attack by the king's sons won the battle, which makes it particularly galling to be uncertain as to whether this was an infantry or cavalry attack.[21] All in all it seems most likely that cavalry was involved at this point. If so, this makes Brémule a good example of the way archers, dismounted knights, and cavalry could all play an equal role in winning a major victory. The French fled, King Louis getting lost in a wood and being led to safety at Les Andelys by a peasant. The French chronicler Suger blames the defeat on the disorderly nature of the French attack compared to the discipline of the Anglo-Normans. He also tends to confirm the conclusion that cavalry struck the final blow by suggesting that it came from a hidden force, which sounds much like the cavalry reserve that we find in other battles of the period.[22] The battle is also a good example of knightly attitudes to killing each other in the twelfth century. Orderic says that of 900 knights in the battle, only 3 were killed: 'They were all dressed in mail and spared each other on both sides, out of fear of God and brotherhood in arms; they were more concerned to capture than to kill the fugitives. As Christian soldiers they did not thirst for the blood of their brothers, but rejoiced in a just victory given by God, for the good of holy Church and the peace of the faithful.'[23] The pious interpretation of Orderic no doubt overlooks the financial gains to be made, but the remarkably low loss of life in these twelfth century battles, as regards to the knights, should be noted. Henry had won a great victory. To commemorate it, he bought Louis' captured standard for twenty silver marks from the knight who had taken it. Henry went on to a joyful reception at Rouen, to the sound of bells ringing and the singing of hymns of thanksgiving.

The Battle of Bourgthéroulde in 1124 was a much lesser affair: no kings were involved, and only a few hundred troops altogether. Nevertheless it has been described in some detail, and the accounts by Orderic Vitalis and Robert of Torigny make it of considerable interest to our discussion.[24] Waleran of Meulan and other lords had rebelled against Henry I in Normandy. They had raided far north to Vatteville, where Waleran wished to

21 Henry of Huntingdon, pp. 241–2, has a foot attack, which must make 'lanceis' spears, and yet 'lanceis inclinatis' sounds like the lowering of lances: 'acies pedestris in qua filii Henrici inerant . . . lanceis inclinatis ex adverso insurrexit'.
22 Suger, p. 196, says the French charge was 'inordinate'; compare *Liber Monasterii de Hyda*, p. 317: 'sine ordine'. Suger also says that part of Henry's force was 'occulte'.
23 Orderic Vitalis, vi, p. 240: of 900 knights, Orderic had been told that only three were killed.
24 The main sources on Bourgthéroulde are Orderic Vitalis, vi, pp. 348–52; Robert of Torigny in William of Jumièges, pp. 294–5.

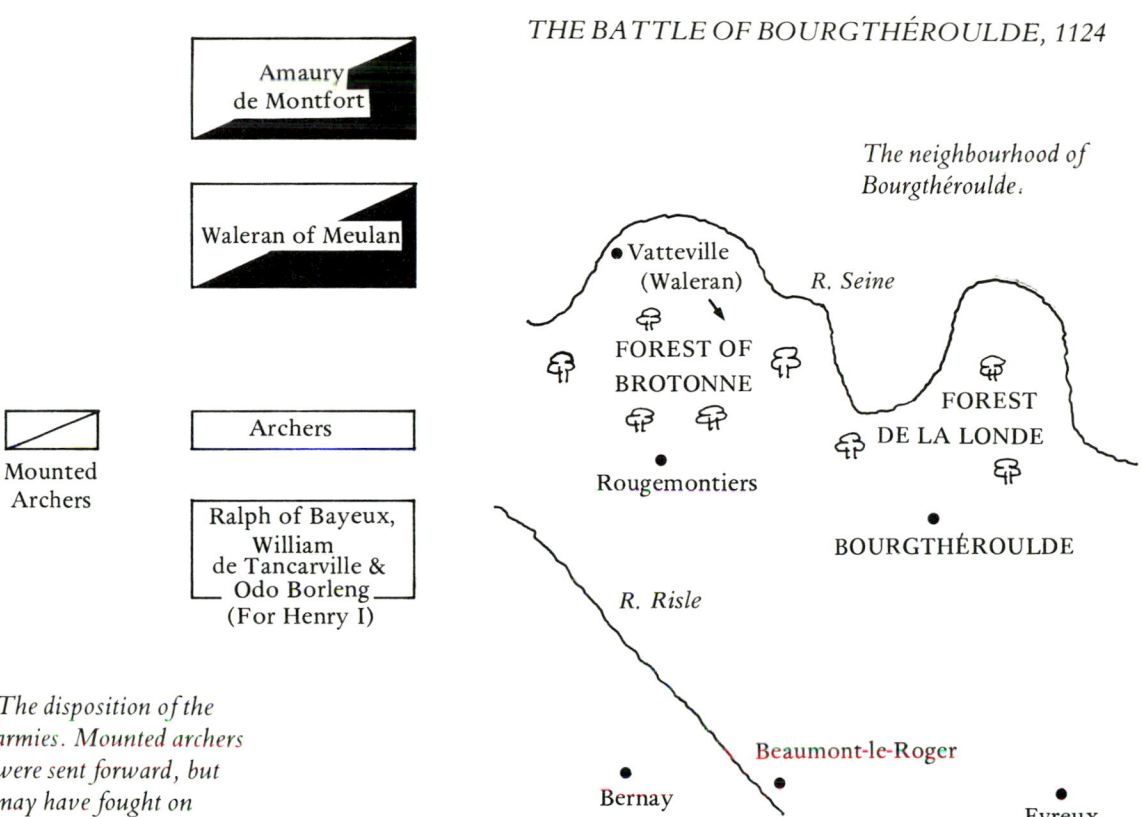

Amaury
de Montfort

Waleran of Meulan

Mounted
Archers

Archers

Ralph of Bayeux,
William
de Tancarville &
Odo Borleng
(For Henry I)

*The disposition of the
armies. Mounted archers
were sent forward, but
may have fought on
foot.*

*The neighbourhood of
Bourgthéroulde.*

• Vatteville
(Waleran)        *R. Seine*

FOREST OF
BROTONNE

FOREST
DE LA LONDE

• Rougemontiers

• BOURGTHÉROULDE

*R. Risle*

Beaumont-le-Roger

• Bernay

• Evreux

provision the garrison. Men loyal to Henry sought to counter this raid. With Waleran in the north, they collected as many men as possible from neighbouring castle garrisons, and blocked the return route of the rebels at Bourgthéroulde. Few in number, the gallant band still made 'a splendid sight as they stood armed with 300 knights'.[25] It is not clear who led the royal force, as the chroniclers credit different knights. Possibly there was no overall leader and the chief men present shared the task. They were Odo Borleng, a captain of Henry I's household troops, William of Tancarville, Henry's chamberlain, and Ralph of Bayeux, the castellan of Evreux. Part of this royal force dismounted, and Orderic gives us a delightful account of the debate necessary to bring this about. Perhaps the authority of Odo Borleng was not sufficient to guarantee the obedience that Henry I himself would have expected. Odo explained to his force: 'the best plan is for one section of our men to dismount for battle and fight on foot, while the rest remain mounted ready for the fray. Let us also place a force of archers in the first line and compel the enemy

[25] Orderic Vitalis, vi, p. 348.

troop to slow down by wounding their horses.'[26] The other knights wanted Odo to set an example by himself dismounting, to which he agreed.

Robert of Torigny says the royal force sent forward a band of mounted archers against the enemy right.[27] It is generally assumed that these men rode to position and dismounted to fight. References to mounted archers in the west in this period are certainly rare. On one occasion, in England, Robert of Gloucester in 1139 made a dangerous cross-country trip escorted by knights and mounted archers.[28] It is at least possible that horse archers were used at Bourgthéroulde.

Whatever kind of archers they were, they had immediate effect in the battle. The rebels, led by the spirited young Waleran, made a cavalry charge. Forty archers shot down the rebel horses, and the charge was halted before it came to grips. Waleran himself was unhorsed. Robert of Torigny says that the archers shot from their side, hitting the enemy where they were not protected by their shields, that is, on their right side.[29] He also says that the archers shot rapidly, without interval. This seems to show that the royal army had placed archers on the flank. The rebels fled. Waleran was captured and imprisoned. William Lovel cut off his hair to disguise himself as a squire, and gave his boots to a ferryman to pay for carriage across the Seine so that he might escape home, albeit bare-footed.

## The Battles of Stephen's Reign

Apart from the skirmish at Bourgthéroulde, there was no major Anglo-Norman battle between Brémule in 1119 and the Standard in 1138. Henry I's victories against his brother and against the French king brought a degree of peace to England and Normandy that would be recognised in the troubled times following his death. Those troubled times were largely caused by the fact that although Henry left countless illegitimate children, he left no male heir. His son William had died at sea, when passengers and crew of the *White Ship* had got drunk, and the ship foundered. Henry's only legitimate successor was his daughter, Matilda. For all the king's efforts to make the barons accept that succession, on his death they preferred the claims of his nephew, Stephen of Blois. Stephen had been at his uncle's court for some years, and had been a regular companion of Henry I on military expeditions. Stephen's character is reminiscent of Robert Curthose's: amiable, courteous, easy-going,

26 Orderic Vitalis, vi, p. 348: 'oportet ut pars nostrum ad pugnam descendat, et pedes dimicare contendat'.
27 William of Jumièges, p. 295: 'et equitibus sagittariis quorum inibi excercitus regius maximam multitudinem habebat in dextra parte hostium, premissis'. Compare Orderic Vitalis, p. 348: 'agmen quoque sagittariorum in prima fronte consistat'.
28 Robert of Torigny, RS, p. 137: 'exinde comes Robertus cum decem militibus et decem equestribus sagittariis'.
29 William of Jumièges, p. 295: 'instantia sagittariorum, qui eam in dextris, ubi carebant protectione clipeorum, absque intervallo sagittabant'.

generous, lacking the more vicious side of Curthose's personality, but lacking also the ruthlessness that had brought Henry I success.[30]

Stephen was not himself present at the first major battle of his reign. He was occupied in the south in 1138 when the Scots made one of their regular incursions over the border. The English chroniclers were united in their condemnation of the barbaric behaviour of the Scots, claiming that they ripped open pregnant women, tossed children on the points of their spears, and butchered priests at their altars. Richard of Hexham says they carried off noble matrons, chaste virgins and other women, whom they herded together naked, fettered and then whipped with thongs.[31]

An English force was raised by the northern prelates under the guidance of Archbishop Thurstan, though the latter was too ill to take part in the battle. He sent priests from his diocese to march with their parishioners, carrying crosses. Ralph, Bishop of the Orkneys, acted as Thurstan's deputy, together with a group of northern barons. This northern army was reinforced by a strong troop of knights under Bernard de Balliol sent by Stephen. The church leaders adopted a practice common in Italy, but not otherwise known in England, and which has given the battle its name. They placed a ship's mast in the centre of a cart, and attached flags of saints to it. On top of the pole was placed a silver pyx containing the host and the banner of St Peter. The standard was to act as a rallying point in the battle.

On the foggy morning of 22 August 1138, the English and Scottish armies met on a broad plain to the east of Northallerton in Yorkshire. Ailred of Rievaulx, a Cistercian monk whose patron Walter Espec was one of the English commanders, and who himself had spent some time at the Scottish court, gives an account of the battle.[33] Ailred says the English force was smaller. Most of the English knights dismounted, keeping the usual cavalry reserve. They sent archers and spearmen to the front. Richard of Hexham says that some of the dismounted knights were mixed with the archers in the front rank.[34]

David, the King of Scots, lacked the decisiveness necessary to a successful commander. Perhaps his authority had been undermined through a recent scandal 'on account of a certain woman'.[35] Unwisely he gave way to a demand by the Galwegians that they should fill their traditional role in the van. They made an aggressive but ill-disciplined attack, which failed, and from which the Scots did not recover. Their ardour had been damped by a hail of English arrows. The chief of the men of Lothian fell,

[30] For example, Stephen allowed the invading Matilda freedom of movement in England; gave money to the invading Henry of Anjou; acted with kindness at the siege of Newbury.

[31] Richard of Hexham, *Chronicle*, RS, p. 159; compare John of Hexham, RS, p. 290; and Henry of Huntingdon, p. 261.

[32] Richard of Hexham, RS, p. 163.

[33] Ailred of Rievaulx, pp. 181–99. Walter Espec is described on p. 183: 'an aged man full of days . . . huge, with black hair, bushy beard, large eyes, and a voice like a trumpet'.

[34] Richard of Hexham, RS, p. 163: 'electissimi mixti cum sagittariis in prima acie'; compare Henry of Huntingdon, p. 263: 'sagittarii equitibus inmixti'.

[35] Richard of Hexham, RS, p. 156; and Richard of Hexham ed. Stevenson, p. 45.

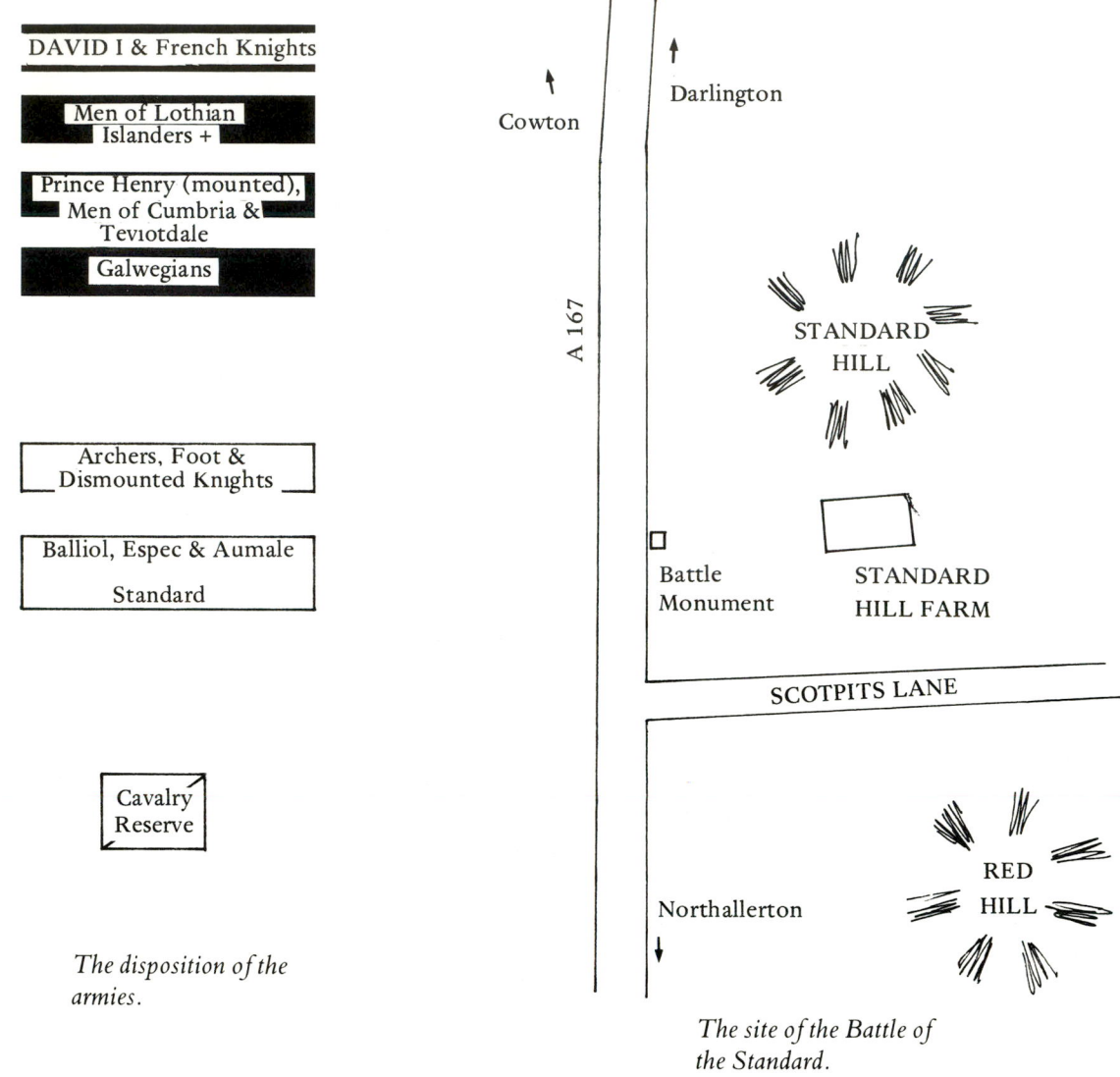

**DAVID I & French Knights**

**Men of Lothian**
**Islanders +**

**Prince Henry (mounted),**
**Men of Cumbria &**
Teviotdale

**Galwegians**

Archers, Foot &
Dismounted Knights

Balliol, Espec & Aumale

Standard

Cavalry
Reserve

*The disposition of the*
*armies.*

Cowton

A 167

Darlington

STANDARD
HILL

Battle
Monument

STANDARD
HILL FARM

SCOTPITS LANE

Northallerton

RED
HILL

*The site of the Battle of*
*the Standard.*

pierced by an arrow. They retreated, according to Ailred: 'like a hedgehog with spines, so were the Galwegians with arrows'.[36] The King of Scots then himself dismounted, and ordered those with him to do the same. They could not halt the flight. The king's son, Henry, led a gallant mounted charge, but it too failed, and the knights retired with wounded horses. The archers and dismounted knights of the English had been so successful

[36] Ailred of Rievaulx, p. 196: 'ut hericium spinis, ita Galwensem sagittis undique circumseptum'.

that their cavalry reserve was never called upon to participate. In this battle, many years before Falkirk or the victories of Edward III, John of Hexham concludes that the Scots were 'destroyed by arrows'.[37] The battle lasted but two hours.

Our set of early twelfth century conflicts is almost complete. There remains only the Battle of Lincoln fought in 1141. Like so many of the fights of this period, it arose from a siege. It ought to have decided the succession dispute between Stephen and Henry I's daughter, the Empress Matilda. Stephen had established himself on the throne by 1139, when Matilda sought to replace him. In the civil war which followed, Matilda made little headway, until the Battle of Lincoln. Ranulf, the Earl of Chester, had turned against Stephen. He entered Lincoln castle, pretending to have come on a social visit. Once inside, with most of the garrison absent visiting the town, Ranulf seized the castle. The citizens of Lincoln appealed to Stephen to regain the castle, so he came to besiege it. Ranulf left to rally a force in its defence, and returned with an army led by Matilda's half brother, a bastard of Henry I, Robert Earl of Gloucester. Stephen would have been wise to heed advice which he was given, to withdraw in order to gather a larger force. Probably he could not forget the reputation of his father, who had abandoned a dangerous situation in the Holy Land, and been branded a coward. Stephen's mother, the Conqueror's redoubtable daughter Adela, had sent the unfortunate Count back to the Holy Land, to redeem himself, and there he had been killed at the Battle of Ramla. Stephen wished to avoid a similar reputation. The anonymous author of the *Gesta Stephani* says that he chose to fight: 'refusing to stain his reputation by the disgrace of flight'.[38]

Stephen chose not to make the battle speech, because, it was said, he lacked a witty tongue.[39] He gave the task to Baldwin FitzGilbert, a scene which is beautifully depicted in the *History of the English* by Henry of Huntingdon. Speeches were made on either side, according to the Huntingdon chronicler, insulting the enemy commanders. For example, Robert of Gloucester was said to have the mouth of a lion but the heart of a hare; Waleran of Meulan was said to be slow to advance but quick to retreat; William of Aumâle's wife was said to have left him because of his intolerable filthiness in behaviour.

Stephen's men tried to stop the enemy earls crossing the Foss Dyke, but failed. The two armies drew up in sight of Lincoln, probably outside the Newland Gate. The earls brought with them knights who had been disinherited through Stephen, and a

[37] John of Hexham, RS, p. 294: 'videntes se confodi et consui sagittis'.
[38] *Gesta Stephani*, p. 112; pp. 110–4 deal with the battle of Lincoln; other sources are Henry of Huntingdon, pp. 268–74; William of Malmesbury, *Historia Novella*, p. 49; Orderic Vitalis, vi, pp. 540–6.
[39] Henry of Huntingdon, p. 271: 'quia rex Stephanus festiva carebat voce'. The illustration is in *BL Arundel MS, 48*, f. 168v. The insults are recounted by Henry of Huntingdon, pp. 269–70, 272.

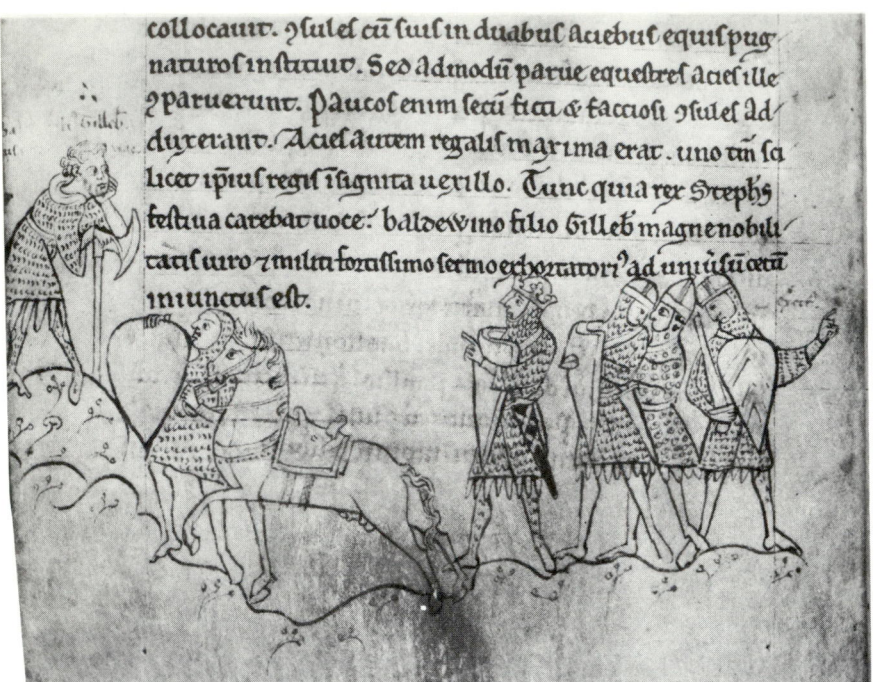

The illustration contains Latin text:

collocauit. 9suleſ cū suiſ in duabuſ aciebuſ equiſ pug
naturoſ inſtituit. Seð admodū parue equeſtreſ acieſ ille
9paruerunt. paucoſ enim secū fieci & faccioſi 9suleſ ad
duxerant. Acieſ autem regaliſ marima erat. uno tñ sa
licet ipiuſ regiſ iſignita uexillo. Tunc quia rex Stephs
feſtiua carebat uoce: baldewino filio Gilleb magne nobili
catiſ uiro 7 militi fortiſſimo sermoe cbortatorʼ ad uniuſ suū ceū
iniuncauſ est.

*This illustration appears on the page of Henry of Huntingdon's chronicle in which the Battle of Lincoln is described. Baldwin FitzGilbert delivers the battle speech from a rise, Stephen listens, crown on head. (British Library, MS Arundel 48 f. 168v).*

force of wild but poorly-armed Welsh, described by Orderic Vitalis as 'barbarians armed with knives'.[40] Some knights on both sides dismounted, including Stephen himself, and Ranulf among the opposing troops. Ranulf was said to have reinforced a brave contingent of foot-soldiers from Cheshire. These latter could have been archers, since Cheshire was to have a great reputation as a source of archers. The first clash destroyed the poorly armed Welsh, but the earls recovered and dealt the decisive blow by breaking the king's cavalry. The flight of William of Ypres, otherwise a valiant and loyal lieutenant to Stephen, suggests the royal army was lacking in numbers. Stephen was left with only infantry forces, surrounded by his enemies. He fought on with his sword till it broke. Then a citizen of Lincoln handed him a battle-axe. Still the king resisted, 'like a lion, grinding his teeth and foaming at the mouth like a boar'.[41] Finally he was hit on the head with a rock, and captured. He spent about a year in prison, but Lincoln was not as fatal for him as Tinchebrai had been for Curthose. Matilda could not establish her position in London or the kingdom. Stephen's wife Matilda and William of Ypres caused the Empress to flee from London, and then again from Winchester. At the latter town, Robert of Gloucester was captured and later exchanged for the king.

[40] Orderic Vitalis, vi, p. 536: Robert of Gloucester raises forces for Lincoln, the Welsh with 'Britonum gladiis'. Compare Henry of Huntingdon, p. 268: the Welsh are 'more daring than trained in arms'.
[41] Robert of Torigny, RS, pp. 140–1: 'rugiens ut leo . . . Stridens dentibus,/ Spumans ore,/ Apri more'.

54

We have examined the main battles for which there is enough material to analyse, and which occurred in the Anglo-Norman lands between 1066 and 1141. Some interesting conclusions emerge. It has been seen that the common method of fighting was to combine dismounted knights with archers, and with cavalry. No one of these three elements should be emphasised at the expense of the others; it was the combination of all three that proved so effective. The use together of dismounted knights and archers should be of especial interest. Is it not in essence exactly the combination that would win so many battles in the Hundred Years' War?

Although archers are not mentioned for all the battles, it is clear that they were prominent in all infantry forces at the time. In the three battles where bowmen are not mentioned, it may still be inferred that they were present. We know that Curthose employed archers on campaign before Tinchebrai. Before Brémule, similarly, we know that Henry I used archers and

*THE BATTLE OF LINCOLN, 2 FEBRUARY 1141*

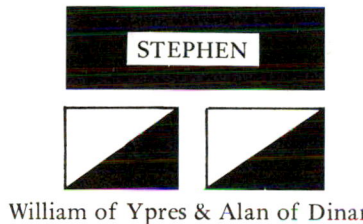

William of Ypres & Alan of Dinan

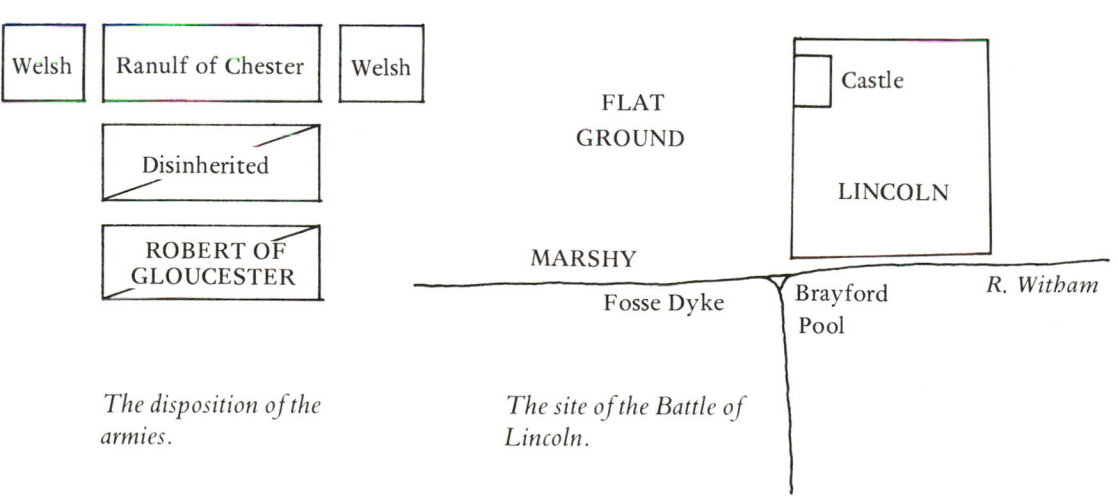

*The disposition of the armies.*

*The site of the Battle of Lincoln.*

55

*Twelfth century illustration showing a concerted charge with knights riding in line abreast.*

crossbowmen in the campaign that led to that battle. As we have suggested, archers probably halted the first French charge. We do not hear of archers at Lincoln, but Stephen commonly used them in his wars, for example, a body of 500 went with Baldwin FitzGilbert to Wales; a large force of archers was used at Plympton; and the important success of Stephen at Faringdon was begun by ringing the castle with archers.[42] It might be noted

[42] For Baldwin's expedition, see *Gesta Stephani*, p. 20: 'uirilis pectoris arcitenentes usque ad quingentos conducens'. For Plympton *Gesta Stephani*, p. 36; 'cum ingenti

56

that when Henry II sought to restore peace after his accession in 1154, one of his actions was to dismiss from the kingdom the mercenaries and archers of foreign nations.[43] In these three battles, therefore, we may presume that archers were present; in the remaining three battles, archers were not only present, but played a significant role. At Alençon they were involved in the successful advance; at Bourgthéroulde they halted the French attack; and at the Standard they virtually decided the whole battle. The likelihood is that archers were present in any infantry force of size at the time, but often overlooked by the chroniclers unless they played a decisive part. At the very least, it is clear that the history of archery in this period should not be over-looked. So much that has been attributed only to a later age may be found in the tactics of this time: archers were used together with dismounted knights; archers were generally placed in the van of the army, and sometimes on the flank.

It might be interesting to speculate on why these tactics appeared in the twelfth century. There is one very reasonable explanation. The great importance of strengthening infantry was that it could then hold a mounted charge. At Hastings, the concerted charge had probably not fully developed. By the time of Tinchebrai, it had. One hears of the effectiveness of such charges during the First Crusade. The author of the *Deeds of the Franks* says: 'all our men together charged the Turks.' Anna Comnena, as has been seen, described this mounted charge as sufficient to pierce the walls of Babylon, especially 'the irresist-ible first shock of the Latin cavalry'.[44] It was this initial charge that had to be countered. Once held, cavalry or other forces could then be used against the scattered enemy. It is not easy to see anything novel in the use of dismounted men-at-arms and archers in the Hundred Years' War. Their role was precisely this: to hold a mounted charge. The tactics of the fourteenth century were certainly adopted anew; there is no clear line of continuity, and they were enormously effective. This does not remove the importance of what has been done by the Anglo-Norman armies in the first half of the twelfth century.[45]

sagittantium cuneo'. For Faringdon, see *Gesta Stephani*, p. 182: 'horrid-issima sagittarum grando'. The same work also has reference to archers on pp. 130, 140, 170.

[43] John of Hexham, RS, p. 331: 'milites con-ductotios et sagittarios exterarum nationum a regno ejici'.

[44] Anna Comnena, pp. 416, 171, 349. Compare the *Gesta Francorum*, p. 19: 'per-tulimus illuc unanimiter gradum'; and pp. 31, 37. Ibn al-Qatansi also writes of the 'charges for which they [the Franks] are famous', see Gabrieli, *Arab Historians*, p. 58.

[45] For a fuller discussion of the general tactics in these Anglo-Norman battles, see Bradbury, 'Battles'.

# Chapter 4

# Robin Hood

No book on medieval archers would be complete without reference to the best known of all medieval archers, Robin Hood. It is, however, not easy to decide where to place a chapter on the outlaw hero. There is still no certain answer to the two most intriguing questions about Robin Hood: when did the real Robin Hood live? was there a real Robin Hood at all? The decision to look at our hero at this point is taken on the grounds that his origins are to be found somewhere in the period between 1200 and 1350. It must be admitted that the ballads about him, on which our knowledge is chiefly based, all belong to the period after 1400. Nor is there any need to apologise for introducing Robin Hood. He symbolises the romance and popularity of medieval archery. In addition, there has been a considerable amount of recent research, both into the Robin Hood ballads, and into documentary records which might provide evidence of a real person behind the legend.[1]

The 'Age' of Robin Hood could take us to any period of time between the twelfth and sixteenth centuries. The bulk of the ballad material was written in the fifteenth and sixteenth centuries. Any attempt to study Robin Hood must begin with this evidence, however unsatisfactory it might seem to the historian. It is probable that a literature and tradition of Robin Hood go back some centuries before the time of the earliest surviving ballads. By the fifteenth century, Robin appears as a folk hero in plays as well as ballads. A letter written by Sir John Paston II to his son in 1473, complains of a servant who has deserted the family after being with them for three years although he had promised to stay for good. He says that the man

[1] A good summary of recent research on the ballads is Dobson and Taylor, *Rymes of Robyn Hood.* A useful collection of historical articles on Robin Hood is in Hilton, *Peasants, Knights and Heretics.* See also Holt, *Robin Hood*; and Bellamy, *Robin Hood.*

had been retained 'to pleye Seynt Jorge and Robynhod and the Shryff off Notyngham, and now when I wolde have good horse he is goon in-to Bernysdale.' Sir John is making light of his loss in suggesting that his own Robin Hood has fled to Barnsdale, the traditional haunt of the outlaw hero.[2]

Whether or not the plays and ballads were based upon the career of an actual outlaw called Robin Hood remains an unanswered question. It is unlikely that there will ever be a positive solution to that problem, and therein lies some of the fascination of the subject. Even the best informed experts have not reached agreement. Those who are in accord over the existence of a real man behind the legend are not agreed upon the period in which he lived, or even upon the century. The most favoured suggestions are the late Angevin period; the time of Henry III; or the reign of Edward II.

## The Social Status of Robin Hood and the Literary Sources

Robin Hood symbolises the significance of the archer in the later Middle Ages, and is a suitable topic to introduce us to this later age. It is a period when infantry forces become increasingly important, more noticed, and more numerous. The Robin Hood ballads demonstrate a new interest in society at large for a social group ignored by earlier literature. The yeoman-archer as well as the knightly warrior becomes a proper subject for romance. To offer a frivolous comparison, one might note the thoughts of Henry of Lancaster in the fourteenth century. He said that he enjoyed the scent of ladies, but preferred kissing their lower class sisters, because they responded more readily.[3] So with archery: social respect grew, albeit grudgingly, because it was earned by the exploits and effectiveness of the archers. The Robin Hood literature is more than a comment upon social change, it is itself a part of the movement of change.

We must first review the main source of our knowledge of the archer-hero. Modern knowledge rests upon the surviving late medieval ballads. The earliest is probably 'Robin Hood and the Monk', which dates from about 1450. The most famous of the ballads, 'A Lyttell Geste of Robyn Hode', survives in five versions, dated from 1500 to 1550, but the original from which these versions come was probably written in about 1400. Two other early works are 'Robin Hood and the Potter', and 'Robin

[2] Davis, *Paston Letters*, i, p. 461, letter no. 275: from John Paston II to John Paston III. A modern English version is in Barber, *The Pastons*, p. 181.
[3] Prestwich, *Three Edwards*, p. 159. Taken from Henry of Lancaster's own treatise, *Livre des Seyntz Medicines*.

Hood and Guy of Gisborne'.[4] Altogether some thirty-eight traditional ballads survive, but the later ones borrow much from the earlier, and move ever further away from any medieval reality. In addition to the early ballads, there are other works which relate to the Robin Hood tales, such as the French pastourelles about Marian and the shepherd Robin. Popular ballads in English only emerged in the late Middle Ages, surviving from the fifteenth century onwards. It has, however, been noted that the earliest Robin Hood ballads use Middle English forms, which are earlier than the fifteenth century. The literature about Robin Hood clearly begins in a period before the surviving works.

This is confirmed by references to literature about Robin Hood made before the literature itself survives. The first is found in one of the best known works from medieval English literature, 'Piers Plowman'.[5] In the B text of this work, Sloth, the unsatisfactory priest, admits:

'I kan noght parfitly my Paternoster as the preest it syngeth,
But I kan rymes of Robyn hood and Randolf Erl of Chestre.'

In other words, Sloth does not know his Lord's Prayer, but he does know the Robin Hood ballads. This text has been dated to 1377, so that the origins of the literature and of Robin Hood himself, must be sought in the years before the death of Edward III. With growing popularity the legend of Robin Hood soon expanded. Both Andrew Wyntoun and Walter Bower testify to the popularity of the tales of Robin Hood and Little John in the fifteenth century.[6] By this time the name of Robin Hood had entered the world of proverbs. It was said, for example, that many men spoke of Robin Hood who had never shot a bow, often with a sexual connotation, as in this 1420 version:

Unkissid is unknowun;
And many men speken of Robyn Hood,
And shotte nevere in his bowe.

Another popular saying is perhaps a little chastening to such as ourselves who find pleasure in the ballads: 'Tales of Robin Hood are good for fools.'[7]

A problem for historians is that the tales are in a genre that encourages little trust in their historical reliability. They are, for a start, later examples of a literature that had flourished for some time, altered and embroidered as such works are bound to be.

[4] Dobson and Taylor provide the best modern edition of these ballads. On the date, see Holt, *Robin Hood*, p. 15.
[5] William Langland ed. Kane and Donaldson, p. 331.
[6] Bower was the continuator of Fordun. He spoke of the story of Robin Hood which the 'foolish populace are so inordinately fond of celebrating both in tragedy and comedy'. See John of Fordun, ed. Hearne, iii, p. 774. Compare with remarks in Andrew de Wyntoun, ed. Amours, pp. 136–7.
[7] For the 'unkissid' verse, see Dobson and Taylor, p. 2; and Heworth, *Jack Upland*, p. 80. For the proverb, see Dobson and Taylor, Appendix III, pp. 288, 291.

The ballad-maker was more concerned with producing a good tale than getting his facts right. When Robin Hood had become a popular subject for ballads, no harm was seen in taking a good story from some other source, and adapting it to fit the current hero. There is no certainty that any of the stories about Robin Hood were original. Parallels for most of the tales can be found in earlier literature. Two strands, in particular, contributed to the Robin Hood ballads: knightly romances and outlaw stories. Some of the favourite Robin Hood characters, as well as the stories in which they appear, were borrowed from earlier works. Maid Marian does not appear in the first Robin Hood ballads. It is thought that the character was borrowed from the French pastourelles in which she was associated with quite a different Robin. We might notice in passing that Marian acquired a reputation, which she seems to have lost again since, for being a loose lady, 'a smurkynge wenche'. Little John, Friar Tuck and the Sheriff of Nottingham are among the characters who probably began life independently of Robin Hood, as subjects of their own ballads and tales. Enterprising ballad-makers incorporated these figures into the Robin Hood corpus.[8]

The best known of the early ballads is the *Lyttell Geste of Robyn Hode*. It is a long work, containing several popular tales. It attempts a more complex structure than the other ballads, giving something like a career to Robin, and fittingly concluding with the story of his death. Close study suggests that it is not in fact a single work, except in the sense that it was compiled by an unknown ballad-maker. It is a skilful working together of several Robin Hood stories, some of which are known independently of the *Geste*. It can be analysed as containing four ballads: Robin Hood and the Knight; Robin Hood, Little John and the Sheriff of Nottingham; Robin Hood and the King; and Robin Hood's Death. It begins with Robin insisting that his men bring a guest for dinner. They return with Sir Richard atte Lee, who proves to be a poverty-stricken knight in debt to the wealthy Abbot of St Mary's. Robin then aids the knight in paying his debt. The second story takes us to an archery contest in Nottingham, and concludes with the killing of the villainous sheriff. This theme is to some extent repeated in the third story, which again involves competition with the bow. The king enters the greenwood in disguise, but is eventually revealed after Robin's unexpected failure with the bow. In the final section, Robin is ill, and goes to Kirklees Priory to be bled. He is betrayed and trapped, but manages to kill the treacherous Sir Roger, before himself expiring.

[8] Dobson and Taylor, p. 42; and Humphrey, King Henry IV Part I, p. 115.

We have to go back to earlier literature in our search for the origins of Robin Hood. Maurice Keen, in his very readable book on 'The Outlaws of Medieval Legend', has assembled the earlier works that have an outlaw theme.[9] His first example is the *Gesta Herewardi*, a tale about Hereward the Wake, written in the twelfth century about the eleventh century hero.[10] Already we meet themes that have become familiar to us from the Robin Hood stories. Hereward makes use of disguise, for example as a potter. He also shows skill with a bow, and kills Earl Warenne.

There are two thirteenth century works upon which the Robin Hood ballad-makers probably drew, both in Anglo-Norman French, about Fulk FitzWarin, and Eustace the Monk.[11] These romances, woven around actual historical figures, deserve careful attention as predecessors of the Robin Hood literature. They might well account for some of the background material and colour that we have come to associate with Robin. In each work King John figures as a villain. In *Fulk FitzWarin* he is said to be hated by all good people, to be lustful, and to have his way with any fair woman he desired. We might note that in the same work Marian de la Bruere appears as a maiden in distress, another possible source for Robin's Maid Marian. Fulk has an argument with John, which results in the latter hitting Fulk over the head with a chessboard. Fulk becomes an outlaw and various forests provide background for his exploits. His band of men are archers, though mainly it seems crossbowmen. Disguise plays an important role in this plot too. Fulk himself puts on the clothes of a monk: 'here is a monk, fat and burly; he has a belly big enough to hold two gallons of cabbage'. Elsewhere he changes clothes with a charcoal burner, in order to lure John to a trap in the forest. There is also a tale about two sergeants who bring a poor knight into the hall for food. The leader of the forces against Fulk is none other than Ranulf or Randulf, the Earl of Chester, and we are reminded of the first reference to Robin in *Piers Plowman*, where Sloth claims to know 'rymes of Robyn hood and Randolf Earl of Chestre'.[13] No independent tales of Ranulf are known, though they might once have existed. Possibly the reference is to Fulk FitzWarin. The role of Ranulf in the Fulk story is similar to that of the sheriff in Robin Hood, and the one may well owe a debt to the other.

It has become an academic game to seek the real men behind the Robin Hood characters: the real sheriff, the real king, and so on. It is not likely to prove a very profitable exercise, since the figures and their roles seem most often to have been taken from other tales and re-moulded. The 'real' figures are far more likely

[9] Keen, *Outlaws*.
[10] This work was included in a compilation by Robert of Swaffham in the thirteenth century. The Latin is printed with Gaimar, RS, ii, pp. 339–404.
[11] Recent editions of these works are for Eustace the Monk, Conlon, *Romans de Wistasse*; and for Fulk FitzWarin, Hathaway, *Fouke le Fitz Waryn*.
[12] Translation in Stevenson, 'Legend of Fulco Fitz-Warin', RS, p. 340.
[13] See Note 5 above.

to have a literary than an historical model, and are most unlikely to have originated from one period of time.

The romance of *Eustace the Monk* is also set in the time of King John. Eustace was a renegade monk, who became a sea captain, serving in turn England and France. He took to an outlaw life, and to piracy. Again themes found in Robin Hood can be detected in this thirteenth century work, including disguises as merchant, charcoal burner, and potter. The story of the Abbot of Jumièges found in *Eustace the Monk* suggests a literary ancestor for Robin's Abbot of St Mary's. Eustace, like Hereward and Fulk FitzWarin, belongs to history, but clearly the stories in which they figure are not all historical. We cannot believe that each of them really went in disguise as a charcoal burner. The fact that these similar works are about real figures adds to the possibility that Robin Hood existed, but the history of the stories suggests that the exploits in which Robin Hood figures were not historical events. They were simply good stories that were used over and over again in medieval literature. The legend embroidered around the name of Robin Hood is mostly formed from the threads of earlier literature. The Robin Hood ballads are romantic fiction. As has been said, it is always summer in the forest.

## The Real Robin Hood

The question remains, was there a real Robin Hood who inspired the ballad-makers to seek out suitable stories to attach to his name? The search for a real Robin has been fascinating, but inconclusive. Some historians are convinced that they have found a solution, but no answer has found universal acceptance. Others indeed believe the search to be a wild goose chase, and that there is no actual Robin Hood to be found, our hero being no more than a creation of literature. So flimsy is the evidence, that such a viewpoint cannot easily be gainsaid.

There may be a clue in the location of the archer-hero. Some of the early ballads seem to contain material that is not common to other works, and within this material are references to places in the relatively narrow geographical region of the West Riding of Yorkshire.[14] 'Robin Hood in Barnsdale stood', was clearly a well-remembered line of the ballads, and often repeated. There is also mention of Doncaster, Kirklees and Gisborne. The reference to 'The Sayles' in the *Geste* is particularly significant, being a

[14] Good recent discussions on the location are in Holt's *Robin Hood*, pp. 83–108; and in Dobson and Taylor, pp. 17–24. References to Robin in Barnsdale are frequent in the early ballads, e.g. stanza 3 of the *Geste*: 'Robyn stode in Bernesdale', Dobson and Taylor, p. 79. Used as a legal maxim, see Bolland, *Manual*, p. 107. On the Sayles, see Dobson and Taylor, p. 22; and in the *Geste*, e.g. stanza 18, Dobson and Taylor, p. 80: 'And walke up to the Saylis'. The 1306 incident was noted by Hunter, *Robin Hood*, pp. 14, 19–20; and see Dobson and Taylor, p. 24, n. 3; and Holt, *Robin Hood*, p. 52. The Sayles robbery was noted by Maddicott, 'Robin Hood Ballads', p. 293. See also Dobson and Taylor, p. 24, n. 3.

63

little known place-name that has been identified as an area on the northern edge of Barnsdale. It has also been shown that Barnsdale was in the Middle Ages a haunt for criminals. Three Scottish ecclesiastics passing through the area in 1306 increased their archer bodyguard from eight to twenty, 'because of Barnsdale'. In 1329 there is also a record of robbery at The Saylles. There are of course place-names in the ballads which do not fit with the West Riding, but the borrowing of other tales and other characters involved also the borrowing of locations. For example, with the sheriff came Nottingham and Sherwood. On the basis of the evidence in the ballads, Robin Hood is more likely to have been in Barnsdale than anywhere else.

Historians attempting to show that there was an actual Robin, have been perplexed by the question of when he lived. This is more difficult to answer than the location problem. The ballads can be taken to point to more than one period in the past. As new generations of ballad-makers embroidered the tales, so material from different periods entered the ballads. It becomes very difficult to identify a period of origin, when only late examples of the process survive.

It is strange that the modern popular concept is of a twelfth century Robin Hood, with John as the villain and Richard the Lionheart as the good king. The earliest ballads give no indication of this period. In fact, being ballads, they are extremely vague over historical background, much vaguer than the earlier prose romances. The ballads are primarily verse tales, with fairly simple plots, intended for recitation or possibly for singing. They do not normally have reference to historical events or to identifiable figures in history. The only time the king is named in the early Robin Hood ballads, he is called *King Edward*.[15] If that is to be trusted, we must rule out the Angevins. And if we abide by our decision to keep to the period before 1377, we are left with a choice between the first three King Edwards, whose reigns span the period from 1272 to 1377. It may be, however, that the ballad reference is not to be trusted. In later ballads the king appears as *King Henry*.[16] There is an obvious explanation of this in that a later ballad-maker up-dated the material to make it topical. Unfortunately that leaves a nagging doubt as to whether such a process had not already occurred, and that 'King Edward' was simply an up-dating of the original.

Some historians have argued that the material in the ballads, their background and tone, is largely late medieval. One of the points made is that the archer Robin must be late in time. Morris wrote: 'No one who has studied the development of military

[15] Dobson and Taylor, p. 104, stanza 353: 'Edwarde, our comly kynge', in the *Geste*; and p. 107, stanza 384; p. 111, stanza 450.

[16] Dobson and Taylor, p. 284, Appendix 1, no. 33: the ballad itself is called 'Robin Hood's Chase; Or a Merry Progress between Robin Hood and King Henry'.

archery could dream of a Robin Hood of the thirteenth century drawing a six foot longbow, a weapon which was only at its beginnings'.[17] One might rather expect archer-heroes in the fourteenth and fifteenth centuries, but it is not a conclusive argument. We shall examine the longbow question in more detail in the next chapter. Suffice it to say now that 'longbows' might well have existed in the thirteenth century, and there seems no reason why a hero of the thirteenth century should not have come to literary popularity in the later centuries. Is it heresy to suggest, especially in a work about archery, that the original Robin might not even have been an archer? The archery themes seem to appear in what is probably borrowed material, for example the sheriff story. In any case, in the early ballads, the bow is never called a longbow. We can only speculate on the length of the bows in the stories. The archery argument carries little weight. The main point to bear in mind is that, even when one finds in the ballads the use of late medieval terms, such as *yeoman*, they might have been introduced by later ballad-makers. They signify little in the search for Robin Hood's period of origin.

The argument of Professor Holt that the ballads contain central material relating to the thirteenth century is more interesting.[18] He suggests that central themes, such as the hatred of sheriffs, the distraint of knighthood, and money-lending abbots, are 'essentially problems of the thirteenth rather than the fourteenth century'. Not everyone has been convinced by his arguments, which are persuasive but not conclusive. In short, the ballads themselves provide no certain foundation for placing Robin Hood in any particular period of time. All that can be said is that the ballads, as we have them, were written down from the fifteenth century onwards; that their form and other evidence argues strongly for at least a fourteenth century origin; and that their content suggests they are based on an earlier tradition and possibly on an earlier hero-original. We are, however, not very much closer to a real Robin Hood.

Another approach to the puzzle has been to comb the historical records. There have been two main lines: to look for situations that would suit Robin; and to search for names that would fit the ballads. The first approach has certainly shown plenty of evidence that medieval outlaws existed, and that they frequented the woods. Robber bands have been found in periods suggested for the original Robin. Matthew Paris, writing in the thirteenth century, has accounts of a band of fifty robbers at St Albans in 1265; and another set of previous supporters of Simon de

[17] Morris, *Welsh Wars*, p. 33; accepted, for example, by Keen, *Outlaws*, p. 142.
[18] See Holt in Hilton, *Peasants, Knights and Heretics*, p. 253.

Montfort pillaging in a wooded valley near Wilton.[19] In the same period, the Bury St Edmunds chronicler describes how men collected in bands in the woods, and seized everything they wanted. This work also mentions their inability to pay off the Abbot, reminding one of Robin's abbot.[20] The unpopularity of sheriffs in the period is shown in songs that have survived:

> Who can tell truly
> How cruel sheriffs are?
> Of their hardness to poor people
> No tale can go too far,

and also how men escaped to the forest to avoid the sheriff: 'I will keep within the woods, in the beautiful shade; there is no deceit there nor any bad law.'[21]

Similar evidence exists for the fourteenth century. A gang under Sir Gilbert of Middleton captured and robbed two cardinals in Northumberland. In 1306 a general order went out to the sheriffs to deal with men 'lurking and dwelling in the woods', and sheriffs certainly remained unpopular. Edward II punished the guilty sheriff, Roger of Elmebrugge. The king 'graciously remitted the penalty of treason and had him hanged'. There is a curious letter, apparently of 1336, from Lionel the King of the Rout of Raveners, leader of a robber band. In the letter he threatened Richard of Snowshill with various punishments unless he paid up protection money. The address given was 'our castle of the North wind in the Green Tower in the first year of our reign'. Brigands seem to have been especially common in the reign of Edward II. In 1332 parliament tried to deal with 'divers persons, in defiance of the law' who had risen in large bands, and exacted ransoms from their victims. Learned articles have taken as their subject the activities of two notorious gangs in the Midlands, the Folvilles and the Coterels. Between them they captured and ransomed a royal judge and killed an exchequer baron. Many of them were nonetheless acquitted in 1333.[22]

By the fifteenth century men were emulating rather than inspiring the Robin Hood tales. Various lawless Robins and Roberts lurked in the forests. A late medieval Star Chamber action was taken against Roger Marshall, who called himself Robin Hood. In Derbyshire, Piers Venables collected a gang, and dressed them in 'his clothing like it hadde be Robyn Hode and his meynee'. In the south, one Richard Stafford took to calling himself Friar Tuck. The Robin Hood ballads may belong to

[19] Matthew Paris, ed. Giles, iii, p. 355.
[20] Chronicle of *Bury St Edmunds*, pp. 34–5.
[21] *EHD*, iii, pp. 917, 919.
[22] Evidence on the fourteenth century. On Middleton, see *Vita Edwardi Secundi*, p. 83; and p. 120 for Elmebrugge. For the 1306 order see *EHD*, iii, p. 522. The letter from Lionel is in *Select Cases*, v, pp. 93–5. On the 1332 parliament, see Keen, *Outlaws*, p. 193. The articles on the Midlands gangs are: Bellamy, 'The Coterel Gang'; and Stones, 'The Folvilles'.
[23] Evidence on the fifteenth century. On Marshall, see Holt, *Robin Hood*, p. 148; and W. K. Boyd, 'Staffordshire Suits', p. 81. For Venables, see Holt, *Robin Hood*, p. 150; and *Rotuli Parl.*, v, 16. For

Stafford, see *Cal. Pat. Rolls*, 1416–22, pp. 84, 141; and 1429–36, p. 10. Both Holt and Dobson and Taylor suggest Stafford could be the original of Friar Tuck, but it seems more probable that he, like the various Robin Hoods, was using a name made popular by literature.

24 For example, Harris, *Truth about Robin Hood*.

25 Translation in John Major, ed. Constable. The Latin is in John Major, *Historia Majoris Britanniae*: 'Circa haec tempora, ut auguror, Robertus Hudus Anglus et Parvus Joannes, latrones famatissimi, in nemoribus latuerunt. Rebus hujus Roberti gestis tota Britannia in cantibus, utitur'.

26 On *Sloane MS*, see Dobson and Taylor, Appendix II, pp. 286–7. Although this is the earliest surviving prose life of Robin Hood, and used by Ritson and others, it seems to be based on a paraphrase of the *Geste*, and material from John Major.

27 Dobson and Taylor, pp. 187–190, no. 14: which prints extracts of Martin Parker, *The True Tale of Robin Hood*, 1632. Parker writes of 'Robert Earle of Huntingdon vulgarly called Robin Hood, who lived and died in AD 1198'.

28 For Bower, see n. 6.

romantic fiction, but they are based upon a real world of forest outlaws, robber bands, ransomed captives, hostility to sheriffs and corrupt authority in general.[23]

The other line of approach has been to look in the records for the originals of the outlaw heroes, and especially for Robin Hood himself.[24] Let us examine the fruits of this labour. Those who have sought in the Angevin period have found nothing. The reign of Richard I still triumphs in the presentation of a fictional Robin, in the films and television of our own age, but it is not favoured by modern historians. Perhaps they dismiss it too readily. The Robin Hoods found in later records have not been found in the twelfth century, but perhaps only because of the lack of records concerning the lower sections of society. It is a period that deserves to be considered. We have seen that there are some parallels with the stories about Eustace the Monk and Fulk FitzWarin, which are firmly set in the Angevin period. The Scottish chronicler, John Major, writing in 1521, favoured the Angevin age. He said that at about this time 'flourished those most famous robbers Robert Hood an Englishman, and Little John, who lay in wait in the woods, but spoiled of their goods those only that were wealthy.'[25]

Why Major believed this to be the correct period is difficult to say. None of the ballads refer to this time, and no archive materials give support. It is true there was a Tudor tradition that Robin was really noble, and a claimant to the Earldom of Huntingdon. That earldom only flourished from 1160 to 1247, having at one time belonged to the Scottish royal family. Perhaps this tradition led Major to his conclusion. The Sloane Manuscript, based on the same sort of late tradition, mentions that Robin was born in the reign of Henry II, and outlawed for debt, a fact which the manuscript claims was in the Exchequer Rolls.[26] Such a reference has never been found. An even later work, by Martin Parker, repeats what is said to be the epitaph to Robin Hood, giving his death in 1198.[27] So far as one can see, the evidence for an Angevin Robin Hood derives from Tudor traditions, but where evidence is so slight, traditions should not be ignored.

A late medieval Scottish writer, Walter Bower, whose work is about a century earlier than John Major's, placed Robin Hood in the mid-thirteenth century. According to Bower: 'the famous murderer Robin Hood rose to prominence among those who had been disinherited and banished on account of the revolt.'[28] In other words, Bower makes him a supporter of Simon de Montfort, outlawed after that hero's defeat. Several modern commentators have favoured this period. Bower is the earliest historian to attach a date to Robin Hood, so one might see this as the oldest tradition. Gutch, who edited the ballads, believed this was the age of Robin, and we have already mentioned Professor Holt's arguments for the thirteenth century. Another early chronicler to favour the thirteenth century was Andrew Wyntoun, who placed Robin and Little John in Inglewood and Barnsdale, apparently under 1283.[29] In this mid-thirteenth century period we also begin to find real Robin Hoods in administrative records. The earliest suitable candidate is Robert Hood, listed as 'fugitivus' on the Pipe Rolls in the period 1227 to 1231.[30] If he were the real Robin, he would be too late for an Angevin, and too early to be a Montfortian.

Currently the most commonly accepted period for a real Robin Hood is the fourteenth century, and especially the reign of Edward II. There are more Robin Hoods to be found in the administrative records, but the multiplication of finds of the name does not make any one of the possessors more likely to be our man. Few can be shown to be outside the law. The increased use of the name might only reflect the popularity of the ballads, and argue for an earlier origin. Nevertheless, the researches of Hunter, Walker, Harris and others have focussed on the reign of Edward II.[31] The earliest ballad name given to the king is Edward, which could rule out the claims of both an Angevin and a Montfortian Robin. Enough circumstantial evidence has been unearthed to allow the construction of a career for Robin.[32] A Robin Hood has been found in the documents as a tenant on the manor of Wakefield in Yorkshire. A Robin Hood has been discovered among the household retainers of Edward II. Other personal names have been noted in the Wakefield records that seem to match those of the merry men. The identification is, however, less convincing on closer inspection. The coincidences with the names have been stretched. There is no evidence to suggest that the two Robin Hoods were other than two separate men. The retainer Robin seems to have retired because of old age. There is no evidence that either of these Robins was ever an outlaw. The argument for a fourteenth century Robin Hood is not as strong as its supporters claim, and Holt indeed sees the case presented by Walker as 'a tissue of errors'.[33] At best the case for Robin in Edward II's reign is no stronger than the Angevin or Montfortian claims.

There is one other possibility that has not to date been examined. The case is no more convincing in any final sense than the others, but it has been ignored. Even though it may do no

[29] For Wyntoun, see n. 6. Modern writers favouring the thirteenth century include Gutch, and Holt, for whom, see n. 4.

[30] *PR 14 Henry III*, p. 274: 'de catallis Roberti Hood fugitivi'; and Dobson and Taylor, p. 16. The entry was noticed by L. D. V. Owen in 1936.

[31] Those favouring a fourteenth century date include Hunter, Walker, and Harris.

[32] The evidence on separate Robin Hoods under Edward II is discussed in Holt, *Robin Hood*, p. 193, n. 17, and n. 23. In the same work on p. 49, Holt suggests that the Wakefield tenant probably died in about 1317; and on p. 193, that the servant was already working for Edward II before the king went to Nottingham, on the basis of evidence in *PRO E.101/379/6*; i.e. that the career for Robin Hood constructed by the above writers is not confirmed by the evidence.

[33] Holt, *Robin Hood*, p. 48.

[34] Langtoft, RS, compares Robert Bruce to Fulk FitzWarin. A literary link from Fulk to Robert Bruce to Robin Hood is not impossible. Langtoft, i, p. 372 compares Robert to Fulk who fed on grass 'en la forest'; and p. 378: 'King Robin still

in moors and marshes/ Wanders in his turbulence'.

35 Barrow, *Robert Bruce*, p. 201: Edward I on the capture of Wallace: 'As the cloak has been made well, make the hood also'. Compare Nicholson, *Edward III*, p. 23, where the Scots insult the English as 'painted hoods, witless'. See also *Cal. Docs. Scotland*, ii, no. 1465. In *Political Songs*, p. 216, the Bruce is called the 'kyng of somere', and 'King Hobbe', and wanders the moors.

36 Walter of Guisborough, p. 259: 'that he should be buried in our house at Gysseburne next to his father'; 'in that year was founded our house of Gysseburne by Robert de Bruys'. Barrow, *Robert Bruce*, p. 29: calls the first Robert Bruce 'essentially a Yorkshireman'.

37 Dobson and Taylor, p. 111, stanza 440: 'I made a chapell in Bernysdale.'

38 Wyntoun, ed. Laing, p. 467: 'Come to Roxburch, qwhen it wes myrk/ And wyth his menyhe thare gert he wyrk/ Wyth help off Hwde, that his men all,/ Wyth leddris clame wp oure the wall'. Compare Barrow, *Robert Bruce*, p. 277; and *Vita Edwardi Secundi*, p. 48, when the Bruce took Roxburgh with ladders. It is possible that Wyntoun

more than confuse the picture even further, let us consider the case for no less a candidate than Robert the Bruce. He is an odd candidate, certainly, and rather distant from our yeoman archer. Barbour's work on Bruce, dating from about 1375, was probably based on some earlier literature. The case, such as it is, depends on the chronicle of Langtoft.[34] Here we meet 'King Robin' lurking wild in the forest. The Bruce was of course in exile for part of his career, and romantic versions of his story are close to the outlaw fiction we have already met.[35] There is also a link between Bruce and England. Apart from the old claims of the Scottish kings to Huntingdon, which Robin Hood inherited according to Tudor tradition, and in which the Bruces had estates, the Bruces had a connection with Yorkshire. Guy of Gisborne is one of the characters in the early ballads, and Gisborne was an alternative name for Guisborough. Guisborough Priory was founded by an earlier Robert Bruce in 1130 and at least two of the Bruces were buried there.[36] The archer-hero of the ballads is said, rather oddly, to have 'made a chapell in Bernysdale of Mary Magdalene',[37] not the action one would have expected of the yeoman outlaw. One could but suggest that a lost work about Robert Bruce as an outlaw hero contributed to the fund of popular stories from which the Robin Hood ballads borrowed. In this case the original Robin Hood could have been no less than King Robin, that is, Robert Bruce. These fragments do not make more than a curiosity, and are not to be built into any substantial argument. Perhaps they will suffice at least to suggest that there are still many mysteries surrounding the way in which the Robin Hood legend has grown.

For all the efforts that have been put into finding him, the real Robin Hood has preserved his anonymity. The only action which might be attributed to a real Robin Hood in the chronicles, is the mention under 1347 by Andrew Wyntoun that Hood took Roxburgh Castle.[38] This fact seems to have been ignored, perhaps because it does not fit with any of the popular theories, though Keen at one point seemed to favour the reign of Edward III for Robin. In any case the Roxburgh description in Wyntoun could well have been confused with Robert Bruce's earlier capture of the same town, also using ladders. If this is not Bruce, the 1347 'Hwde' remains a candidate for the historical Robin Hood. Yet another Robin Hood was imprisoned for a forest offence in Northamptonshire in 1354.[39] Edward III might seem a more suitable candidate for the hero-king of the ballads than Edward II, hardly a hero-figure by any reckoning, but it is not our intention to construct another fictionalised career for Robin based on isolated pieces of evidence. All that we can show is that it is possible to build some sort of case for placing Robin in several different periods of time, none of them entirely convincing. and none of them conclusive. At present Robin Hood must remain a figure of legend and literature rather than of history, but no doubt the search for a real Robin will continue.

has confused the two episodes.
39 Dobson and Taylor, p. 12; and Chambers, *English Literature*, p. 130.

# Chapter 5

# The Advent of the Longbow

## The Origins of the Longbow

[1] *EHD*, iv, p. 69, translates 'arrows from long bows' for Geoffrey le Baker, p. 68: 'sagittarum de arcubus'. The first *OED* reference to longbow is under 1500 AD, but for use in *Paston Letters*, about 1448, see Chapter Eight, n. 22. Even in Ascham, *Toxophilus*, the word longbow is never used, though one does find 'long bow' and 'longbow' in Smythe, *Discourses* in 1590. The word 'longbow' is used in the eighteenth and nineteenth centuries for example, in Barrington, 'Observations'; and Roberts, *English Bowman*; but only to mean the ordinary wooden bow such as was used at Hastings. Thus Smythe, p. 2: 'our peculiar and

Everyone associates the longbow with the Hundred Years' War. But how long had that weapon been in existence when the war began in the 1330s? It is as difficult a problem as those we met in the previous chapter, and cannot be answered with much more certainty. Before the question can be pursued, we must define the weapon under consideration. What was a longbow? It may be surprising to find that the answer is not as obvious as one might have supposed. For a start, the word 'longbow' was never used in the age with which we always link the weapon. Nor was there any special word in Latin or in French until the very end of the middle ages. Even then it was only called 'longbow' to distinguish it from the crossbow or the shortbow proper. It is a very modern concept to use 'longbow' as something distinct from the shorter ordinary wooden bow.[1] So far we have ducked the question of what is the real difference between the longbow, and what we have continued to call the 'ordinary wooden bow'. A good deal of confusion has come from the failure to recognise that in all fundamentals the longbow is the same thing as the ordinary wooden bow. It is made from a single wooden stave, often though not always of yew. The stave is rounded rather than flat, with the central part shaped in a 'D' section, tapering towards the extremities. The elastic sapwood is used on the outer side of the stave, the resilient heartwood facing the archer. Thus the stave is given a natural spring which provides the tension

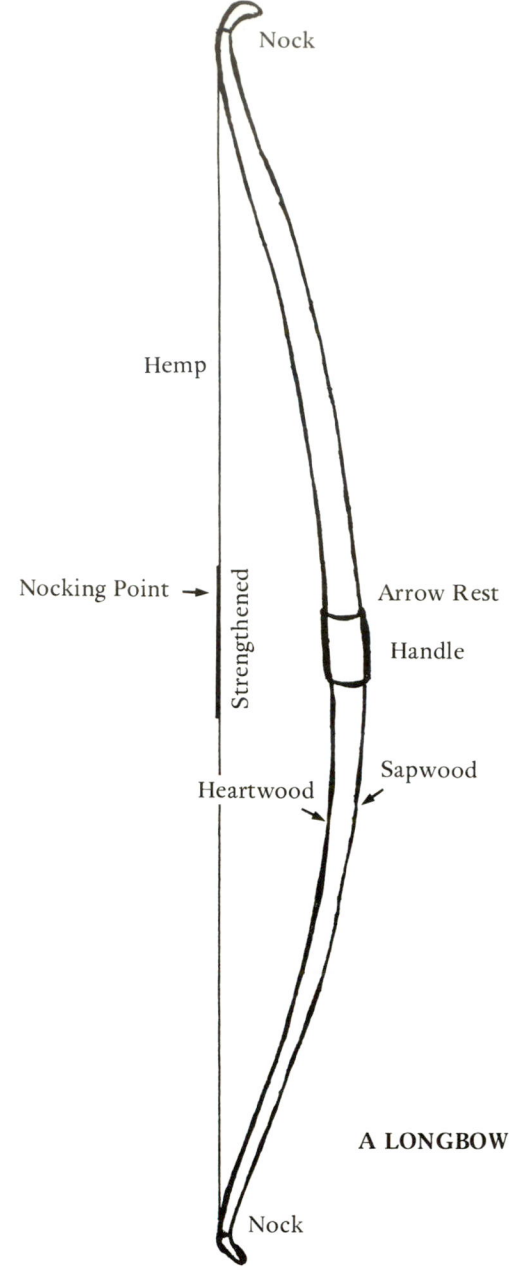

Nock

Hemp

Nocking Point →

Strengthened

Arrow Rest

Handle

Heartwood

Sapwood

**A LONGBOW**

Nock

necessary to propel the arrow. The centre of the stave has a grip for the left hand, while the right hand draws the string. The string was normally gut, looped over each end of the stave. Horn pieces, or nocks, were usually added to the ends of the stave, to hold the string in place.

Some bow-staves and fragments of staves survive from the Middle Ages, mainly from the last century of the period. In recent times we have been overwhelmed by the finds in the Tudor warship *Mary Rose*, which contained a large number of nearly perfect bows and arrows. The *Mary Rose* bows seem to differ little if at all from the bows used in the Hundred Years' War, and we now have a fairly clear idea of the late longbow. Unfortunately, for the early part of the war, and for the period immediately before it, there are no clearly identified surviving staves. Nor are manuscript illustrations much more useful for this period. It is only in the fifteenth century that an art style developed which presents us with fairly accurate representations in size and proportion. Earlier drawings give an impression, but cannot be entirely relied upon as regards to length.

72

Some historians have tried to define the longbow not by its length, but by the way it is used: by the stance or the draw. They would argue that it becomes a longbow when the archer takes a sideways stance, and when he draws the string to his ear. These features may certainly be seen as consequences of the length of the bow, and may give an indication of the kind of bow, but they can hardly be used as definitions. A single bow might be used in two different ways, yet it would remain the same bow for all that. In short, is there a way to distinguish between the longbow and the shorter ordinary bow which is sometimes incorrectly called the 'shortbow'? J. E. Morris obviously saw some clear difference. He believed that the longbow was a new weapon discovered in Wales by Edward I and then introduced to English warfare. He declared that the Edward I longbow could be 'improved up to the standard of Crécy and Poitiers', whereas the 'short bow, drawn to the chest, does not admit of improvement'.[2] And yet, if one tries to discover what is the vital difference, one is left puzzled. The two bows are each made of a single stave, both strung in the same way, both made of the same kind of wood. There is no need to use the bows in a different manner. There is nothing to prevent one drawing the shorter bow to the ear. Even the shortbow proper could be used in this way. A late Roman source explains:

'The bow is drawn sometimes to the ear, sometimes to the neck, and sometimes to the breast. . . The first of these is the strongest shot'.[3]

In fact, there is only one difference between the longbow and the shorter ordinary bow: its length. Where then does one draw the dividing line? What is the magic measurement, above which an ordinary wooden bow becomes a longbow, and below which it is the 'short bow' which can never improve? The problem is brought into focus if one applies the question of length to medieval manuscript illustration. How long are the bows on the Bayeux Tapestry, or on the Luttrell Psalter? The art styles concerned do not aim at accurate representation. At best we can make an approximation by relating the weapon to the man. And that is the point. An average longbow might be from about 5' 8" upwards, but there is no perfect length. The bow is perfect only in relation to the archer. The span between the left hand grip on the bow and the right hand pull on the drawn string varies from man to man. One man's 'longbow' is another man's 'short bow'. The greater the length of the stave, the greater the force of the

singular weapon the Long Bowe'; Roberts, p. 13: 'the English Long-bow', used by Richard I, 'in contra-distinction to the bows used by most of the Eastern Nations'; Barrington, p. 46: 'the Normans are represented as drawing the *long* bow'. The modern usage of 'longbow' as opposed to a shorter ordinary wooden bow belongs to the late nineteenth century.
[2] Morris, *Welsh Wars*, p. 100.
[3] McLeod, 'Ancient Treatise', p. 10: suggests from the second century AD.

bow, but if the bow goes beyond the capability of the archer it will lose efficiency. If what is a 'longbow' in one man's hands, can become a 'short bow' simply because it is held by a larger man, where is the vital distinction? Clearly there is none. The ordinary wooden bow is nothing less than the embryo longbow.

We have already agreed that the impression from manuscript illustrations, unreliable as it may be, is that wooden bows are rather shorter in the eleventh century than they became in the fifteenth. We shall maintain that the ordinary wooden bow probably increased gradually in average size throughout the medieval period. Perhaps constant practice built muscle able to cope better with a bigger weapon. The physical deformation of some of the bodies on the *Mary Rose* might support this. Even so, bow-staves of full longbow length are not new in the

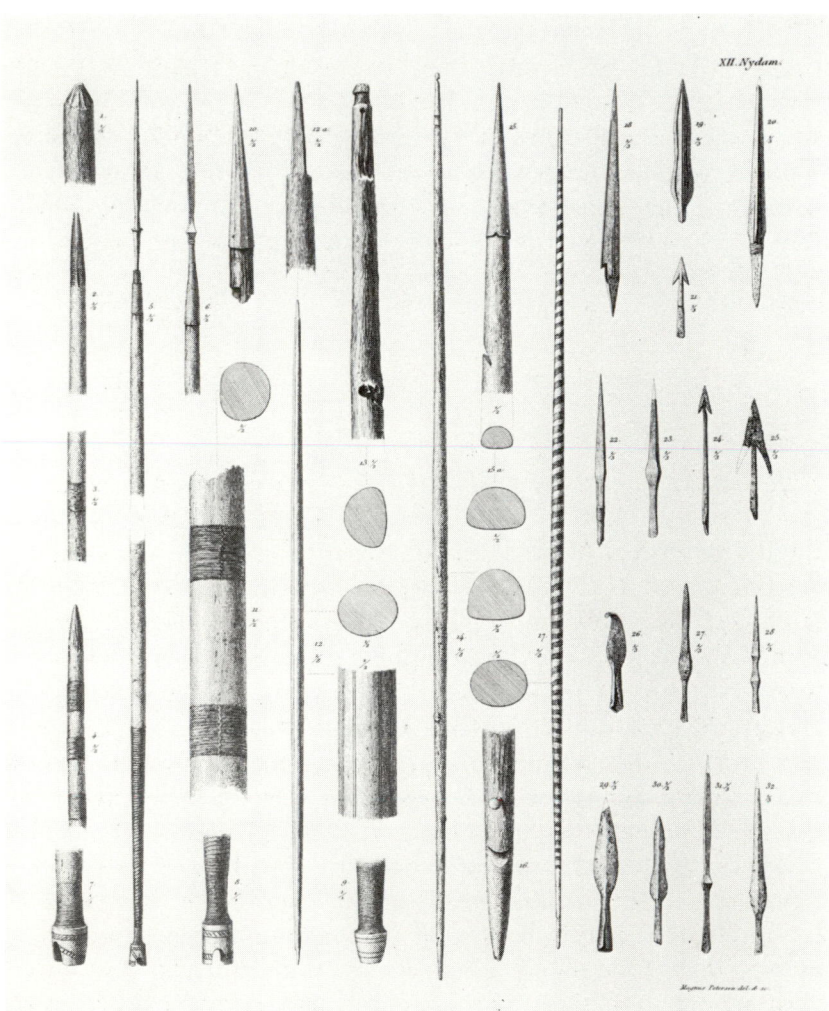

*Bows from the Nydam excavation dating from the late Roman period. Many are made of yew and are of longbow length.*

fourteenth century. Longer bows were used by at least some archers in earlier periods. The thirty six bow-staves from the Nydam excavation date back to the late Roman period. They measured from 5' 7" to 6', and many of them were made of yew. Bows from Lupfen in the eighth century, and Ireland in the tenth were of longbow length, as was the bow-stave on display in the Viking Exhibition at the British Museum.[4] Overall it is impossible to be dogmatic about the length of longbows in the twelfth and thirteenth centuries, since there is no clear evidence to support any conclusion. A reasonable suggestion might be that in those centuries bows were used which did not differ fundamentally from longbows of the fourteenth and fifteenth centuries, but that average length probably increased slightly. It is unlikely that military bows would have been very much smaller, since their force depended upon their length, and they would need to be effective. That bows were effective in battle, from Hastings on, we have already seen. Let us stand by our previous estimate: that longbows in the eleventh century might have been about 5' in length, gradually increasing to become about 6' by the fifteenth century. In the century before the Hundred Years' War, it is unlikely that bows were notably different from those used in the war. There is no need to seek for the invention of a new weapon, and there is certainly no evidence that a new weapon was developed.

## Evidence of English Archery before the Hundred Years' War

There are other aspects of the history of the longbow before the Hundred Years' War that need to be examined. Important conclusions have been reached about the role of Edward I as the 'father of the longbow', and the Welsh as 'inventors' of the weapon.[5] The relevant contemporary evidence needs careful examination to see if these claims are justified. The most obvious source for such information would be the narrative chronicles, but they are almost silent on the later twelfth and thirteenth centuries. The twelfth century evidence of Gerald of Wales, which we considered earlier, is important but should not be exaggerated.[6] It shows us that the South Welsh were skilled archers, but does not prove that the English were not. In fact, he shows a lordly Anglo-Norman family in Wales much concerned with bows. After this, there is something near to silence. Some

[4] Hardy, *Longbow*, pp. 29–30. See Ch. 1, n. 26. The bow in the Viking Exhibition at the BM in 1980 was exhibit no. 115, from Hedeby.

[5] For example, Hardy, *Longbow*, p. 41: Edward I 'the father of the military longbow'; compare Oman, *Art of War*, 1953, p. 119: 'To Edward I the longbow owes its original rise into favour'. On the Welsh, for example, Warner, *Battlefields: South*, p.836: 'the Welsh, who were the inventors of the longbow'.

[6] See above, chapter one. In Gruffydd ap Cynan, p. 132, and see p. 172, n. 5, the Welsh leader has 'foreign' soldiers, probably archers, who have their right thumbs broken after capture.

historians have taken this to show that the bow disappeared as a weapon of importance, which is almost certainly a false conclusion. It has also resulted in giving Edward I a role in the history of archery which he probably does not deserve.

It is a curious fact that thirteenth century chroniclers, with rare exceptions, do not mention archery in battles. The omission takes on a different significance, when one realises that they rarely mention any kind of weapon. No less than their earlier counterparts, these writers scorn the role of lower ranks in war. It was not a lack of interest in warfare that explains the omissions, but a decline in the attention they give to weaponry and tactics. Perhaps the growing criticism of unjust war by the church had some effect on clerics who composed chronicles. Certainly one seems to find more concern with diplomacy and peace-making, which might be presented as more suitable interests for clergy in the new climate of opinion.

Not that archery is altogether missing from the chronicles of the twelfth and thirteenth centuries. In the Angevin period, there are frequent references to the bow in ordinary daily use. Killings with the bow are common enough to make one realise that it was a weapon in everyday use. In 1163, for example, the Abbot of Lagny was shot by an arrow in the eye. In 1209 a woman was shot by accident by men practising with the bow.[7] There is evidence for the bow in war. Archers took part in the invasion of Ireland: seemingly, on occasion, in formation with dismounted men, and once with some mounted archers. As usual, it is difficult to know when ordinary bows rather than crossbows were used; but, for example, when Jordan Fantosme described action with archers and crossbowmen, it is clear that both were still to be found. In the Barons' Wars of Henry III, one hears of archers active in the Weald of Sussex. It is difficult to put much trust in a sixteenth century source about the Battle of Lewes in 1264 which says that the Londoners were forced back by 'the sharpe shot of arowes', but the earlier *Melrose Chronicle* also mentions that crossbowmen were present.[8]

One does gain an impression that crossbows came into more common use in the thirteenth century. But it is a conclusion that depends partly upon the fact that there are special words for crossbow and none for the ordinary bow. Nevertheless it is true that armies often contained specialist stipendiary forces, and these were more likely to be crossbowmen. In Poitou arbalesters 'bent their bows' in 1242 in a crisis in which Henry III was invited to intervene; and three years later in Wales one of the king's archers who died is named as Raymond the Gascon, 'of whom the king

[7] For the Abbot of Lagny, see Robert of Torigny, ed. Stevenson, p. 759. For the 1209 incident at Oxford, see Tucker, 'Archives', p. 192.

[8] The bow in war. For Ireland, see Gerald of Wales, RS, v, p. 230: 'sagittariis quoque pedestribus quasi trecentis', which suggests there may also have been mounted archers; and see Morris, *Welsh Wars*, p. 18. On the siege of Wark, see Jordan Fantosme, p. 89: 'archiers' and 'arbelastiers'. For the Weald, see Roger of Wendover, ii, p. 176: 1000 archers were collected against Louis of France: 'congregatis ad mille sagittariis'. For Lewes, the later source is John Rastell, p. 186; the earlier source is the *Chronicle of Melrose*, translation in Stevenson, p. 217; from the original: 'inter quos erant multi balistarii et fundibularii', see *Chronicle of Melrose*, Bannatyne, p. 194; see also Langtoft, ed. Hearne, i, p. 217, n. 1.

*A thirteenth century crossbowman from Matthew Paris's Chronica Minora.*

often used to make fun'.[9] It is generally thought that crossbows were not commonly used by English kings, yet William the Breton writing in the early thirteenth century claimed that Richard the Lionheart brought the crossbow into France. The crossbowman who killed Richard is given the bolt by one of the Fates, and she says:

> 'This is how I want Richard to die, for it was he who first introduced the crossbow into France.'[10]

It is difficult to see how this claim could be true, but perhaps it at least reflects the degree to which crossbowmen were associated with the Angevin king. Throughout the twelfth and thirteenth centuries, English kings employed trained bands of crossbowmen in their armies. Richard I used crossbows to land in Cyprus, and in the battles and sieges of the Third Crusade in the Holy Land. At Jaffa his crossbowmen were employed in pairs: one to load, and one to shoot. The English chronicle of Bury St Edmunds goes so far as to attribute the crusading defeat of 1250 to the lack of compact formation, and to the crusaders being 'without crossbowmen'. Not long before this, at Damietta, when Reginald d'Argenton fought on till his arms and legs had all been cut off, a force of three hundred crossbows was used. And if Matthew Paris, in his chronicle, rarely mentions bows in battle, he nevertheless has illustrations showing them, and sometimes calculates distances in crossbow shot lengths.[11]

[9] Matthew Paris, RS, for Poitou, iv, p. 178: 'Pictavis arcubalistis protensis'; translation in Matthew Paris ed. Giles, i, p. 394. For Raymond, RS, iv, p. 483: 'quidam Guasco arcubalistarius Reymundus, de quo saepe rex ludere consuevit'.

[10] Gillingham, *Richard the Lionheart*, p. 12; from William the Breton.

[11] Gillingham, *Richard the Lionheart*, pp. 67, 165, 213–4. For 1250 see *Chronicle of Bury St Edmunds*, p. 16: beaten because 'scattered [or few ?] and without crossbowmen'; 'sparsi et sine balistariis'. Matthew Paris, ed. Giles, has reference to Damietta, i, p. 63; 'about a crossbow shot from Hertford', i, p. 360; 'about a crossbow shot wide' between the English and Welsh, ii, p. 110.

Despite the reticence of the chronicles, we need have no doubt about the continued use of bows in war and peace. It is fortunate for the historian, that at the moment when narrative sources show less interest in archery, other records survive in greater numbers and allow an understanding of the bow's continued importance. The wealth of administrative records available defies a brief analysis. We cannot here attempt an all-inclusive survey, but will sample the evidence, to show in how many different ways evidence does in fact exist for archery in the period before the Hundred Years' War.

The Angevin period sees the beginning of the survival of regular records for the financial business of the crown. A single Pipe Roll remains from the reign of Henry I, but with Henry II we have a continuous series. They show the king regularly employing archers. Payments are made to individual archers, or to bodies of them, for example to the garrison of the castle of Roger de Powis; or to the named Ralph de Bure, and Hubert the 'king's archer' in Torfeia. With Isaac *arcuarius*, or Robert *le archier*, it is possible we have surnames rather than a description of occupation, and with Alice *le archier* this would seem to be so.[12] But even the latter was the widow of an archer, and in most cases the description of archer or crossbowman still seems at this time to reflect occupation. From the very frequency of the name, we can be sure that archers were not thin upon the ground.

In the thirteenth century Assize of Arms of Henry III, unlike that for England in the reign of Henry II, specific mention is made of archers. We are shown the social group from which they are drawn. Michael Powicke considered Henry III's Assize to be 'truly revolutionary', because it saw 'the recognition of the bow as the national weapon'.[13] This is perhaps going too far. The continental Assize of Henry II had included archers. The failure to mention archers in the 1181 Assize does not mean that Henry II did not draw on them for his armies. Nevertheless the thirteenth century evidence does confirm the recognition of the value of the bow, and shows us the middling group of society, including forty shilling freeholders, from which the archers come.

Legal records from the thirteenth century give glimpses into everyday life not available in earlier periods, and the bow often features. In 1267 William de Stanegate was walking along a Sussex road with his crossbow slung over his shoulder. He bumped into the widow Desiderata. She asked if he had been ordered to catch lawbreakers, and jested that she would be a match for three such as him. She caught him by the neck with

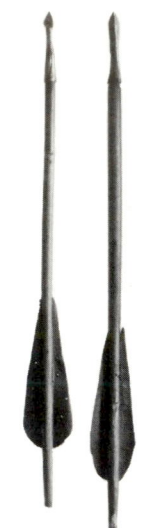

*Crossbow bolts and right, an early sixteenth century quiver made of wood and pigskin.*

[12] The early Pipe Rolls of Henry I and Henry II, ed. Hunter. For Ralph, see 19 Henry II, p. 121; 22 Henry II, p. 62; 23 Henry II, p. 126; 24 Henry II, p. 21; 25 Henry II, p. 3. For Roger, see 19 Henry II, p. 107, 'Et x. Archarii qui fuerunt in castello Rogeri de Powis'. For Hubert, see 22 Henry II, p. 26: 'Huberti sagittarii regis in Torfeia'; and 25 Henry II, p. 73. 'Ysaac arcuarius' is 34 Henry II, p. 96; 'Robertus le archier' 3 Henry III, p. 29. For Alice 'quo fuit uxor Roberti le Archer', see 28 Henry III in *Rotulorum Originalium*, p. 5.
[13] Powicke, *Military Obligation*, p. 88.

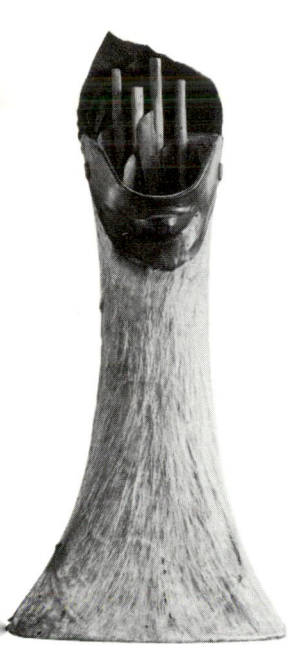

her arm, crooked her leg behind him, and tripped him over. She fell upon him, but landed on the crossbow bolt tucked in his belt, was pierced to the heart, and died on the spot. The verdict was death by misadventure. Only a year after that incident, the *Calendar of Inquisitions Miscellaneous* gives details of another unfortunate affair, this time at a wedding. The guests had become rather drunk, and attacked a group of locals. In the skirmish one man drew his bow, and wounded William Selisaule. The said William had enough strength left to jump at his attacker as he was preparing a second shot. He hit the archer on the arm, causing him to loose prematurely, so that the arrow hit Adam de Auwerne and killed him. The verdict was mischance rather than malice aforethought.[14]

Land tenure records reveal another aspect of the history of the archer. Feudal tenure had once been the province of the knight. Now tenures grew up to use land in order to raise archers. From Mendlesham in Suffolk, John de Cornedbeef (or possibly Cordebof), held 'by serjeanty of staying with his crossbow in the army for forty days at his own cost'. Similarly a virgate in Northamptonshire was held of the king 'by serjeanty of archery'. In the north, William le Areblaster held four carucates 'by crossbow service and doing guard at York Castle in time of war for forty days at his own cost, and if longer at the king's cost, and conducting the king's treasure through the county at the king's cost'. In Shropshire, at Chetelton, Isabel de Broc had to find 'one man to go with the king into North Wales with bow and arrows when necessary'. This last case is not unusual, and it is clear that when the English kings went on Welsh campaigns they used English archers. Another Shropshire reference makes early mention of a crossbow winch, when the archer is obliged to take with him a winch and three bolts, which having been used 'if he has to remain longer, it shall be at the king's cost'. From the far side of England, the Patent Rolls provide an interesting arrangement against expected invasion in East Anglia. Archers and crossbowmen were to be gathered in 1264, it being stressed that no excuse for absence would be acceptable, whether because of the harvest, or because of domestic matters.[15]

By the fourteenth century there are references that make it clear bows were used in large numbers. There are details relating to the storage and transport of bows and arrows. Against the Scots in 1304, for example, London supplied 130 bows and 200 quivers of arrows; Lincolnshire, 286 bows and 1200 arrows; Yorkshire, 320 bows. In the army besieging Berwick there were four men employed full time in making arrows. In 1298, in the

[14] *EHD*, iii: for Desiderata, see p. 827 [from *Cal. Inqu. Misc.*, i, no. 82133]; for Selisaule, see p. 828 [from *Cal. Inqu. Misc.*, i, no. 359].
[15] *Cal. Inqu. Post Mortem*, i, p. 49, no. 196 for John de Cornedbeef; p. 51, no. 205 for Alan; p. 95, no. 351 for William le Areblaster alias Arblastarius de Geveldale; p. 99, no. 365 for Isabel. The winch reference is *Cal. Inqu. Post Mortem*, iii, Edward I, p. 61, no. 87: to find a man with a bow and three arrows, 'cum troculo', 'to be with the king in Wales in time of war'. The East Anglian reference is *Cal. Patent Rolls*, Henry III, 1258–66, p. 360.

*An archer operating a windlass to draw the bowstring; detail from an illustration in Froissart's* Chronicles.

inventory for the weapons in the store at Berwick Castle, we find seven crossbows with winches having old cords; six crossbows for two feet (presumably meaning that two feet were used to load it), one of which lacked a nut; eight crossbows for one foot; 189 wings of geese for feathering bolts. Bolts were listed separately for the three different grades of crossbow, and were presumably of different sizes. The records also give details of garrisons, for example, at Roxburgh Castle in 1297 were 20 crossbowmen and 92 archers.[16] At the same time, the writs of array make clear that specific demands were made to raise archers rather than other infantry. In 1295, for example, 20s. was allowed to Thomas Turbeville to buy arrows, and he was instructed deliberately to find archers. Sometimes mention is made of protective clothing. In 1316, in addition to weapons, each vill had to provide a man with haketon and bacinet. In 1334 mounted archers are required.[17] Taken together all this suggests a rise in the respect and demand for archers, leading to the archer's own steady rise in society.

A very useful piece of information about the bow itself comes from the De Banco Roll of 1298.[18] It concerns an incident in the previous year, when Simon de Skeffington had been killed by a barbed arrow. His brother Geoffrey had then accused one John

[16] Prestwich, *War, Politics and Finance*, for 1304, p. 106; siege of Berwick, p. 106; Roxburgh, p. 74. For the Berwick store see *Source Book of Scottish History*, p. 201; compare also on same page the store of Edinburgh Castle, which included 'a great parcel of packthread for crossbow strings'.

[17] Thomas Turbeville in Prestwich, *War, Politics and Finance*, p. 106 [from *PRO E.101/ 351/9*. The 1315 and 1334 references are in Prestwich, *Three Edwards*, p. 69.

[18] The Latin is in Cottrill, 'Bow and arrow', pp. 54–5. The shot was 'de una sagitta barbata . . . longitudinis arcus unius ulne et dimidie'. Translation by Farnham & Skillington, 'The Skeffingtons', pp. 74–128.

de Tilton of responsibility for the death by harbouring the unknown archer-assailant. The accusation contained a detailed description of both the bow and arrow. It was stated that Simon had been shot:

'with an arrow from a bow, the arrow being barbed with an iron arrow-head 3" long and 2" broad, and the fletch of the said arrow was made of ash three-quarters of an ell long and 1" thick, the said fletch being feathered with peacock feathers, and the bow being of yew and the bowstring of hemp, the length of the bow being one ell and a half and in gross circumference 6" thick, with a length of bowstring of a fathom and a half, and in thickness half an inch, and with that arrow gave him a blow on the left side of the breast, 3" from the said breast, descending 2" and the depth 6", so that he immediately died of the blow.'

The unnamed felon had then fled to the house of John de Tilton. John appeared at the hearing, and declared himself to be a clerk and a member of Holy Church. Apparently this was

*The 1298 'De Banco Roll' which records the Skeffington case over a killing by bow and arrow.*

accepted, and no judgement was recorded. As to the bow, at first sight we seem to have irrefutable evidence of the existence of a longbow. Traditionally a cloth ell would be a yard and a quarter, or 45", thus giving the bow a length of 67½", and the arrow would be almost 34" long. This might well compare with the traditional 'clothyard' shaft of 37". Though there is some dispute over the length of the ell in this passage, the use of the ell in measurement, with its special connection in measuring cloth, is interesting alongside the tradition of the clothyard shaft. In any case we seem to have discovered a longbow in England during the reign of Edward I.

There was still some feeling against hired archers. One wonders if the Assize was intended to associate archery with a respectable layer in society. At any rate, when the Lords Ordainers gained power over Edward II they expelled the king's archers: 'Robert Lewer, archers, and such manner of ribaldry, shall be removed from the king's pay, and not stay in his service, except for war.'[19] The possession of such a dangerous weapon by the common people was certainly feared. It would appear in the hands of the rebels in 1381, but already in the reign of Edward II, one hears of popular riots in Bristol: barricades were raised in the streets, mills were attacked. The rioters threatened the castle by shooting arrows and quarrels.[20] But effectiveness in war assured that whatever the dangers, archery must be maintained. The Luttrell Psalter shows us archers at practice in the age before the Hundred Years' War.

Arrangements had to be made to raise archers and to conduct them to war. In 1324 Thomas le Botiller and William Walsh

[19] *Chronicles of the Reigns of Edward I & II*, i, p. 199: 'Item qe Roberd le Ewer, archers et tieu manere de reibaudaille, soient oustiez des gages le roi', in about 1311.
[20] *EHD*, iii, pp. 869–70, no. 227, on rioting in Bristol in 1313. From *Cal. Patent Rolls*, 1313–7, pp. 68–9.

*Target practice in the fourteenth century* Luttrell Psalter.

from Petworth were commissioned to select 300 foot archers from the Forest of Dean and elsewhere, and see that they reached Portsmouth and so went on to Aquitaine against the French. The men that Thomas Turberville raised were organised in units of twenty under a vintenar. Each man was paid 2d a day, and the vintenar 4d. These were then grouped in units of a hundred under a mounted centenar. Payment for the army at war was normally the task of the Wardrobe. Sometimes the payments were not made promptly, as in 1301, when it resulted in a mutiny by the archers and crossbowmen led by a household knight, Walter de Teye.[21]

The scale of pay could vary, but a general pattern emerges. It is instructive to note that the English archer was normally considered worth more pay than his Welsh counterpart, just as the crossbowman was paid more than the ordinary archer, and the archer more than the ordinary infantryman. The mounted archer was treated on a par with the serjeant. Perhaps pay and inducements were not enough to entice the best men on all occasions. One political song claimed that 'the strongest shall stay at home for ten or twelve shillings, and send forth a wretch that cannot help himself when he needs'. In 1315 John de Botetourt had to complain that his company consisted of 'feeble chaps, not strong enough, not properly dressed, and lacking bows and arrows'.[22]

## The Bow in the Welsh and Scottish Wars

It is clear that the longbow was important in England through the period before the Hundred Years' War, and not only after the Welsh Wars of Edward I. English kings used English archers when they went to war in Wales. English kings had also made use of Welsh infantry long before the Scottish Wars of Edward I. There is no evidence that the Welsh under Edward I, or any king before him, were mainly archers, or that they were especially effective. If they were superior to the English archers, it is odd that they should be paid less. If anything, it is likely that Edward I still gave preference in archery to his Gascon crossbowmen. At Falkirk, always quoted as proof of the importance of the Welsh archers, there is no evidence of any great numbers of Welsh archers, or of any importance at all for them in the battle. According to Gerald of Wales, again always quoted to support the case, only the South Welsh were accomplished archers.

[21] Thomas le Botiller in *EHD*, iii, p. 611, no. 132, from *Cal. Patent Rolls*, 1324–7. Turbeville is in Prestwich, *War, Politics*, p. 69; and 1301, p. 166, from *Cal. Documents of Scotland*, ii, no. 1223; compare *Vita Edwardi Secundi*, pp. 135–6.
[22] For the song, and Botetourt, see Prestwich, *Three Edwards*, pp. 68–9.

Although many thousands of Welsh infantry were raised for the Falkirk campaign, possibly not as many thousands as the round figures given, only 1000 of them came from Glamorgan in South Wales.[23] In Edward's army, apart from his Gascons, were 1000 men from Cheshire and 1000 from Lancashire, both areas renowned for producing archers. According to all accounts of the battle, the Welsh took little part in it — odd support indeed for an argument to make Edward the father of the longbow that was invented by the Welsh! Of course the Welsh possessed archers, and skilled archers, and would make an important contribution to the English battles in the years ahead, but there is no reason to see them as any more accomplished than their English, or indeed their Scottish, counterparts. The longbow does not belong to any one area in particular. Bowmen were to be found in any region that encouraged the use of the bow, especially in wild and forested regions South Wales, the Weald, the Forest of Dean, Selkirk.

In order to make a fair assessment of Edward I's contribution, we must consider the tactics that he used, and the role that was found for archery. Much has been made of the tactics of two minor English victories during the Welsh Wars, at Yrfon Bridge and Maes Moydog. More has been made of these affairs than they deserve, and in any case Edward himself was not present at either. In 1282 John Giffard was the victor at Yrfon Bridge, using we are told 'new and momentous tactics'.[24] The Welsh were positioned on a height guarding the bridge over the Yrfon. A ford was betrayed to the English, which enabled them to cross the river and capture the bridge. English archers and cavalry in combination made a successful assault on the Welsh position. There is little that is new in such a combination. In 1295 it was the Earl of Warwick who defeated the Welsh at Maes Moydog. Warwick's army included archers and crossbowmen, and in a defensive position he 'placed one crossbowman between two cavalrymen'.[25] The Welsh made a frontal attack, but it failed. Here the tactics were interesting, but not novel, and not in a pattern that would be much followed. A more telling parallel for the future would have been of archers acting in groups on their own. Since longbowmen did not feature much, nor Edward at all, in this battle, it is difficult to see how it contributes to the picture of Edward as the innovator of the tactics to be used in the Hundred Years' War.

The use of archery in the Scottish wars has received much attention. To see its real significance we need to look beyond Edward I into the reigns of his son and grandson. We also need

[23] Morris, *Welsh Wars*, p. 96; compare Prestwich, *War and Politics*, p. 95.
[24] Jenks, *Edward Plantagenet*, p. 191.
[25] Trivet, p. 335: Warwick 'assumpta secum electa militia cum balistariis et sagittariis . . . qui fixis in terra lanceis cuspides . . . sed comes inter duos equites posito uno balistario, ac jaculis balistarum magna parte eorum, qui lanceas tenebant, prostratis'; and see Edwards, 'Maes Madog', pp. 1–12; and William of Rishanger, ii, p. 148.

to look not at the archers in isolation, but at the role of the archers in the overall pattern. We must not allow our interest in archers to exaggerate their part. At Dunbar, for example, in 1296, archers were present, but seem to have taken no major part in the victory which was won chiefly by cavalry. If the English had now perfected longbow tactics in the Welsh wars, it is odd to see them failing so soon in a major battle against the Scots at Stirling in 1297. In fact it would probably be true that the Scots had developed tactics that were more revolutionary than anything tried in England or Wales. England was developing a major infantry arm with the archers, but had not yet organised the army to make maximum use of them. The infantry revolution does not begin in England, but rather in Scotland and in Flanders. Here trained infantry forces were used in mass, and the armies were built around them. The Flemish found the change easier to accomplish, in that citizen militia played a large role in their armies and their whole force had a far less aristocratic nature than the armies of the French or the English. The Scots, forced into desperate straits through the English invasion, turned to a leader from the people in William Wallace, and to tactics that were fundamentally based upon infantry. The Scots at Stirling, like the Flemings at Courtrai, showed the worth of the infantry pike. At Stirling the English encountered the Scottish schiltroms, or hollow squares of pikemen. The English army under Warenne, again in the absence of Edward I, crossed the Forth near Stirling. Wallace allowed half the army to cross, and then attacked. The English never recovered. Warenne fled, but Hugh de Cressingham was less fortunate: he was slain, and his skin stripped off from head to heel to make a sword-belt for Wallace.[26]

At Falkirk in the following year the English gained their revenge. The tactics employed by both sides are of considerable interest, and have sometimes been misinterpreted. Wallace took a defensive position, with four great schiltroms of pikes at the heart of his army. Archers were placed on the flanks of the schiltroms, and the position was defended by fixing stakes in the ground, and tying ropes and cords 'to impede the entrance of the English'. As we have pointed out earlier, however many Welsh were taken to Falkirk is of no great moment, for they did not give Edward any aid in the battle. The chronicler William Rishanger warned Edward: 'if you place any faith in the Welsh, you are making a mistake'. Rishanger and Walter of Guisborough agree that the Welsh went over to the Scots, according to Rishanger because of their hatred for the English. Another

[26] *Chronicon de Lanercost*, ed. Stevenson, p. 190: Cressingham 'de cujus corio ab occipite usque ad talum Willelmus Waleis latam corrigiam sumi fecit, ut inde sibi faceret cingulum ensis sui'. Translation in *Chronicle of Lanercost*, ed. Maxwell, p. 164.

writer, Langtoft, sums it up: 'the Welsh gave no assistance in the battle'. Archers did play a part in the battle. English crossbowmen and archers helped to break the schiltroms, but cavalry formed the greater part of the army, and cavalry completed the victory. What proportion of the army the crossbowmen and longbowmen formed is impossible to know, but Edward had called up large numbers of infantry. It is also impossible to see how Edward disposed his archers in this battle.[27]

Geoffrey le Baker's comments on the English defeat at Bannockburn in the next reign (1314) do allow a retrospective glimpse of Edward I's tactics. Geoffrey criticises Edward II's disposition of his army, and suggests what would have normally been done. Bannockburn is generally seen as the key battle in the Scottish War of Independence. After a single combat and some skirmishing on the first day, the battle was engaged in earnest on 24th June. The Scots had taken a defensive position, with marshy ground in front of them. According to Geoffrey, the English had cavalry in the first division, foot and archers in the second. His words are worth quoting: 'the phalanx of archers did not have its usual apt position, but was stationed to the rear of the armed men, not on the flank as was usual'.[28] The Earl of Gloucester made a gallant but hopeless charge against the schiltroms. The English never recovered, and many drowned in the burn that has

[27] On Falkirk, impeding, see Rishanger, ii, p. 187: Wallace 'longos palos in terram figens, et cum funibus nectens, et cordis, ut ingressum Anglicorum ad suos impediret'; and also on the Welsh: 'Rex Edwarde, fidem si des Wallensibus, erras.' Compare Walter of Guisborough, pp. 325–7: Scots 'Inter circulos illos erant spacia quedam intermedia in quibus statuebantur viri sagittarii . . . viros sagittarios de foresta de Selkyrk.'
[28] Geoffrey le Baker, pp. 8–9: 'in secunda vero pedites cum sagittariis . . . falanx sagittariorum non habencium destinatum locum aptum, set prius armatorum a tergo

*THE BATTLE OF BANNOCKBURN, 24 JUNE 1314*

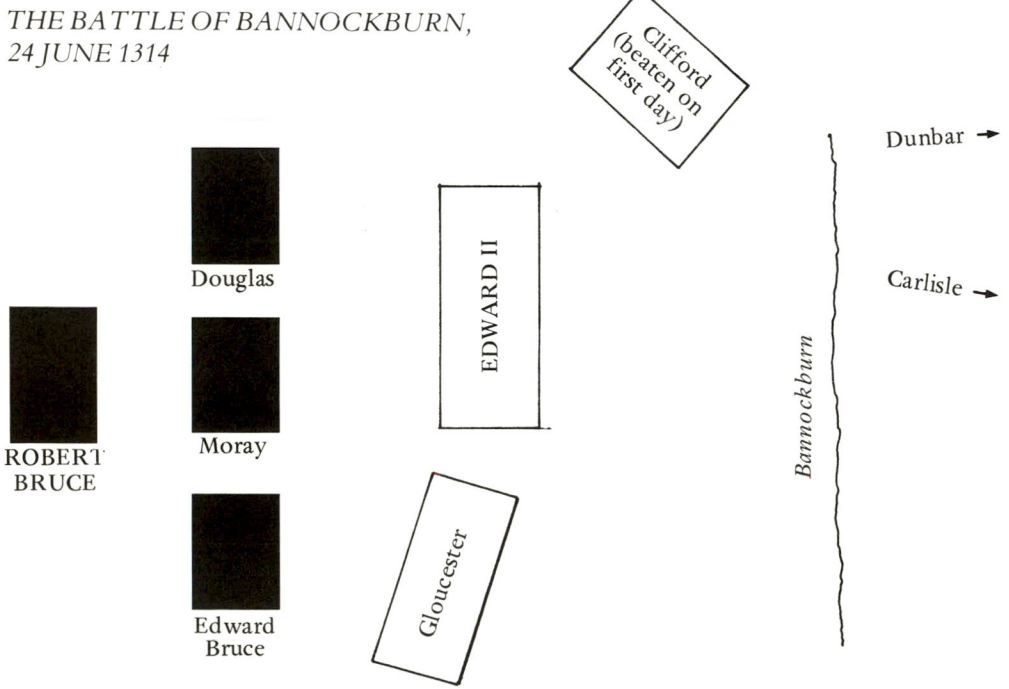

given the battle its name. The English archers had little opportunity to show their abilities, but even so the Scottish chronicler Barbour thought that they shot 'so fast that if only their shooting had lasted it would have been hard for the Scots'.[29] As it was, the archers were scattered in an attack by the Bruce. Geoffrey le Baker's comments seem to imply that Edward I normally used his archers on the flanks, a perfectly acceptable suggestion. It places Edward in the long tradition of English commanders, but does not hint at anything startlingly new, hardly enough to make him the 'father of the longbow'.

In Edward I's battles we do not see men-at-arms dismounting to form infantry blocks alongside the archers. This does not necessarily mean it never happened, but again makes it difficult to view Edward I as developing the tactics of the Hundred Years' War. In any case dismounting men was not a new development. We have seen it commonly employed in the twelfth century.

There is nothing revolutionary about the later battles of the Scottish War of Independence, or indeed about that of Boroughbridge in England, but the parallels with tactics used in the Hundred Years' War are closer, and dismounted men-at-arms fight alongside groups of archers. The fact that both sides dismounted at Boroughbridge, suggests there was nothing very novel about the idea. The battle was fought in 1322, when the rebel earls of Lancaster and Hereford were retreating towards Scotland, and were intercepted by Sir Andrew Harclay acting for Edward II. Harclay occupied the northern bank of the River Ure to prevent the rebels from crossing. The Lanercost Chronicle provides a telling account: 'he sent all the horses to the rear, and posted all his knights and some spearmen on foot at the northern end of the bridge. Other spearmen he formed in a schiltrom, following the manner of the Scots, to resist the cavalry and horses'. The rebel earls tried to cross the river. The Earl of Hereford was killed on the pikes, and although Sir Roger Clifford escaped, he was badly wounded by pikes and arrows. The rebel cavalry could not cross the Ure, 'because of the number and density of the arrows which the archers shot against them and their horses'.[30] It is odd that Boroughbridge has been taken as a model for later tactics. It is certainly an interesting pointer, but it seems clear that Harclay was doing no more than borrow the methods of the Scots.

This is not to deny the significance of the Scottish Wars in the development of English tactics, but to place them in a proper perspective. There is no sudden emergence of marvellous new weapons and tactics, but a gradual welding together of archery

stancium qui nunc a latere solent constare.'
[29] John Barbour, p. 77. On Bannockburn, see Oman, 1924, ii, p. 95; Morris, *Bannockburn*; Christison, 'Bannockburn'.
[30] *Lanercost*, p. 243: 'et dimissis retro equis suis et suorum statuit in pedibus omnes milites et quosdam lancearios'; at the ford 'posuit alios lancearios in scheltrum secundum modum Scotorum ad resistendum equitibus et equis': 'Sagittariis autem praecepit ut venientibus, inimicis spisse et continue sagittarent'; the earls 'comites . . . cum comitiva sua praecederent in pedibus.' See also *EHD*, iii, p. 275, and Tout, 'Tactics', pp. 711–5.

and other forces into an army where the balance moves towards an infantry basis. The dismounting of men-at-arms is not new, nor is it necessary to all situations; it is to be looked for whenever the army is placed in a defensive situation. The one development that is new, and deserves far more emphasis than it is usually given, is the sheer increase in the number of archers employed. This came partly from a growing interest in the bow and a realisation of its capacity and partly from the improved organis-ation of larger armies. The increase in numbers explains the impact. It was possible to use mass archery and to place large groups of archers together in positions of tactical importance. When placed in good positions, and shooting in mass, the effect of archery made itself felt, and commanders increasingly recognised its value. This development can be seen through the century before the Hundred Years' War, and not least during the later stages of the Scottish War.

The Battles of Dupplin Moor and Halidon Hill are rightly seen as signs of things to come. In these two northern battles the gradual changes of the previous century emerge in a pattern that will be crystallised in the conflict with France. Dupplin in 1332 arose from an expedition of the disinherited, encouraged from England, to regain their estates in Scotland. Again this should remind us of the importance of Scottish influence upon English tactics. The Scottish pikemen drove the Engish back, but were in turn halted by the English archery. This was a small English army, with only 500 cavalry and men-at-arms, and 1000 foot including archers. It necessitated a defensive attitude, and led to the dismounting of men-at-arms. The placing of the archers is not so certain as some commentators have assumed, but probably they were on the flanks. The *Bridlington Chronicle* in fact says that 'squadrons and archers were placed so that they could attack the "collateral" wedges of the enemy', which seems only to mean that the Scots had schiltroms placed alongside each other. It does not allow us to give the English archers any definite position, except for a forward one, and is not enough to demonstrate a 'standard formation' to be followed on later occasions. In fact, from Jean le Bel, it might seem that the men-at-arms, rather than the archers, were on the wings. Dupplin then is hardly a model battle, but it is significant. Archers, dismounted men-at-arms and cavalry had routed a larger Scottish army in much the same way that would be repeated in the war with France.[31]

The parallel comes even closer in the Battle of Halidon Hill in 1333, which after all is only a few years before the Hundred

[31] On Dupplin, see *Bridlington Chronicle*, ii, p. 106: 'Dispositis itaque turmis sagittariis suis, ut collaterales cuneso hostium invaderent'; and *EHD*, iv, p. 54. On standard formation, see Prestwich, *Three Edwards*, p. 70. On wings, see Prince, 'Campaign of 1327', p. 301; and Jean le Bel, i, p. 53.

Years' War begins. Again the English were faced by a large Scottish army. Edward III chose to defend a position on a 500' height, two miles north-west of Berwick. The king sent the horses to the rear, and archers were posted on each wing. It is not certain that the wings were composed entirely of archers, but this may have been the case. That knights dismounted is clear: Edward III himself, having addressed his men before the battle, leaped down from his horse, and placed himself with his men in the second division. The Scots attacked, but 'were able to sustain neither the force of archers, nor the arms of the knights'. They broke and fled. According to the *Bridlington Chronicle* many Scots were slaughtered, but of the English only one knight, one squire, and a few footmen. The combination of dismounted cavalry with the archers is significant, and it was presumably this that Geoffrey le Baker intended when he said that the English 'fought on foot, contrary to the ancient custom of their ancestors', although as we know that is not entirely accurate. So far as we can see the experiment of Harclay at Boroughbridge in using schiltroms was not followed. From Geoffrey's viewpoint though, the English were adopting Scottish tactics. The Scots at Halidon also fought on foot, the men-at-arms dismounting to support the pikes, and according to the *Brut*, the Scottish lords were 'alle on foote'. In the battle the value of the archers was made perfectly clear. The *Eulogium* written at Malmesbury states

HALIDON HILL

*THE BATTLE OF HALIDON HILL, 19 JULY 1333*

bluntly that the Scots were 'beaten by the English archers'. And we need have no doubt that this was mass archery. The sheriffs of London alone were instructed to send 4680 arrows, and in the battle the arrows appeared 'as thik as motes on the sonne beme'.[32]

Before we leave the Scottish War, let us move on to the Battle of Neville's Cross in 1346, a late battle against the Scots which provides useful information on tactics. The Scots had invaded England, and were faced by an army raised chiefly in the north. This presses home the point about the large numbers of archers now available to English armies, when one realises that these were men left at home by Edward III's great expedition to France. Neville himself at the northern battle had archers from the county of Lancashire. The Scots formed schiltroms, King David standing as if surrounded by a round tower. The English archers fought in the van of the army, protected by the men-at-arms, and again were primarily responsible for the victory.[33]

The Scottish Wars have an important place in the emergence of English archery history. The tactics that emerge are those found again in France, though their development is a long story, and not a case of novelty. The use of archers at the front of an army and on the wings goes back at least to Hastings and the twelfth century. The dismounting of cavalry forces to fight as infantry, and even the combination of them with archery, can be seen in the twelfth century. But given this, the Scottish Wars saw the forging of a system that did not simply use archers but depended upon them for success. The most significant change was probably in the numbers of archers used. The great impact that archers now made upon military history was not due to the appearance of a revolutionary new weapon, but to the use of large numbers of archers, operating together from well-chosen tactical positions, and able to produce a devastating hail of arrows against man and horse.

[32] Halidon Hill. Archers on the wings, see *Bridlington Chronicle*, p. 114: 'Sagittarii alis singulis deputantur'; and *EHD*, iv, p. 57. Compare Geoffrey le Baker, p. 51. That Scots could not sustain, see *Bridlington Chronicle*, p. 116: 'Sed nec sagittarum copiam nec arma militum sufferentes'; and numbers killed on same page. On the foot, see Geoffrey le Baker, p. 51: 'contra anti-quatum orem suorum patrum, pedes pugnare'; and *Brut*, p. 285, Scots 'alle on foote'. Beaten by the archers, see *Eulogium*, ii, p. 291. On arrows, Nicholson, *Edward III*, p. 135, n. 3.

[33] Neville's Cross, see Geoffrey le Baker, pp. 87–8: 'cum sagittariis de comitatu Lancastrie'; 'Steterunt nempe in modum rotunde turris glomerati.'

# Chapter 6

# The Triumph of the Longbow

The longbow as a weapon, and the tactics which made it effective, had emerged before the beginning of the Hundred Years' War. Although several secondary works seem to indicate otherwise, there is no reference to suggest that the French believed themselves to be faced by a new weapon. Nor, as we have seen, was the combination of archery with dismounted men-at-arms entirely novel. It was not a tactical lesson learned by the French at Crécy, as some historians seem to believe.[1] French armies had begun to learn the effectiveness of strong infantry at the hands of the Flemings at Courtrai in 1302. In the battles during the early stages of the Hundred Years' War before Crécy, the French dismounted to fight on foot as often as the English.[2] The picture of incurably stupid hordes of French cavalry riding endlessly to their doom is clearly false. They did not fail for want of recognising the nature of the Scottish, Flemish and English tactics, nor even for want of trying them. Their real failure was to find a type of infantry that could match the pikemen and archers of those other nations.

In the early medieval period it was, at times, difficult to find sufficient evidence for the history of archery. With the opening of the Hundred Years' War, our problem becomes one rather of an embarrassment of riches. Several chronicles deal with the war at considerable length. There are no less than fifteen volumes in the standard Luce edition of Froissart, even though it is not yet complete. The Johnes edition of Monstrelet similarly extends to thirteen volumes. On the battle of Poitiers alone there are some twenty sources.[3] Despite, or perhaps because of, the mass of

[1] For an older view, see Oman, 1898, and 1924.

[2] The French dismounted at Morlaix 1342, St-Pol-de Léon 1346, La Roche-Derrien 1347, Taillebourg 1351, Ardres 1351, and Mauron 1352 — all before Poitiers which some have seen as the first time the French used this tactic.

[3] The standard edition of Froissart, still in progress, is ed. Luce and others. The standard edition of Monstrelet is ed. Douët-D'Arcq. For general comment on the sources for Poitiers see Burne, *Crécy War*, p. 310; and for more recent thoughts, Barber, *Edward, Prince of Wales and Aquitaine*, pp. 110–48.

sources, there are few modern accounts of the actual warfare. Present day historians have tended to shy away from battles and tactics, in favour of subjects that were once neglected, such as diplomacy, or the social effects of warfare. It is true that war is more than battles, but it still seems strange to find, for example, that the excellent volume on the Hundred Years' War, edited by Fowler, which deals with so many aspects of the war, has nothing on the fighting.[4] Warfare without battles, in the words of Henry V is like 'sausages without mustard'. Certainly it is important to us to consider the tactical use of archers in battle in the Hundred Years' War, and little has been added to the discussion since the publication of Burne's *The Crecy War* in 1955. The lack of interest in the warfare itself is very much a modern attitude, not shared by those who lived at the time of the conflict. Contemporaries did not question the significance of military victory. Froissart pointed out that 'the English will never love or honour their king unless he be victorious and a lover of arms.'[5] There are many who would agree with Michael Prestwich's assessment of the English monarch who supervised the victories in the first phase of the war as 'one of the greatest of English war leaders'.[6] For us, this is the period that saw the great age of the medieval archer, and merits study in some detail.

The fourteenth century saw the emergence of the archer as an essential component in the English armies, and in their victories. In consequence one sees a gradual rise of the archer in society and in literature. A real Robin Hood might belong to an earlier age, but it was now that he became a popular figure in literature. To take another example, Lawrence Minot writing in the mid fourteenth century could present as his hero John of Doncaster, a Master Archer.[7]

Our concern in this chapter is the role of the archer in the military campaigns of Edward III and of his son, Edward the Black Prince. The Hundred Years' War lasted over a century, from 1337 to 1453. Indeed, if one sees it as the war for control of the geographical area of Western France, then it could be said to have started in 1066 when a Duke of Normandy became also King of England, and to have ended in 1558 when Calais was finally taken by the French in the reign of Mary I. The concept of a 'Hundred Years' War' is a later and rather artificial one, based on the idea that it was a conflict to determine the succession to the French throne. No one in the fourteenth century could view it as a Hundred Years' War, and it is doubtful that Edward III saw his claim to the French throne as the main objective. He was prepared to surrender the claim as a negotiating point, even after

[4] Fowler, *Hundred Years' War.*
[5] On Henry V's comment see, for example, Seward, *Hundred Years' War*, p. 161. For Edward III, Fowler, *Hundred Years' War*, p. 130.
[6] Prestwich, *Three Edwards*, p. 165.
[7] Laurence Minot, ed. Hall.

a series of military victories.[8] If one looks back on the war from the present, it still does not make much of a unity. It may be true that sporadic warfare continued through most of the hundred years and even beyond, but it can hardly be viewed as one continuous war. It makes more sense to consider the war in fairly distinct phases.

The first phase was the war of Edward III, marked most obviously at its conclusion by the making of the Treaty of Brétigny in 1360. It was in this war that the significance of archery in English and European warfare became clear. As we have seen, the use of the longbow, and suitable tactics for its use, were not a new development in the late 1330s. In fact, by 1363 some men already believed that the golden age of archery had passed. In that year sheriffs were instructed by the king to enforce archery practice: 'Whereas the people of our realm, nobles as well as commons, usually practised in their games the art of archery leading to honour and profit for the realm ... and we gained not a little help in our wars ... now the art is almost totally neglected and the people amuse themselves with dishonest games so that the kingdom, in short, becomes truly destitute of archers'.[9] The people were enjoined to practise on feast days. It seems a strange outlook to us, fifty years before the Battle of Agincourt, yet it is true that the success of English archery abroad depended upon development, organisation and practice at home. The 1363 instruction does show recognition of the importance of regular training, and it is worth noting that nobles as well as commons are included in the order. There is an interesting illustration in the *Luttrell Psalter*, dated about 1341, at the beginning of the Hundred Years' War, showing just such an archery practice. It shows two solid targets, with one individual just having scored a bullseye, and perhaps rather smugly encouraging the others to follow suit.[10]

There is good evidence at this period for the importance attached to archery for warfare, over the provision of bows and arrows and their storage, and over the raising of large numbers of archers. The *London Calendar Book* for 1337 to 1352, covering the period of the Battle of Crécy, asks for 500 archers from London. Nor were commanders necessarily satisfied with mere numbers. There were complaints about the physique of men provided. There were also fears that the French would emulate the English achievement with archery, and in an attempt to prevent this development, proclamations in 1357 and 1369 forbade the export of bows and arrows, and in 1365 archers were forbidden to leave England without royal licence. In 1341, before

[8] On Brétigny and the succession, see Palmer, 'War Aims'; and Prestwich, *Three Edwards*, p. 169.
[9] *EHD*, iv, p. 1182, no. 694.
[10] Harris, 'Archery', p. 20.

any major land battle had been fought in the Hundred Years' War, Edward III ordered the collection of 7,700 bows and 130,000 sheaves of arrows. The Tower of London was the major storage centre. The country was scoured for these weapons. In 1356, the year of Poitiers, it was claimed that no arrows could be found in all England, since the king had taken them all. The Black Prince even had the fletchers of Cheshire arrested in order that he could be sure of obtaining their services. The completeness of the operation of collecting archers is suggested by a new attempt to raise men in Rutland in 1356, when it was claimed that practically none could be found fit to serve, only one wounded man and two without equipment, since the Earl of Warwick had taken the best men already. In 1347, for the siege of Calais, the government decided to release criminals to fill the ranks, and 1800 men were set free, men such as Robert White, accused of 'homicides, felonies, robberies, rapes of women and trespasses'. Of such heroic material were the armies of Edward III! Various methods were tried to find archers for the armies. In 1347 it was laid down that every £30 landholder must find one man-at-arms and one archer, though the king promised that this measure would not be treated as a precedent. At the same time the contract system was developing, and was particularly useful for foreign wars. So, for example, in 1345 Henry de Grosmont agreed to go to Gascony with a force of 2000 soldiers, including 1000 infantry. In general, although the armies included released criminals, unwillingly pressed men, those who served primarily for reward, the quality of the English armies was good.[11] Jean le Bel commented that the English troops were prepared to fight even when they were not paid their wages. No doubt success made them more content, fulfilling the hopes of wealth and plunder. The chronicler Walsingham refers to the vast amount of stuff sent home by the English soldiers, to the extent that almost every woman in England had received something: 'clothes, furs, bedcovers, cutlery, tablecloths and linen, wooden and silver bowls'.[12]

During this period there was an important development in the composition of the archer sections of the armies, with an increasing emphasis upon mounted archers. The beginnings are not easy to distinguish. Some infantry in the armies had been mounted as far back as the Anglo-Saxon period, and it is often difficult to know which men were horsed for travel, even if they fought on foot. There are occasional mentions of mounted archers in the twelfth century. Morris has argued that the hobelars were the forerunners of mounted archers.[13] These were

[11] Tucker, 'Archives', p. 192. Prestwich, *Three Edwards*, pp. 192, 194, 225.
[12] Prestwich, *Three Edwards*, p. 202.
[13] Morris, 'Mounted Infantry', p. 80.

94

[14] Wrottesley, *Crécy and Calais*, pp. 4, 204; and compare p. 191; see also *EHD*, iv, p. 498.

[15] *EHD*, iv, p. 85, and Prince, 'Strength of English Armies', pp. 362–3.

[16] Jean le Bel, i, p. 127: 'Aussy bien et assy noblement est maintenant arme ung povre garchon, qu'est ung noble chevaliers'; and i, p. 156: 'Or ont ilz sy apris les armes au temps de ce noble roy Edowart, qui souvent les a mis en oevre.'

[17] For usual view on meaning of *herce*, see, for example, George, 'Archers at Crécy'; Lloyd, 'The "Herse" '; Burne, *Crécy War*, p. 38, for Froissart's use of the word see Froissart, ed. Luce, iii, p. 175: 'mis leurs arciers à manière d'une herce, et les gens d'armes ou fons de leur bataille'; iii, p. 416 (Rome MS) : 'et missent les archiers tout devant en fourme de une erce, et les gens d'armes ou fons'; and on Poitiers: v, p. 22: 'et ont mis leurs gens d'armes tout devant yaus leurs arciers à manière d'une herce dont cest trop sagement ouvre'; and v, p. 252 (Amiens MS): 'deux hayes d'archiers devant yaux, à manière d'une herce'. For a useful discussion on the term, see Wylie, *Henry V*, ii, pp. 148–9, n. 10.

the horsed infantrymen referred to in the Scottish wars. It is said they were brought from Ireland, where their horses were known as 'ubinos' or 'hobinos', seemingly meaning horses that are quick or nimble. They were, in other words, troops riding horses that were lighter and less expensive that the destriers of the knights. Increasingly the commanders sought to obtain mounted archers. It seems unlikely that these men fought on horseback, in the manner of Eastern archers with their shortbows. The mounted archers of the Hundred Years' War almost certainly dismounted to shoot their bows on foot, but their horses gave them valuable mobility on campaign. At the siege of Calais Edward III had 20,076 archers, and 4,025 of them were mounted.[14] It might be noted in passing that here as elsewhere the Welsh were listed separately, and not with the archers. For the Scottish campaign of 1347, we have the lists of mounted archers in the retinues: thus, for example, Lord Percy and Lord Mowbray each took 100 mounted archers, Sir Thomas de Lucy and Sir Thomas de Rokeby each took 50.[15] This greater use of mounted archers might be seen in connection with Jean le Bel's remarks on the improved standards of men used as retainers. He commented that 'the poorest retainer is now as well and as smartly armed as a noble knight'.[16] He said this improvement had come during his own lifetime, that is between 1290 and 1370, and also offered an explanation, suggesting that it was the result of the efforts of Edward III himself, who had 'done much for their training', and whose victories caused a change in European attitudes towards the military capacities of the English. The English were now, he thought, the best fighters you could meet.

## The Tactical Meaning of Froissart's 'Herce'

The way in which Edward III won his battles is of interest to us. It is generally agreed that his archers played a significant role, and we shall not quarrel with that conclusion. But it seems to be assumed that the archers' role took one form in every battle. That view is based upon the interpretation of Jean Froissart's description of a particular archer formation which he enigmatically described as a *herce*.[17] It is doubtful that the term *herce* can be interpreted with any certainty to its original meaning. But some historians have developed an interpretation which has come to be treated as if it were a factual description. Even more oddly, this interpretation of a phrase which only Froissart uses, and only very rarely uses, has been taken as a correct view of how archers were used in every battle of the Hundred Years' War. This current orthodoxy deserves to be challenged at both levels: both at the level of interpretation of the meaning of *herce*; and at that of its application to the war as a whole.

We can take two lines of approach: an investigation of the meaning of *herce*; and an examination of other evidence of archer tactics in the war. There can be no question that Froissart is a chronicler of importance, and that any description by him relating to archer tactics is of note. When, therefore, he writes of a tactical formation with archers placed 'in the manner of a *herce*', it should be a useful clue to how the English archers were used on those occasions when he uses the term.

Froissart was born in about 1335 at Valenciennes in Hainault, and thus was a fellow countryman of Edward III's queen, Philippa of Hainault. He came to England and entered the queen's service, returning home on her death. In later life he entered the priesthood, and formed connections with men who had fought against the English in the Hundred Years' War: the Count of Blois, whose father had been killed at Crécy; and the Duke of Luxembourg, whose father, the famous King of Bohemia, had suffered a similar fate.[18] Froissart revised his chronicle, and the later changes reflected a more favourable attitude to the French. It is interesting that this third version has been little used for translations of Froissart's work into English. Most editions have been based on Froissart's first redaction, which is the one used in the standard Luce edition, and that translated by both Lord Berners and Johnes.

A second point to bear in mind with Froissart's work, is the degree to which, especially in the early sections, he was dependent upon other sources. There is no intention of diminishing the value of this great work, but simply of placing it in its proper perspective. Froissart himself claimed that he wrote: 'so that the honourable adventures and noble feats of arms achieved in the wars of France and England may be memorably set down and recorded in perpetuity', and that in so far as he was able, he had 'sought out the truth'. He was justly proud of his own work, and having presented a copy to the King of England, Richard II, he claimed that the king had read it 'with pleasure, as well he might'. He also believed his work would survive: 'When I am dust and ashes, then this grand and noble history will be in great demand'.[19] Who are we to deny that expectation nearly six centuries after his death? However, the term in which we are interested appears in the earliest version of his chronicle, and in a

[18] For an outline of Froissart's life, see Froissart, ed. Jolliffe, introduction; and for recent discussion on the chronicler, see Palmer, *Froissart*.

[19] Froissart ed. Luce, i, p. 1; Froissart ed. Jolliffe, pp. 362, 281.

section on the Crécy campaign which has been shown to borrow considerably from the chronicler Jean le Bel. Jean le Bel had been raised as a noble in Liège, and as a youth had borne arms and ridden in tournaments. He was therefore familiar with the conditions of warfare, and a valuable commentator. Unlike Froissart, he was also an adult at the time of Crécy. And unlike many of the writers upon whom we have relied in this history, he was a man of the world, marrying the noblewoman Marie des Pres, by whom he had two sons.[20]

Let us first consider what Froissart himself said, when describing English battle formations. At Crécy he said that the English archers were placed: *à manière d'une herce*. In the Rome manuscript, the phrasing is similar: the archers were placed *tout devant en fourme de une erce*; and at Poitiers, the English had *mis leurs gens d'armes tout devant yaus leurs arciers à manière d'une herce*; or in the Amiens Manuscript, in a version not always looked at in full: *deux hayes d'archiers devant yaux, à manière d'une herce*. Clearly Froissart saw this formation as rather unusual, and sought an original simile to explain it.[21] Unfortunately, what was clear to Froissart, and probably to his readers, is not at all clear to us, or at any rate to some of us. In England, historians from George and Oman down to Burne, have refined an interpretation of *herce* to the point where one meaning seems to be universally accepted as correct.[22] Burne expressed this conclusion in terms of there being a formation with triangular wedges of archers with the apex of the triangle facing the enemy, each wedge being placed between separate divisions of men-at-arms fighting on foot: 'hollow wedges, in conjunction with the archers of the next division. These were easily and simply constructed: each body inclined diagonally forward, pivoting on the flank of its own men-at-arms, where the two contiguous lines of archers joined up an apex was formed. The effect was that a bastion-like formation was created in the intervals between the divisions, and the flanks of the army were similarly enfiladed'.[23] All this on the basis of the one word, *herce*!

This view of the meaning of Froissart has been built on a gradual acceptance of the translation of *herce* as harrow, and of harrow as meaning triangular. George saw the formation as: 'alternately pointed wedges of archers and straight lines of men-at-arms'; and Oman similarly accepted alternate squares of men-at-arms and triangles of archers. This has become current orthodoxy, as, for example, expressed recently: 'a standard battle formation had been developed, with each battalion of dismounted men-at-arms flanked by wings of archers'.[24]

[20] Jean le Bel's life, see Jean le Bel, i, pp. l–lxv, by Viard.
[21] See n. 17.
[22] See n. 17, and Oman, *Art of War*, 1924, ii, p. 137, n. 2.
[23] Burne, *Crécy War*, p. 38.
[24] Prestwich, *Three Edwards*, p.870, and cf. p. 197.

A. H. BURNE'S VERSION OF THE HERCE

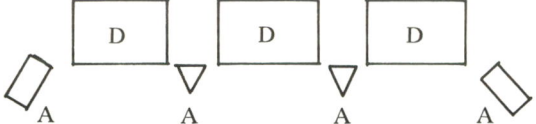

D = DISMOUNTED KNIGHTS
A = ARCHERS

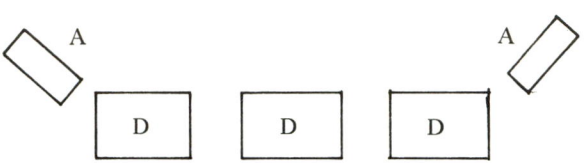

THE USUAL ENGLISH FORMATION
IN THE HUNDRED YEARS WAR

*A. H. Burne's interpretation of the 'herce', with triangular wedges of archers between the blocks of dismounted men-at-arms. It is not likely that the English often, if ever, used this formation. The more common formation is also shown with archers on the flanks only.*

This interpretation has been extended to battles which Froissart did not describe in the same way, or did not describe at all. J. E. Morris congratulated George on tracing 'a permanent system through the whole of the Hundred Years' War'. Thus we can find writers such as Burne and Heath describing *herses* of archers at Agincourt, and in every battle of the war.[25]

The most fundamental basis of all this interpretation is so uncertain as to make such a concrete superstructure appear unwise. What in fact did Jean Froissart mean by *herce*? It is a very uncommon word, Froissart himself only uses the term on one other occasion. Sixteenth century uses are not reliable, because they are themselves interpretations of Froissart, though not without interest. In the fourteenth century the word had several possible meanings, and it is far from certain which of them Froissart intended.[26] Let us, however, for the moment, suppose along with George, Oman, Burne, et. al., that Froissart actually did mean harrow. What would that meaning imply in military terms? We cannot, for one thing, be sure of the nature of a fourteenth century harrow. Most commentators seem to accept it as being triangular, and yet no triangular illustration is known.

[25] Morris, 'Archers at Crécy, p. 427; and, for example, Heath, 'Agincourt', p. 8.
[26] Meanings of *herce*, see Du Cange, iii, under 'hercia', 'hercius', and 'ericius'.

The harrow in the *Très riches heures* appears to be either rectangular, or else slightly narrowing, but certainly not triangular.[27] It would certainly be reasonable to argue that a harrow might be rectangular rather than triangular. The meaning in terms of shape therefore is not conclusive. In any case, if Froissart wished only to describe a simple thing like a shape, why choose an obscure simile? It could be that if Froissart meant harrow he was thinking of other things than shape. We might consider it as a board-like object with spikes underneath it, that would break up the earth. What this would imply in military terms must remain uncertain, but should not be ignored. It is the kind of simile that can register only with those who recognise what the actual formation was like. In the twentieth century, we can only speculate, or seek for other evidence.

In speculation, what are the other meanings of *herce*, and what might these imply? It could, for example, mean a candelabrum. Whatever a formation like a candelabrum means, it hardly suggests anything triangular, though this is what Du Cange seems to accept. It would seem more likely to point to a horn-shaped projection on the wings of an army. But it may well be that *herce* or *erce* is closer to its derivation from *ericius*. *Ericius* means a hedgehog, and is the most obvious term to connect with a military meaning, since several other military terms are based on it, all suggesting something with spikes: a defence bristling with pointed stakes, a portcullis with pointed beams. This would provide a perfectly acceptable interpretation of Froissart as meaning archers in some kind of defensive formation, perhaps using stakes for protection, or pikemen giving them cover — both of which formations are to be met with in the medieval period. *Herce* certainly seems nearer to terms such as *herissé* or *herisson*, and is probably best translated as 'like a hedgehog', or perhaps as 'hedged in'.

Another approach to the problem is to examine Froissart's sources for Crécy, and see if there is anything similar to his comment. As we have seen Froissart, only nine at the time, depended on others for his account of the battle. There is in fact a striking similarity of phrasing in the *Valenciennes Chronicle*, where the formation is described as being 'in the manner of a shield'.[28] Froissart may well have taken this simile, and tried to improve on it. 'Shield' is perhaps clearer than *herce*, but could also be taken to mean either shape or shelter, indeed it may be a dual meaning which made both similes seem appropriate.

Then again we need to examine other accounts of Crécy and Poitiers to see if there are independent accounts of the battles

[27] *Très Riches Heures*, ed. Durrieu, pl. x.
[28] Froissart ed. Lettenhove, v, p. 478: 'deux batailles d'archiers à deux costes en la manière d'un escut'.

*Three illustrations showing the harrow as rectangular rather than triangular.*

Très Riches Heures du Duc de Berri, *fifteenth century.*

which give their own description of the archer formations, and might throw light on Froissart's meaning. Before we examine the individual battles, it must be said that as one moves through the war, it becomes clear that the English archers are not used in

*English fifteenth century harrow.*

*Fourteenth century* Luttrell Psalter.

just one type of formation at all times. Thus Froissart might well be describing a particular formation that was used on some occasions and not on others, and which again might call for an original simile.

ll gueran dit contes deu et de richemout
vey comment et plusieurs autres bons
par vug deu capitames le conte de se
dedy francois yssueut do/me et autres officiers

*Longbowmen in combination with pikemen, from a French manuscript.*

We must turn to the war itself for further information about the use of archers. The various political and economic conflicts between Edward III and Philip VI, the first of the Valois kings, finally moved to open warfare in 1337. The first major clash came not on land, but at sea off Sluys. This was an unusual battle, and one that deserves our attention, since it was fought almost as if it were a land battle, and the English archers were employed in a manner that can be compared with their use on land. A chronicler was later to see Sluys as one of the three great battles of the war, the others being Poitiers and Agincourt.[29] Both longbowmen and crossbowmen featured in the battle. The French were said to have 20,000 of the renowned Genoese crossbowmen; the English had both types of bowmen, since Geoffrey le Baker mentions 'an iron shower of bolts from crossbows, and arrows from bows'.[30] There had been some talk of a French plan to invade England in these early years of the war, but, in the event, it was an English fleet that sailed, and the French who had to try and prevent a landing. The two fleets collided in June of 1340, the English having the advantage of the wind. Neither of the French admirals, Quiéret and Béhuchet, were seamen, and they chose to hold their position and fight at close quarters, their ships chained together and barricaded with planks. They placed captured English ships at one end of their line, with crossbowmen on board. They also had crossbows elsewhere in the line.

[29] *Gesta Henrici Quinti*, p. 122: 'Primo videlicet in bello navali de Sclus.'
[30] Geoffrey le Baker, p. 68: 'ferreus imber quarellorum de balistis atque sagittarum de arcubus'.

The English ships were organised in four squadrons: a squadron of men-at-arms took the centre, with a squadron of archers on either side, and a fourth squadron in reserve. From the very beginning of the war we note what had already become common in English armies, the use of archers on the flanks. Edward III waited and then advanced with the tide, attacking the French ships, which were like 'a line of castles', at their moorings.[31] The English archery shot with effect, not for the last time in the war, and the English men-at-arms were able to board the enemy ships. Edward used arrows, bolts, stones and lime, and sent divers to bore holes in the French vessels, and though the king's own white boots were bloodied in the conflict, it was a conclusive victory for him. The French admirals were both taken and executed. It was said, from the fact of so many Frenchmen being sent overboard, that if fish could speak they would have been able to learn French.

A main theatre of the early part of the Hundred Years' War was Brittany. On the death of Duke John III in 1341, there was a succession dispute in which both England and France took an interest. John de Montfort, the half brother of the deceased duke, had the support of Edward III. His rival, Charles of Blois, was married to the deceased duke's niece, Joan of Penthieve, and was also the nephew of Philip VI of France. The French king, not unexpectedly took up the case of his nephew. In 1342 an English expeditionary force was sent under the command of Walter Manny, a Hainaulter, and it was soon joined by the Earl of Northampton. They were soon engaged in the first main land battle of the Hundred Years' War, at Morlaix in 1342. The English force took up a defensive position in front of a wood, and astride a road. Dismounted men-at-arms took the centre, with archers on each flank. Charles of Blois also dismounted his men-at-arms, and ordered an attack. This in itself is worth note, and is sufficient to dispel the myth that the French always fought on horseback because they were too proud to dismount and too disdainful of infantry tactics. It is true that, on the whole, they made greater use of cavalry than the English, only to be expected since in the majority of cases they had greater numbers of troops to call on; but it is not true that they failed to appreciate a lesson in tactics taught them by the English. If Morlaix be taken into consideration, then they had learned the lesson pretty early in the war, and in fact, if one examines the battles in the early stage of the war, the French dismounted to fight on foot in just as many battles as did the English.[32] At Morlaix, the English archers defended themselves by making ditches, but an outflanking

[31] Geoffrey le Baker, p. 68: 'quasi castrorum acies ordinatam'.
[32] See n. 3 above, and Tout: 'Neglected Fights', p. 726.

103

movement by the French caused the Earl of Northampton to retreat some hundred yards to the line of the wood. A. H. Burne's unconscious comment on archer tactics in this battle are of ironic interest. He suggested that they formed 'what we now call a "hedgehog", a defensive line along the edge of the wood and facing in all directions'. It may well be that this is the simple meaning of the *herce*. Not for the last time in the war, the Genoese crossbowmen on the French side were outshot. The Genoese captain, Grimaldi, admitted the fact in a letter written soon after the battle. In the very first land battle of the war, the English archers were placed on the flanks of the army, made artificial improvements to their defences, and fought successfully in combination with dismounted men-at-arms.[33]

33 On Morlaix, see Burne, *Crécy War*, p. 71; and Geoffrey le Baker, p. 76, compares Bannockburn with Halidon Hill. The 'hedgehog' comment is in Burne, *Crécy War*, p. 74, with the Grimaldi letter on p. 76.

*The Battle of Crécy; an illumination in a copy of Froissart's* Chronicles.

## Crécy

Crécy, one of the two great battles of the war, occurred in its early stages, with Edward III still at the height of his powers. His expedition in support of Lancaster resulted in the taking of Caen in Normandy, where 105 Normans were painfully killed when they unwisely exposed their backsides insultingly towards the English archers. Edward III moved northwards, tracked now by a larger French army, and was finally brought to bay at Crécy-in-Ponthieu. It was a battle that caught the contemporary imagination and was much described. There is some conflict in the details, but a fairly clear account emerges. The greater problem is to rescue the contemporary description from the accretions of later historians. We must rely on comments we can understand rather than on interpretations of the *herce*, and must accept that we do not know precisely where the battlefield was and so cannot base our descriptions on the nature of a site that we have chosen.

The English took a defensive position in three divisons on ground that sloped down towards the River Maie. Edward III chose as his vantage point a height with a windmill on it. A hedge separated the armies, and Edward III seems to have constructed a kind of defensive enclosure for the supply wagons, perhaps with the wagons themselves.[34] The French fought with the sun in their faces, and since the hour was late they were presumably facing west.

Nowhere are we told that the archers were placed in separate wedges across the field. The interpretation of *herce* and even of *escut*, as we have seen, is far from certain. The phrasing of the *Valenciennes Chronicle* suggests that the forward positions were on the flanks: Edward III placed 'two divisions of archers on the two sides in the manner of a shield'.[35] This very much reminds us of one of Froissart's phrases, when he describes at Poitiers *deux hayes d'archiers devant yaux, à manière d'une herce*. This may be translated as 'two hedges of archers before them in the manner of a *herce*'. Geoffrey le Baker gives a similar impression. We have already met Geoffrey as a chronicler of the Scottish wars, and he gives no indication that the formation used in the Hundred Years' War was in any way novel or exceptional. Describing the formation at Crécy, he says: the archers were placed 'not close to the men-at-arms, but on the sides of the king's army, as if they were wings, and thus they would not impede the men-at-arms or clash with the enemy head on, but could shoot their arrows from the side'.[36] The English army was in three divisions: under the

[34] For wagons, see *Chronique Normande*, p. 81: the English 'saillirent hors de leur charroy', and 'lors yssi le roy Edouart de son charroy'. The windmill is mentioned in Froissart ed. Luce, iii, p. 416 (Rome MS).

[35] See n. 28 and n. 17.

[36] Geoffrey le Baker, pp. 83–4: 'Sagittariis eciam sua loca designarunt, ut, non coram armatis, set a lateribus regis exercitus quasi ale astarent, et sic non impedirent armatos neque inimicis occurrerent in fronte, set in latera sagittas fulminarent.'

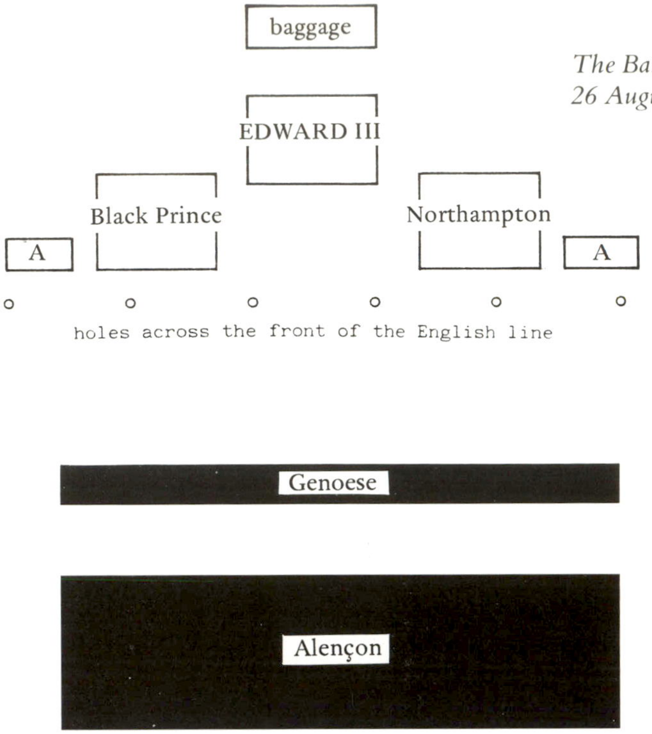

*The Battle of Crécy,
26 August 1346.*

baggage

EDWARD III

Black Prince

Northampton

A

A

o     o     o     o     o     o

holes across the front of the English line

Genoese

Alençon

*EDWARD III'S ROUTE TO CRÉC*

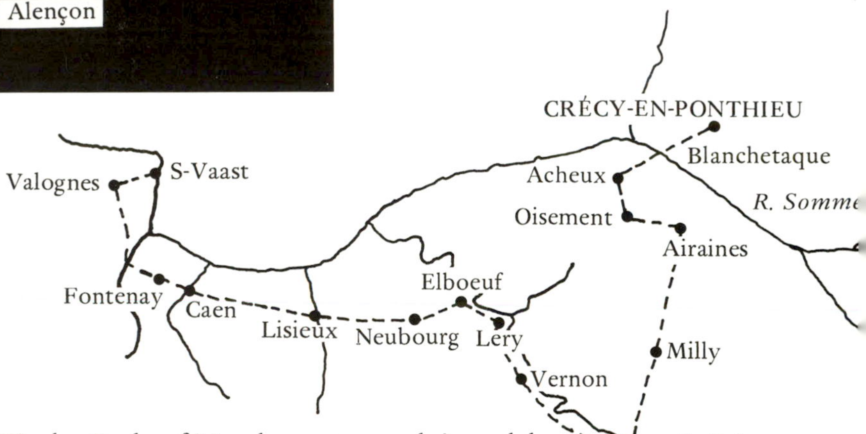

CRÉCY-EN-PONTHIEU

Blanchetaque

Valognes    S-Vaast    Acheux    *R. Somme*

Oisement

Airaines

Elboeuf

Fontenay    Caen    Lisieux    Neubourg    Léry    Milly

Vernon

*R. Seine*

Poissy

command of Edward III; the Earls of Northampton and Arundel; and the Black Prince, referred to by one chronicler as 'Edward IV'.[37]

The French army was larger, and was not deployed with precision; there is no agreement even on the number of the French divisions. It is, however, agreed that the Genoese crossbowmen were sent forward and opened hostilities. They seem to have lacked the range of the English archers, since the English arrows began to strike the French, but the crossbows 'were not harming the English at all'. Perhaps too much notice should not be taken of this point, since several sources suggest that rain before the battle adversely affected the crossbows. Some modern historians have queried this development, but it seems

[37] *Anonimalle Chronicle,* p. 22: 'Edward le quart prynce Dengleterre et de Gales avoit lavaunt garde.'

106

38 Burne, *Crécy War*, p. 177 on number of French divisions. On relative effect of bows see Geoffrey le Baker, p. 83: 'incoaverunt balistarii Francorum, quorum quarelle nullum Anglicorum attigerunt set ceciderunt a longe corum eiis.' For Genoese failure, see Jean de Venette, p. 43. On the English advance, Froissart ed. Luce, iii, pp. 185, 187.

39 On disdain for archers see Froissart ed. Luce, iii, p. 177: 'tues toute ceste ribaudaille: il nous esonnient et tiennent le voie sans raison'. Compare Geoffrey le Baker, p. 83. For the hedge of archers, see Froissart ed. Luce, iii, p. 180: 'une si grande haie d'arciers et de gens d'armes au devant que james ne fust passes'.

well authenticated. Jean de Venette says the crossbows 'were soaked by the rain and shrank', whereas during the storm the English had 'protected their bows by putting the strings on their heads under their helmets'. The Genoese, he says, 'could not stretch the cords to the bows so shrunken were they ... they could not shoot a single bolt'. According to Froissart, the Genoese advanced in three stages, each time giving a shout when halting to shoot.[38] The English archers then stepped forward and shot together, so that their arrows fell like snow upon the heads and arms of the Genoese, who had never experienced such archery. Some cut the cords of their crossbows, some flung them to the ground, some fled. Philip VI then exclaimed: 'they are getting in our way and they serve no purpose, this rubbish'. The French rode through and over their own crossbowmen, but were halted by the English archers. The Count of Alençon is described as riding past the English archers, which again confirms that they were in a forward flanking position. On the other hand, it does not seem as if all the archers were forward, since the French found 'a great hedge of archers and men-at-arms in front of them that had remained unbroken'.[39] One black horse, given to its

*The Battle of Crécy from a late fourteenth century copy of the* Grandes Chroniques de France.

owner by Philip VI himself, was driven to panic by the arrows. It bolted and threw its unfortunate rider into a ditch, from which he extricated himself and returned to the fray. He was luckier than some. Jean le Bel says the French horses under the archery attack were felled, and 'piled up like a litter of piglets'.[40] The English army showed its discipline by refusing to break ranks, even to take prisoners who would be valuable for their ransoms. Wave upon wave of French cavalry advanced into the evening sun, only to break on the hedge of English archers and men-at-arms. Presumably they were hampered by the one foot deep pits that Edward III had ordered to be dug in front of the English position. Fifteen attacks were made, and every one of them failed. Blind King John of Bohemia, brave amongst his unsuccessful French comrades, had himself led forward to the conflict, perhaps the only combatant not affected by the declining light. He died bravely, but ineffectively. In the heat of the battle, the young Prince of Wales came under severe threat. He was knocked down, but was sheltered by his standard bearer. Edward III supposedly made the famous remark about his son: 'I want them to let the boy win his spurs'. Nevertheless he sent twenty knights to help the Black Prince. As Froissart expressed it: 'That day the English archers gave a tremendous advantage to their side. Many say that it was by their shooting that the day was won'.[41] Philip VI himself had been wounded in the neck by an arrow. It is interesting to note, despite the solid evidence for the significance of the archers in the battle, that the victorious king made not a single reference to them in a letter written soon afterwards about the engagement. Today, as then, the French see Crécy as 'le désastre'. According to Geoffrey le Baker, there were 4000 French knights killed, and 'no one troubled to count the others'. Edward III had lost very few of his men, and rode on triumphantly to Calais.[42]

In the years between Crécy and Poitiers the fighting continued, especially in Brittany. These lesser known campaigns and conflicts should not be ignored, for they add to our knowledge of how the archers were used. In 1347 Sir Thomas Dagworth replaced the Earl of Northampton as commander in Brittany, and at once moved to the attack. Charles of Blois, the French king's nephew, was besieging La Roche Derrien. At the approach of the English he levelled the countryside around in order to destroy possible cover for the archers, so that they could not gain advantage from hedges and ditches. He also dug large entrenchments around his position. His French force was not lacking in archery, possessing 2000 crossbowmen, and 600

[40] Jean le Bel, p. 103: 'comme pourcheaulx a tas'.
[41] On number of attacks, Geoffrey le Baker, p. 84: 'quindecies nostris insultum dederunt', with a sixteenth on the following day. On winning his spurs, Froissart ed. Luce, iii, p. 183: 'je leur mande que il laissent a l'enfant gaegnier ses esporons'. On archers giving the advantage to the English, Froissart ed. Luce, iii, pp. 185, 187.
[42] For the letter, see Barber, *Life and Campaigns*, p. 23. For the modern comment, Favier, *Guerre de Cent Ans*, p. 117. The remark on counting is in Geoffrey le Baker, p. 85: 'et plures alii, quos Gallici capti et inquisiti nescierunt nominare'.

108

'archers of the countryside'.[43] These measures all indicate the use of artificial and natural defences both as protection and as cover for archers. The French commander's actions were unavailing. The small English army of about 5000 men, some 4000 of whom were archers, was reinforced by a sortie from the besieged garrison, and together they overcame Charles, who was also taken prisoner.[44]

At Mauron on the Breton frontier the fate of Brittany was settled for this first phase of the war. In this battle, as in others during this campaign, the French as well as the English, dismounted some of their men-at-arms. The only French to remain mounted were a small force of some 720 men, who were deliberately intended to charge against the archers. The English used a hedge for protection, and had archers on both flanks, by far the most common position for English archers in this war. The English won the battle, but not all the archers acquitted themselves well. Thirty archers who had fled at the height of the battle, 'frightened by the numbers of the French' were beheaded on the next day.[45] It reminds us both of the vulnerability of archers in close fighting, and of the disdain felt for them by the nobility. It was not unknown for cavalry to break and flee, but how often does one hear of executions afterwards?

## Poitiers

The second great land battle in this phase of the war was fought near Poitiers in 1356.[46] It is one of the best known of all medieval battles, yet we know less about it than we believe. From reading modern accounts and looking at modern representations of the battle plan, one would think we knew exactly where the battle took place, and exactly how the armies were arranged. In fact there is considerable doubt about both these matters. The chronicles do give information that allows us to unravel something of the battle tactics, but as we have already seen, we cannot allow speculation over the meaning of *herce* to convince us that the English army had a particular formation.[47] Nor, since we cannot place the site precisely, can we allow considerations about a site which some historians believe to be correct to influence an interpretation of tactics. In other words, we must rely only on the contemporary evidence. This will give us the order of the march, and some indication of battle positions, but, as usual in this period, it is not certain or complete. For example,

[43] Murimuth, RS, p. 388. The comment is in a letter from Dagworth. Charles of Blois has 'des archiers du pais'. The same source has Charles making 'graundes forteresces de fosses entour luy', and destroying 'toutz maners dez fossez et des hayes, par quei mez archiers ne puissent trover lor avauntage sur luy'.
[44] On Mauron see Burne, *Crécy War*, p. 236; Geoffrey le Baker, p. 120; Robert of Avesbury in Murimuth, RS, p. 415; *Chronique Normande*, p. 105, in which the English 'descendirent à pie et se mistrent le long d'une haie, laquele ilz mistrent derrière leur dos, et mistrent leurs archiers sur leurs costez'.
[45] Geoffrey le Baker, p. 120. Walter Bentley; 'iussit triginta sagittarios decapitari, qui in maximo belli fervore territi a Gallicorum immensitate fugam inierunt'.
[46] On Poitiers see Burne, *Crécy War*, p. 275; and 'Battle of Poitiers'; together with Galbraith's review of Burne in *EHR*; Hewitt, *Black Prince's Expedition*; and Barber, *Edward, Prince of Wales and Aquitaine*, pp. 110–148.
[47] See n. 17 above.

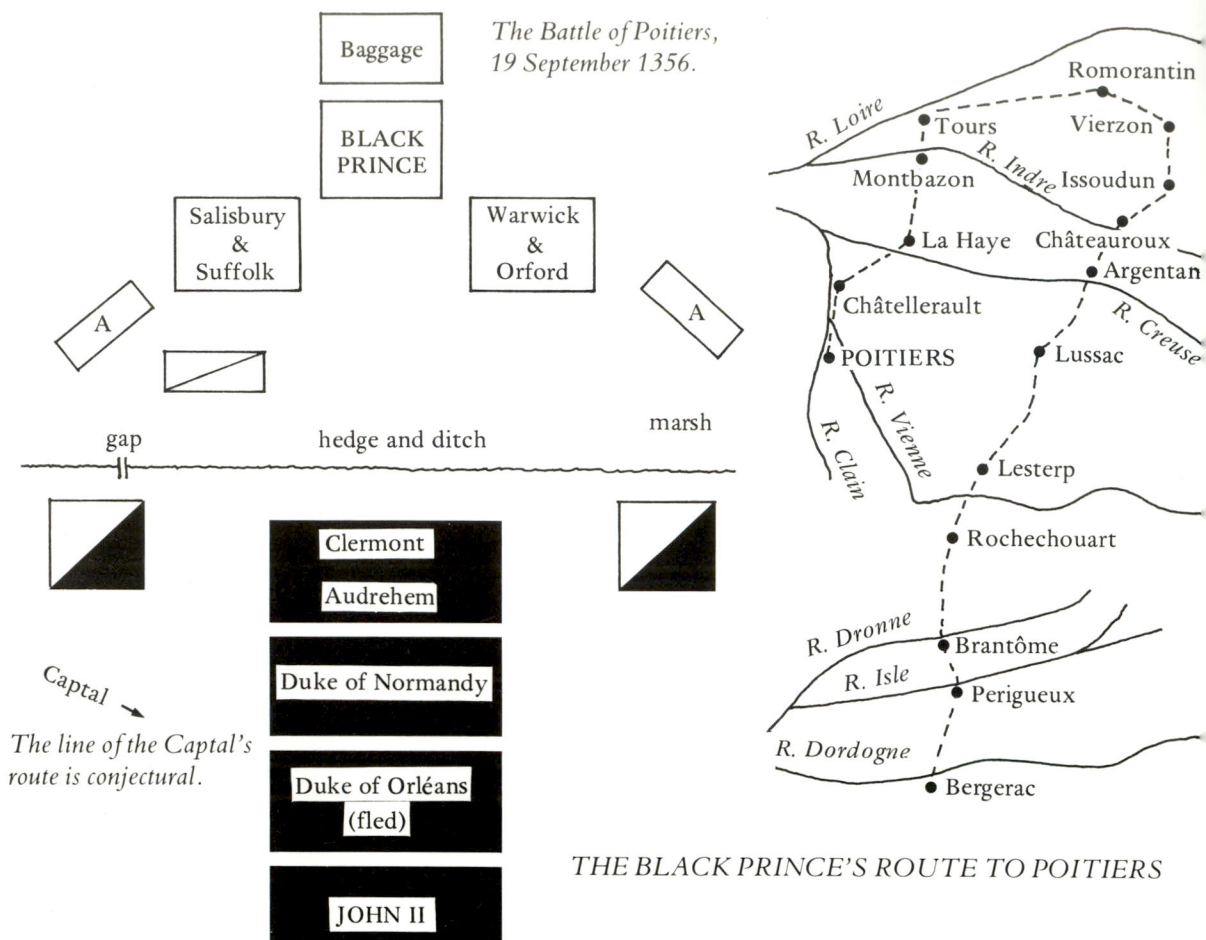

The Battle of Poitiers, 19 September 1356.

Baggage

BLACK PRINCE

Salisbury & Suffolk

Warwick & Orford

A

A

gap | hedge and ditch | marsh

Clermont

Audrehem

Duke of Normandy

Duke of Orléans (fled)

JOHN II

Captal →

*The line of the Captal's route is conjectural.*

**THE BLACK PRINCE'S ROUTE TO POITIERS**

Romorantin, Tours, Vierzon, Issoudun, Montbazon, La Haye, Châteauroux, Argentan, Châtellerault, POITIERS, Lussac, Lesterp, Rochechouart, Brantôme, Perigueux, Bergerac

R. Loire, R. Indre, R. Creuse, R. Vienne, R. Clain, R. Dronne, R. Isle, R. Dordogne

we have some details of the Captal's vital manoeuvre in the middle of the battle, and we know that he used a hill to give cover for the move, but even the side of the field on which he was positioned is uncertain. To show his route on a battle plan, and to mark in an actual hill is no more than conjecture. Nor, apart from what Geoffrey le Baker tells us, is there any assurance about the line of the famous hedge. We must be cautious about Burne's identification of an actual site and hedge.[48] He places the 'gap' as the position of a road, but chronicle accounts suggest more a temporary hole broken through the hedge. There is also room for doubt over the identification of Maupertuis with La Cardinerie. With all these caveats, let us try to reconstruct the battle from the contemporary sources, so that we can view the role played by the archers.

[48] Burne, *Crécy War*, pp. 316–9.
[49] Geoffrey le Baker, pp. 146–7, describes the field, and the gap in the hedge: 'Talia dicens, prospexit quod erat e vicino lateraliter mons quidam sepibus et fossis ad extra redunitus, ad intra vero distinctus quippe ex una parte pascuus et ibi dumis

condensus, ex alia vero vineis consitus, et ex reliqua sacionalis; in cuius vigo sacionali coortem Francorum perpendit residere. Inter nostros et monetem erant ampla profundaque vallis et mariscus, torrente quodam iriguus'; and on the hedge separating the armies: 'sepe longa subterfossata cuius alterum extremum declinavit in mariscum prefatum'; with the gap: 'a declivo bene remota, fuit temesis quedam patula vel hyatus, quem bigarii fecerunt in autumpno.' On the gap, compare *Eulogium*, p. 224: 'Fuit ibi una porta quae vocata in lingua Anglicana lipzet.'
[50] Burne, *Crécy War*, p. 295, accuses the French of 'inventing an English retreat'. A counter view is Galbraith, 'Poitiers', pp. 473–5.
[51] Geoffrey le Baker, p. 143: 'Primo cohors exercitus nostri comitibus Warewici et Oxonie committebatur.' *Prince Noir*, pp. 70–72, on p. 72: 'garderez le cariage'.
[52] On order for French to attack the archers, Geoffrey le Baker, p. 143: 'preterquam quingentos ferro contra sagittas coopertos, quorum assessores iussit invadere sagittarios in principio certaminis'. The advice of Douglas is also Geoffrey le Baker, p. 143.

Geoffrey le Baker gives a graphic description of the field.[49] He tells us that there was a hill to one side, with hedges and ditches around it. Between the English and the hill was a valley with a stream running through it, making the ground marshy. By the English van and centre stood a hedge and ditch, which curved down to the marsh. Near the top of the hill was a gap in the hedge, made so that carts could get through it in the autumn.

The movements of the English army just before the engagement are disputed. French historians, with a little English support, argue that the Black Prince was in retreat when brought to battle. Most English historians have argued against the retreat.[50] Objective decision is not easy since the evidence is not clear. The Black Prince had certainly been trying to evade the French army in his march, just as had Edward III before Crécy. The Earl of Warwick seems to have had to re-cross a stream in order to fight, and his division is described as being in the van, though rather oddly according to Chandos Herald, Warwick was also asked to guard the wagons which one would not expect to be placed in the van.[51] It may however be correct, and reflect rapid arrangements made to re-organise an army where the division which had been in the van on the march found itself the last to deploy for the battle when an attack was made against the army's rear. Galbraith bravely supported the French, pointing out that the *Anonimalle Chronicle* seemed to suggest retreat, and that Burne had not considered this work in his case against a retreat. Probably the Black Prince did attempt to escape from the position, and the French attack on his rear provoked the English to turn, causing Warwick to be re-called over the stream he had already crossed. The English army then assumed a defensive stance, using the hedge and the marsh for protection.

The order of the French army seems reasonably clear. They had a fairly small advance force of cavalry which was led by the Marshals, Audrehem and Clermont. This force had been instructed 'to attack the archers at the beginning of the battle'. There were then three large divisions led by the Dauphin, the Duke of Orleans, and finally King John II. The French were advised by the Scot, Douglas, to fight on foot. The advice was taken, though, as we have seen, it was far from being the first time that the French fought in this manner.[52]

The English order is less clear. There were probably three major divisions: the van led by the Earls of Warwick and Oxford, the centre by the Black Prince, and the rear by the Earls of Salisbury and Suffolk. It seems that the conflict began when the English were passing alongside the hedge. The French tried to break through the gap, and this brought them up against the rear of the English army, which was forced to turn and fight. As Chandos Herald puts it: 'We who were the rear, should now be the front'.[53] The English van was near the marsh and stream, which they had been compelled to re-cross. The position of the Black Prince is not entirely clear. On the march his division was the central one of the three. During the battle he is said to issue from the *charroy*, which probably means the baggage wagons, and may imply that the wagons were arranged in a kind of defensive laager.[54] This may mean that the Prince's division was placed to the rear, where one might expect to find the baggage. It is, however, possible that all three divisions kept roughly in line. The Prince and those with him dismounted. As commander, he addressed himself first to the men-at-arms, and then to the archers. The speech may be an invention of the chronicler's, but up to this period so little note had been taken of the significance of the archers, either by princes or by chroniclers, that it deserves to be recorded here.[55]

'Your courage and your faith are well known to me, for in many great dangers you have shown yourselves as not unworthy sons and kinsmen of those who, under the lead of my father and forefathers, the Kings of England, found no labour too impossible, no place too difficult to take, no mountain too hard to climb, no tower too strong to win, no army unbeatable, no armed host too great. Their efforts tamed the French, the Cypriots, the Syracusans, the Calabrians, and the Palestinians, and overcame the Scots, the Irish, and the persistent Welsh. Occasion, time and danger is wont to make bold men out of timid, quick-witted men out of dull. Honour and patriotism, and the hope of the rich spoils from the French, call you as much as my words, to follow in the footsteps of your fathers. Follow the standards, obey without question, in action and thought, the commands of your leaders, so that if we live to see victory, we shall continue as comrades together, always of one heart and one mind ... Again, if envious fortune decrees, which God forbid, that in this present labour we should go the way of all flesh, your names will not be soiled with infamy, but I and my companions will drink the same cup with you. To conquer the French will be glorious, to be defeated, which God forbid, misfortune and disaster, but not disgrace.'

[53] *Prince Noir*, p. 77: 'Que nous estoias mes derere,/ Et nous seirons tout li primere.'
[54] *Chronique des Quatre Premiers Valois*, p. 49: 'et se hourda de son caroy'.
[55] Geoffrey le Baker, p. 146; for a translation see *EHD*, iv, p. 96.

56 *RIS*, xiv, p. 415: 'innanzi al suo carreggio'; 'seciono due parti de'loro arcieri . . . a destra e a sinestra a in verso'. *Chronique Normande*, p. 114: 'les Englois avoient fait deux ailes de leurs archiers sur les costez de leur bataille, et estoient embatailliez en un grant champ de vignes, clos de haies, ou il avoit pluseurs breches.' *Prince Noir*, p. 77: archers 'sur les deux costes'.

57 *Chronique Normande*, p. 114; Froissart ed. Luce, v, p. 36.

58 Geoffrey le Baker, p. 148: 'comes Oxonie descendit a principe et sagittarios ductos in obliquum iussit.'

59 Froissart ed. Luce, v, p. 29: 'et fisent fosser et haiier leurs arciers autour d'yaus, pour estre plus forte'. And on the volley, Froissart ed. Luce, v, p. 36: 'tout desroute et desconfite par le trait des arciers'.

60 Froissart ed. Luce, v, p. 24: 'le retaillassent au volume de cinq pies'.

61 On the wretches, Geoffrey le Baker, p. 150: 'sagittas a miserrimis semivivis'; on Warwick and Salisbury holding the attack, Geoffrey le Baker, p. 148; and the Captal's route, pp. 150–1.

62 Geoffrey le Baker, p. 150: 'Tunc princeps iussit suum signiferum, dominum Walterum de Wodelonde, versus hostilia signa se movere.'

The Black Prince noted the significance of the hill, and sent a force to occupy it. The position of the archers is not completely clear. The main placing seems once again to have been on the flanks. Villani says there were archers on the right and left, and the *Norman Chronicle* speaks of two wings of archers.[56] During the battle, archers are mentioned lining a hedge, which seems to be at right angles to the French and may therefore not be the hedge that ran across the field.[57] Archers played a major role during the battle. First the Earl of Oxford came from the Prince with orders to lead a band of archers off at an angle, so that they could shoot against the rear of the French cavalry.[58] Perhaps this was into the marshy ground, where archers were certainly stationed on patches of dry ground. The group led by Oxford, however, was used as ordered and then returned to its original position. Some of the archers, at least, defended themselves with earthworks. Froissart says they built 'mounds and ditches around themselves'.

Archers were also important in defending the gap in the hedge which the French tried to break through. The French cavalry attacked head on, but archers and men-at-arms together prevented them from exploiting this weakness. Froissart records that the Marshals' cavalry was 'routed and discomfited by the volley of arrows'.[59]

The bulk of the French force seems to have dismounted. Chandos Herald mentions that when the French cavalry adapted to infantry fighting, they shortened their lances to make them more manageable, and also removed their spurs.[60] The major French divisions attacked in turn, or at least two of them did, since the division under Orleans, the king's brother, seems to have left the field without engaging. But again the French army was larger, and victory was not to be easy. The archers ran out of arrows, and had to run forward to pull arrows from 'wretches who were only half dead'. It seems that Warwick and Salisbury held the main atttack, and this does suggest that the Prince's division was to the rear. Late in the battle a vital part was played by the Captal de Buch, the Gascon ally of the English. He led a reserve force under shelter of the hill to attack the French from the rear.[61] His appearance had an immediate effect at the crux of the battle. The Captal's force certainly included archers, but it seems likely they were Gascons and therefore crossbowmen rather than longbowmen. At this same moment, the Prince ordered his standard bearer, Walter Woodland, to signal the advance, at the same time as bows were shot.[62] The French broke, and were pursued to the gates of Poitiers. The battle,

which had begun at about nine in the morning, was over by noon. The French king had been made a captive, and was to be imprisoned in the Tower of London until ransomed and released.

If Crécy was a disaster for the French, what was Poitiers? It had been a closer fought battle, and the French had successfully forced the English into the fight, but it was in the end a crushing defeat for them. It may be that between 1356 and 1360 Edward III had to moderate his demands to some extent, but from the English point of view, the Treaty of Brétigny was a satisfactory conclusion to this first phase of the Hundred Years' War. The success of the archers was beginning to be more widely acknowledged by chroniclers, and perhaps even by princes.

By 1360 it seems reasonable to attempt some assessment of the evidence relating to archery tactics in the Hundred Years' War.

*The Battle of Poitiers, from a manuscript of Froissart's* Chronicles.

114

[63] Froissart ed. Lettenhove, xv, p. 311: 'Tout
son ost estoit en elles, en
manière de une herche,
et comprendoient bien
ses gens plus d'une
grande lieue de terre . . .
Et les deux elles de
l'Amourath-Bacquin
estoient ouvertes ou
front devant et estoient
estroites derrière, . . . et
les deux elles, lesquelles
estoient toutes ouvertes,
quant les chrestiens
seroient entres dedens,
se devoient devant
clorre et par grant
puissance de poeuple
tout estraindre et con-
fondre quanques ils
trouveroient et encontre-
roient et enclorroient en
leurs elles.'

If, for the moment, we set to one side the meaning of the obscure term *herce*, what have we found? It has become clear that in the great majority of cases, the chroniclers describe a formation where the archers are placed on the wings of the army. It would be wise to see this as the normal manner of employing archers at this time. It also suggests a continuation of the English tactics in the Scottish Wars of Independence to the war against France. We can be more certain of our conclusion if we read on a little in Froissart's *Chronicle*. Froissart does in fact use the term *herce* for one other battle apart from Crécy and Poitiers, and that is the battle of Nicopolis fought in 1396.[63] The details of the battle need not concern us, but the use of the phrase here is decisive. The Luce edition of Froissart has yet to reach this period, and commentators on tactics seem not to have noticed this battle, with its important additional comment. Froissart writes that the army of the Turks under Bajazet was 'in wings, in the manner of a *herche* . . . and the two wings were open at the front in advance, and were closed at the rear . . . and the two wings, which were fully opened, when the Christians had entered within them, were closed up'. Whatever the precise meaning of *herce*, the tactical implications are here made clear: the archers were placed on the wings, forward and fanning outwards, so that when the enemy attacked against the main body in the centre, the archers were able to close on them from the flanks. This then is what we should take to be the normal use of archers in the Hundred Years' War.

# Chapter 7

# Agincourt

## *Preparations*

There can be little question that the Battle of Agincourt deserves a place of honour in the history of medieval archery. It has long been a symbol of English military heroism: from the days when Shakespeare's play filled the Globe, to our own times when the same play enlivened by the magic of Olivier has drawn crowds to the cinema. Agincourt is better known even than Crécy and Poitiers, and is associated even more readily with the achievement of the archers. It was not the last victory for an army using longbows as a major element in its composition, but it is seen now as the apogee of military archery, and no victory after Agincourt has claimed the popular imagination in the same way. After 1415 one somehow feels that the greatest day of the longbow has passed.

Agincourt was born from an attempt to revive English fortunes in France. The Black Death and the fourteenth century depression had left their mark on both England and France, and had contributed to the social and political disturbances of the age. In England the Peasants' Revolt had coincided with the minority of Richard II, and had been followed by the first real break in the dynasty since William the Conqueror, when Henry IV had seized the throne. The new Lancastrian dynasty was far from secure when the young Henry V succeeded. His own early days, at least according to some accounts, were not calculated to inspire confidence. The tale of the tennis balls, sent by the Dauphin to insult Henry, grew in the telling, and is unlikely ever to have happened.[1] It does, however, remind us of Henry V's youthfulness, the point of the story being that he was too young to think about war, too young to do anything except play ball.

[1] On tennis balls, Nicolas, *Agincourt*, pp. 9–11. This remains a valuable source book for the battle. For example, Nicolas quotes Lydgate: 'A tonne of tennys ballys I shall hym sende.' The story becomes embroidered with tennis terms such as 'Fyftene before', and 'let'. On Henry's age, see John Strecche, p. 16: 'quia iuvenis erat'.

French commentators have always blamed the Hundred Years' War on English ambitions. The chronicler of St-Denys suggests that the English king was pushed on by 'the impatient ardour of his subjects'.[2] Accusations against Edward III are repeated against Henry V. Fenin says that he had always intended to conquer France.[3] This may be so, but Henry's actual plans are not easy to recover. Agincourt was far from being a battle that Henry planned and sought. The outcome of the expedition, the way in which it developed may well have been very different from the original intentions. It is true that Henry did turn his eyes to Normandy, and chose to focus initial attention on the Norman port of Harfleur, but his idea seems rather to have aimed at Paris or southwards. In the agreements that Henry made before the campaign in order to obtain the force he needed, it is clear that an expedition to the south figured in Henry's plans. Frequently the agreements specify what wages will be paid should the soldiers be called upon to go to southern France.[4]

As with the start of the Hundred Years' War, there is no simple single explanation of the reopening of the war in the fifteenth century. No doubt Henry was ambitious, saw the possible benefits of success in France, and recognised the need to divert attention from problems at home. Certainly he did revive claims to the French throne, though it is doubtful that he placed great hope in fulfilling them, since he was prepared to abandon them in 1418.[5] It was, however, a deliberately planned expedition, involving a large land and sea force. Henry set about restoring English naval strength from the moment he ascended the throne. The royal fleet had virtually disappeared in the fourteenth century, and at Henry's accession consisted still of a mere handful of ships. Within a few years Henry built a fleet of some strength.[6] Henry also put every effort into raising as powerful an army as possible. One French writer was much impressed by the size of the expeditionary force, including its archer contingent, considering it the best ever to be sent from 'that maritime region at the end of the earth'.[7] It might seem that Henry acted hastily in committing himself to a major campaign after being on the throne for less than two years, but he was an opportunist, and saw the possibilities of attack against a divided France in alliance with Burgundy. Nor, to be fair, was the expedition entirely without provocation: there had been French raids on the English coast. The early popularity of the war in England, and the amount of financial support Henry received from the gentry, demonstrates that it was far from just personal ambition on the king's part.[8]

[2] *Chronique du Religieux*, v, p. 498.

[3] Pierre de Fenin, p. 378.

[4] Nicolas, *Agincourt*, p. 14; Hewitt, 'Organization of War', pp. 78–80.

[5] Le Patourel, 'Origins of the War', p. 71.

[6] Richmond, 'War at Sea', a good summary of this subject, see p. 112.

[7] *Chronique du Religieux*, p. 498: 'Vallidioremque sagittariorum manum' from this maritime region 'orbis fere extremo angula'.

[8] On aristocracy and the war, see Powicke, 'Aristocracy'.

*A fifteenth century pavise from Bohemia.*

In his preparations, Henry gave much attention to the raising of archers, and the collection and production of bows and arrows. In 1413 an order was made that bows and arrows should not be sold to the Scots, and in the same year Nicholas Mynot was made Master of the King's Arrows in the Tower of London. The effort of 1415 in using every possible bowstave, is shown by the fact that in the following year staves were being imported. New bows were made and damaged ones repaired. A writ survives addressed to the bowyer Nicholas Frost, requiring him to find workmen to make and repair the king's bows, at the king's charge, and to get wood from anywhere he could, except from church property.[9]

By the fifteenth century the need was for archers by the thousand. Prestwich suggests that armies in this century became 'a few loyal magnates leading a mass of bowmen'.[10] A Militia Roll from Kent in about 1415, concerned with an anticipated French invasion, shows archers being raised from the boroughs, together with pavisers. The pavise was a shield, generally placed in front of an archer to give him protection. These are usually associated with crossbowmen, who needed more time to load, and it may be that the Kentish archers were crossbowmen.[11] The indenture agreements for the French campaign also include some

[9] Wylie, *Henry V*, like Nicolas an old but useful source. On Scotland and Mynot, see Wylie, *Henry V*, i, p. 161. On imports, ii, p. 354, and for the Frost writ, Nicolas, *Agincourt*, p. 18.

[10] Powicke, 'Aristocracy', p. 128.

[11] Hull, 'Militia Roll', *JSAA*, p. 12. The document itself is printed in *Archaeologia Cantiana*, lxviii, 1954, pp. 159–166, where it is dated 'about 1415'. Men from the boroughs have to provide archers, of whom 44 are named, for example, 'Robertus Warener archerarius'; in some cases, the archer provided is one of the group who provides him, for example, Laurence Newlonde.

crossbowmen, but they are a minority. There is also a significant proportion of mounted archers, for example, in the indenture made between the king and Thomas Tunstall, a squire. Tunstall had to serve with five other men-at-arms, and eighteen mounted archers. Tunstall himself would receive 2s a day, the men-at-arms 40 marks a year, the mounted archers 20 marks. If they went to France, the men-at-arms would get 12d a day, twice as much as the archers. If they had any profits from the war, the king should receive a third of them. Sixpence a day was the normal pay for archers on this expedition. Many indentures mentioned the possibility of going to Guienne, and in this

*Pavises in action at the siege of Caen in a fifteenth century drawing.*

eventuality, archers would receive a reward of 20 marks.[12] Henry gambled his wealth for success. In some agreements, he pawned crown jewels as security for his side of the bargain. The king also checked on the retinues being raised. Richard Redeman and John Strange were ordered to inspect the men-at-arms and archers raised for the Duke of Clarence, and to report on their numbers and on the standard of their equipment.[13] We can in fact obtain some details of the composition of the expeditionary force, since copies of retinue lists have survived. For example, in Harleian MS 782, the Earl of March took 102 archers, the Earl of Huntingdon 35, Lord Camoys 49. Occasionally archers are named, such as William Buteler, Gryffen de Hesketh, and John de Syngleton. The 209 archers of the Earl of Lancaster were among those assigned to the king's retinue. At the foot of this manuscript, it is noted that 8600 archers went from Harfleur to Agincourt. The Sloane MS has lists of mounted and foot archers in the retinues. For example, the Duke of Gloucester had 600 mounted archers, the Earl of Oxford 100 on foot. It is a little odd that in all cases the magnate has his archers either all on foot or all mounted. The figures show that Henry's army had a very large proportion of bowmen in it, and that the bulk of these were longbowmen, half of whom were mounted. Also listed are those craftsmen whose services were essential to the archers on campaign: the fletchers like Robert Mitchell, and the bowyers including Nicholas Frost. It seems that the original manuscript listed the archers by name, but sadly the copies have chosen to name the higher ranks, but with rare exceptions simply to give numbers for the archers.[14]

## Preliminaries

Henry assembled his force on the south coast. When they sailed for France, swans swam around the fleet, which the anonymous author of the *Deeds of Henry V* took for 'a happy augury'.[15] They embarked a few miles west of Harfleur. Henry probably did not envisage a lengthy siege, and it was already fairly late in the campaigning year. The French had not expected this particular move, and Harfleur was not especially well garrisoned. The town possessed excellent natural defences, the Rivers Seine and Lezarde together with marshland. In the event the garrison held out for over five weeks till the 22nd of September. English archers had figured prominently in the siege. They had dug the

[12] See n. 4; and Nicolas, *Agincourt*, App. p. 8. But compare Nicolas, p. 43, where according to a contemporary ordinance, two yeomen are to make a pavise, one holding it while the other shoots — which seems to refer to longbowmen.

[13] On the king's efforts, see Wylie, *Henry V*, i, p. 159, and n. 7; on pawning the crown jewels, Nicolas, *Agincourt*, p. 23, and App. p. 13; and on the inspection, p. 33.

[14] These are printed in Nicolas, *Agincourt*, pp. 327–89: *Harleian MS 782*, and *Sloane MS 6400*. The same work, on p. 389, suggests that the original manuscript contained the names of archers, from a reference in *Ashmolean MS 825*: 'cum tamen sagittariorum nomina omittuntur'.

[15] *Gesta Henrici Quinti*, a major source for the campaign, by an anonymous eye-witness. Attempts to identify him have not been convincing. The reference to the swans is on p. 20.

*A retinue list for the Agincourt campaign including numbers of archers at the end of each entry.*

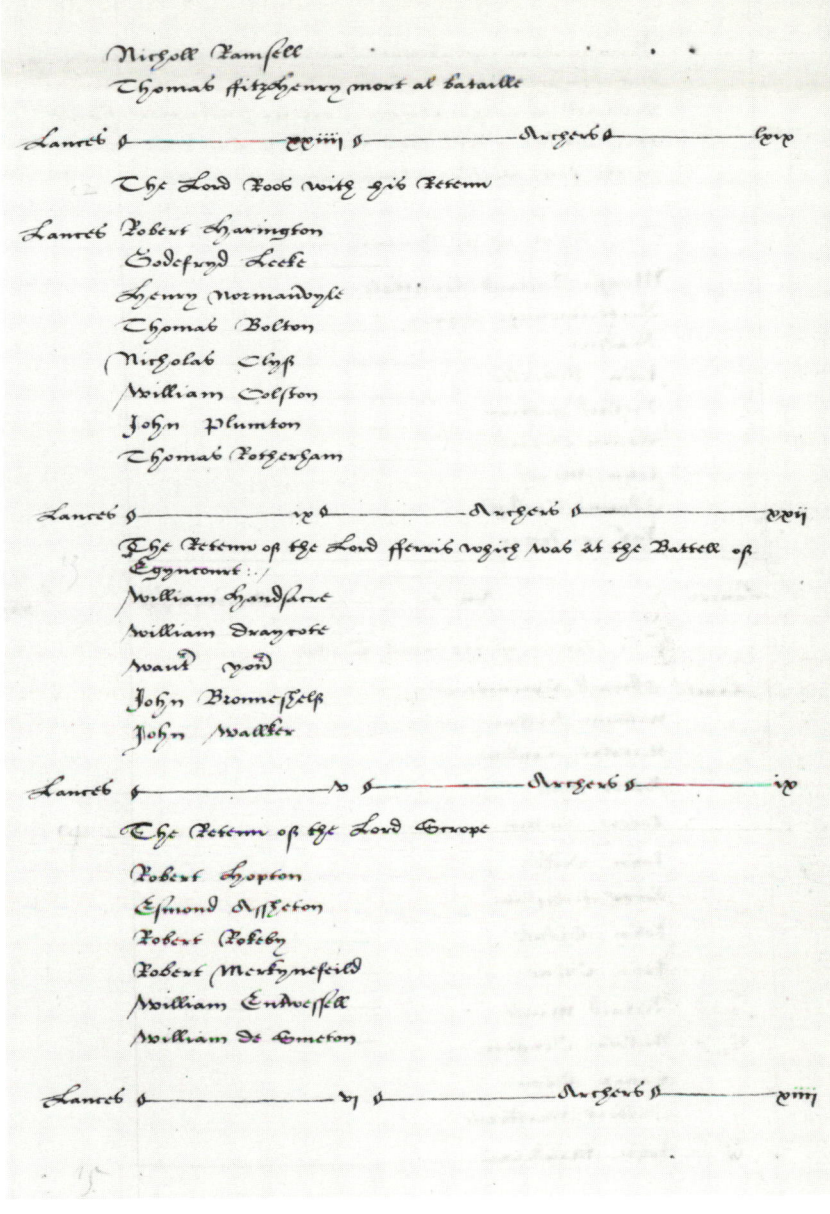

16 *Gesta Henrici Quinti*, pp. 26–30, describes the defences of Harfleur in detail; and the siege on pp. 34–54; and says that after taking the town, Henry left a garrison which included 900 'sagittariis stipendariis'.
17 Favier, *Guerre de Cent Ans*, p. 429.

trenches around the English position, and fire-arrows had finally set alight the barbican before the final assault and surrender.[16]

That Henry had persevered so long in the siege, argues for its significance in his plans. He had not set off simply on a *chevauchée*, where destruction and provocation were all that mattered. Henry had sought and gained a base on the Seine. According to Favier, Harfleur was the 'key to the navigation of the Seine'.[17] It was a threat to Paris itself, as well as a useful springboard for the reconquest of Normandy. The author of the *Deeds of Henry V*, who was himself on the expedition says categorically that Henry sailed 'in order first to recover his duchy of Normandy which belonged by right to William the Conqueror'. One also notes that Henry made efforts to ingratiate himself with the people of Normandy, keeping strict discipline in the army, and hanging a soldier who stole a copper gilt pyx from a church. Henry clearly did have long term intentions regarding the control of Normandy, and the taking of Harfleur established a base for the reconquest. A French chronicler suggests that the local people were ready to accept Henry after the ill treatment handed out to them by the agents of Charles VI.[18]

It was autumn by the time Henry began his march from Harfleur for Calais. It is unlikely that he sought a major battle against a large French army. Probably he intended to round off the campaigning season by what amounted to a *chevauchée*, angering the French, demonstrating the inability of the French king and nobles to protect the populace, and returning safely to Calais. Nevertheless, there was an element of risk, and those with Henry advised him against such a march. In the sense that Henry did not avoid the French army, he was proved wrong in his decision. There seems little doubt that in his march, the intention was to avoid battle, to prevent his army being trapped 'like sheep in a fold'.[19]

[18] *Gesta Henrici Quinti*, p. 16, suggests that Henry set out to conquer Normandy; and tells the pyx story on p. 68. Nicolas, *Agincourt*, p. 69, says that to ingratiate himself further with the populace, Henry forbade his men to search priests 'or the bosoms or heads of the females'. *Chronique du Religieux*, p. 536, says that the French royal agents had treated the people badly.

[19] *Gesta Henrici Quinti*, p. 60: 'velut oves in caulis verisimiliter concluderent'.

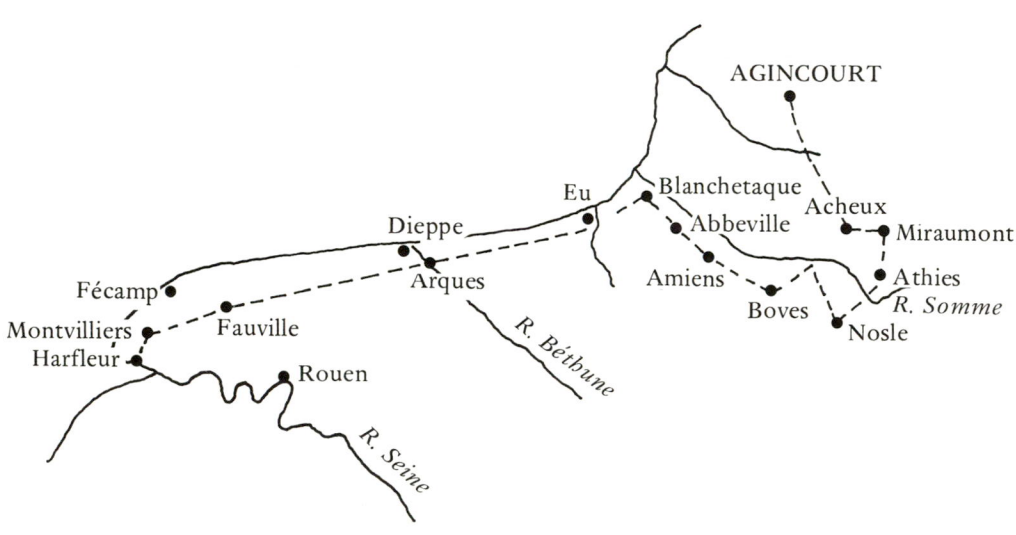

*HENRY V'S ROUTE TO AGINCOURT*

To begin with, he headed northwards along the coast as far as Arques. When, on 13th of October they reached the Somme, it was to find the crossings guarded, and a French army waiting over the river. Henry headed eastwards, searching desperately for a crossing, with the French shadowing him on the opposite bank. He only managed to get over by literally stealing a march, cutting across a bend in the Somme while the French on their side had to follow round the long bend in the river. Henry found and restored the causeways at Bethencourt and Voyennes. Two hundred archers were the first to be sent over, in order to clear away the few defenders and establish a bridgehead. Henry himself supervised the men as they were shuttled across one of the crossings, while the baggage went by the other.[20]

It was necessary to rest the army before proceeding. For all Henry's efforts, the French still managed to get ahead and block his route to Calais. Henry had advanced as far as Maisoncelles, when it became clear that, unless he retraced his steps, he must fight. Just ahead lay the villages of Tramecourt and Agincourt, and a large French army. There was no real possibility of returning to Harfleur, and there would be much loss of face in trying. Henry did attempt negotiation, and was apparently willing to give away Harfleur in return for a safe journey. According to one French writer, Henry was 'like a man who advances fearlessly to the brink of a precipice, but draws back suddenly when he sees the depth of the abyss'.[21] Henry was certainly trapped, and battle seemed inevitable, but there was no question of his courage. He had tried to evade his pursuers and had failed, but having failed he was prepared to fight.

The French had assembled at Rouen. Charles VI had taken the oriflamme, but he did not take part in the operations against Henry, and the Dauphin was prevented from engaging. Nevertheless a large force began to congregate. The vanguard combined the forces of the Constable Charles d'Albret, and Marshal Boucicaut. They had joined forces at Abbeville, and it was their force that had stalked Henry along the Somme.

A remarkable document has come to light, which informs us on the plans of the French at this point.[22] It has been discovered by a research historian, examining a manuscript in the British Library for quite different purposes. He realised the importance of the document, and it has now been published in the *English Historical Review*. It is the most exciting new material relating to the Agincourt campaign to have come to light for many a year. It is a plan of battle, both the formation and the instructions for manoeuvres. It was not the plan for the whole French army at

[20] Recent accounts of the campaign include Burne, *Agincourt War*; Hibbert, *Agincourt*; Keegan, *Face of Battle*, and Seward, *Hundred Years' War*. There is an excellent account of the campaign in Philpotts, 'French Plan', which the author kindly allowed me to read in manuscript before publication. On crossing the Somme see *Gesta Henrici Quinti*, pp. 60, 72.

[21] On negotiation, see Seward, *Hundred Years' War*, pp. 96–7. Thomas Basin, i, p. 40, suggests that Henry was prepared even to bargain Calais. The comment about the precipice is in Labitte, 'Agincourt', p. 133.

[22] Philpotts, 'French Plan'. The MS is *BL Cotton MS Caligula Dv* ff. 43 to 44v. The only similar document is dealt with by Verbruggen in 'Plan de Bataille'; and in Vaughan, *John the Fearless*, pp. 148–150.

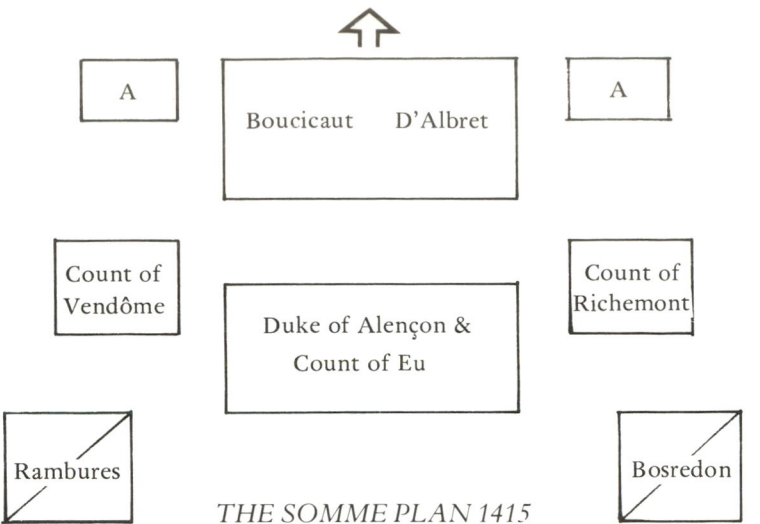

THE SOMME PLAN 1415

*The French plan for the disposition of their army to meet Henry V when he crossed the Somme. It was never put into practice, but makes an interesting comparison with Agincourt.*

Agincourt itself, but for the vanguard alone, and so it must relate to the time when Henry was crossing the Somme. It shows the French were prepared to fight a pitched battle at this stage, with an army that was probably smaller than Henry's, and was only about one fifth the size of the French force that eventually engaged at Agincourt. They were prepared to fight with this vanguard alone to prevent Henry reaching Calais. No wonder the French, with their much greater army, felt so confident of victory at Agincourt.

It is interesting to note that the paper on which the plan is written has a bow and arrow motif for the water-mark, and can be dated to the fifteenth century in North East France. The plan compares closely with what actually happened at Agincourt, but there are also some interesting differences. It is unusual to possess this kind of medieval battle plan, more precise and trustworthy than chronicle accounts. Only one other such plan survives, but our present example relates to one of the most famous of all medieval battles. The document provides, in words, a detailed account of the French formation to be employed against Henry, and instructions on how the army was to fight. The force was to be divided into two divisions: the van to be commanded by Boucicaut and d'Albret together, their banners side by side in the centre, with their men respectively behind them left and right. The second main division was to be under the Duke of Alençon and the Count of Eu. If the English faced them without dividing into divisions, these two main French divisions were to combine into one larger unit. In addition, there would be two wings of dismounted men-at-arms: that on the right commanded by the Count of Richemont, that on the left by the Count of Vendôme. All the archers from the whole force, were to be placed 'in front

124

of the two infantry wings', under the command of Richemont and Vendôme respectively. There was also provision for two units with more freedom of movement, both mounted. The first of these was a force of 1000 men-at-arms, together with half of the valets mounted on their masters' best horses. It was to be commanded by the Master of Crossbows, the Lord of Rambures, and was to be stationed to the rear of the main army. They were to 'fall upon the archers, and use their force to break them'. When the Master of Crossbows ordered this force to move, it was also to be the signal for the infantry wings with their archers to attack. It is not clear from which side this unit would attack, but coming from the rear it would clearly have to make a flank attack, and this fact together with the placing of their own archers on the wings very much suggests that the English archers were also on the flanks. The second mounted unit was smaller than the first, consisting of 200 men-at-arms and the other half of the valets mounted on their masters' horses, under the command of Louis de Bosredon. They were instructed to 'go behind' the English, and attack the valets with the baggage. This unit was also to set off at the time when the Master of Crossbows began his cavalry attack against the archers.

The plan shows that chronicle accounts of battles tend to prolong and separate moves that must often have been designed to coincide. There is a clear intention to make one major effort, that would strike at vital points, at the same time engaging all the English forces so that there could be no reinforcement against a successful breakthrough. The planned attack on the baggage is also of interest, since there was a similar move in the actual Battle of Agincourt, which has generally been taken to have been unofficial. Neither of the mounted units were given precise directions of movement, and this suggests a flexibility that would be advantageous in battle. The instructions for the main divisions to combine in a certain situation, also shows that battle plans took into account possibilities in the battle itself. Overall the document adds to the growing evidence that medieval battles were not just crude charge-and-hammer events.

The plan may have been drawn up in relation to the English crossing of the Somme near Péronne, when Henry was issued a challenge to battle. We know that it was never put into operation. Henry moved on, and the French chose to unite the van with the main army at Bapaume. They moved parallel with the English for a while, and then, as we have seen, moved across the English route at Agincourt, blocking the way to Calais.

Battle surely now was inevitable. The French wished to fight, as they had not always done in the past. They must have been confident in the massive size of their enlarged army, led by the same men who had been prepared to fight on the Somme. They knew of the problems the English had faced: disease, rapid and long marches, shortage of supplies. They had outmanoeuvred Henry, and had caught him in the trap he had sought to avoid. Henry, on the other hand, could not have been eager for the battle, but had little option. Attention must now be given to the site where the battle would take place.

The two armies faced each other at about a mile distance, though several chroniclers suggest they were closer.[23] They formed the triangle around the three villages of Agincourt, Tramecourt and Maisoncelles, just a few miles away from Hesdin and Boulogne. The French were based at Agincourt and Ruisseauville, the English at Maisoncelles. Between them lay farmland and woods, described by several chroniclers.[24] Perhaps, though, we should not be too certain that we can locate the actual battle site. The woodland is not the same now as then, and a nineteenth century account refers to recent clearance.[25] It should also be noted that woodlands are mentioned in front of the English, as well as to the sides. Another warning lies in the name given to the battle. From the site generally thought to be the battlefield, it is further to Agincourt than to Tramecourt. whereas contemporary accounts make it clear that the battle was named after the nearest fortress.[26] It is not good enough to simply call this a mistake, since among those who gave the information to Henry were the French heralds. As with most medieval battles, it is better to follow the contemporary accounts than to let one's description depend upon a chosen, and possibly incorrect site.

The chronicles make it clear that the battle was fought over muddy farmland that had recently been sown with corn, between the villages of Agincourt and Tramecourt. The accounts also suggest that the woodland on either side created a funnel which affected the course of the battle. Chris Philpotts, who discovered the Somme plan, suggests that the French may not in fact have chosen the site for the battle, and that it was simply the point at which the English made contact with the French flank.[27] This might be an answer to why the French selected a site that was apparently to their own disadvantage. However, it may be that the disadvantage was less apparent before than during the battle. In any case, Burne is probably right in believing that the site offered no real advantage to either side.[28] It could hardly be

[23] Nicolas, *Agincourt*, p. 107. Monstrelet, ed. Douët-D'Arcq, iii, p. 101, has 'trois trais d'arc ou environ'; Pierre de Fenin makes it four bowshots; and Titus Livy 250 paces.
[24] Descriptions of the ground in Monstrelet ed. Douët-D'Arcq, iii, pp. 101, 108; *Gesta Henrici Quinti*, p. 78; Thomas Basin, i, p. 44; Jean Juvenal, ii, p. 519; Jean De Waurin, p. 210; and the 'Vita', in *Memorials of Henry V*, p. 43.
[25] Labitte, 'Agincourt', p. 133, n. 1.
[26] Mazas, *Vies*, v, p. 633, suggests that the heralds said Agincourt was closest because Tramecourt was hidden by woods. Mazas, although an early nineteenth century work, deserves consideration because the author had access to a now lost source on Agincourt by a lord of Tramecourt. On this, see Belleval, *Azincourt*, pp. 88, 120, who says that the manuscript was used by a peasant at the time of the French Revolution to swat flies and wasps which were after the grapes!
[27] Philpotts, 'French Plan'. See n. 20 and n. 22.
[28] Burne, *Agincourt War*, p. 79.

argued that the French suffered from the disadvantage of having more men. If they found themselves in difficulty because of the ground, it was through tactical errors in the way they used their forces.

Henry sent a small force to the rear of the French army, which fired a barn and house belong to the priory of St George at Hesdin.[29] This move may have been a last attempt to encourage the French to depart, or (more likely) was intended to divert some of their troops from the main battle. In the event it seems to have had little effect.

The outcome of the battle was to depend on the tactical use of their forces made by the respective commanders, and it is therefore important to try and understand how they deployed their armies. The French formation can be viewed in the light of our new knowledge about their plans for a Somme battle. They now possessed a much larger army to deploy in a more restricted position. They were facing eastwards, since the morning sun was in their eyes. They chose now to divide the army into the traditional three divisions. The van was led by the Constable d'Albret together with the Dukes of Orleans and Bourbon. According to Ursins there were two lance throws between the first and second divisions, but it may be that, as in the plan when

[29] Monstrelet ed Douët-D'Arcq, iii, p. 105.

THE BATTLE OF AGINCOURT,
25 OCTOBER 1415

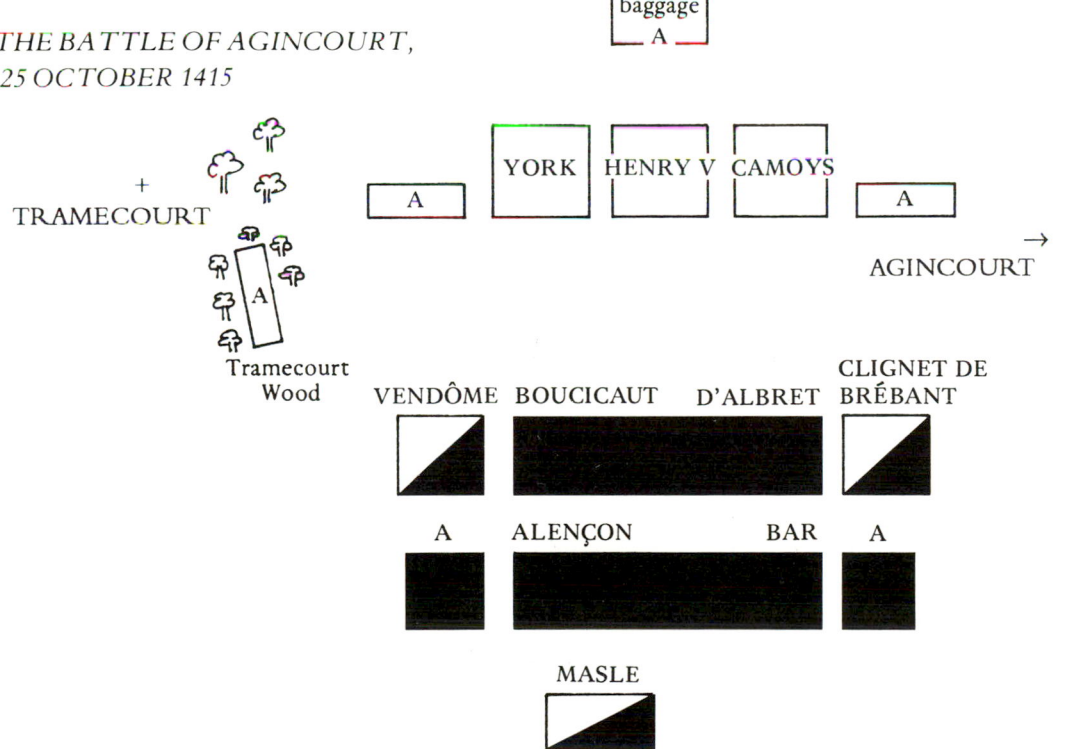

127

they saw the English in one division, they closed up these two divisions.[30] The second division, like the first, was dismounted. It was led by the Dukes of Alençon and Bar. The third division, under the Count of Masle was mounted. At Agincourt, unlike on the Somme, the wings were to be of cavalry, perhaps because the larger army could be less defensively minded, but probably also because on the restricted field the flanks could not be blocked by infantry and room must be left for the cavalry manoeuvres.

The cavalry wings were intended to destroy the English archers, again suggesting that they were to be found on the flanks.[31] It is probable that by this period the French were emulating the tactics that had earlier brought success to the English. Livy says that the French had two projecting wings, like horns.[32] That on the right was led by Clignet de Brébant, that on the left by the Count of Vendôme. Bosredon was also on the flank, as he had been on the Somme plan, and he was indeed the only leader named on that plan who fought at Agincourt and was neither captured nor killed.[33] (Not that he survived long: he was drowned in the Seine in 1417 on the orders of Charles VI for having an affair with the queen.)

The French seem to have made an error in the disposition of their archers. In the Somme plan the archers were placed at the front on the wings. This could not be done at Agincourt if there were to be cavalry wings with room to manoeuvre. D'Albret at Agincourt seems to have made the same error that Edward II made at Bannockburn, placing the archers in a position where they could have little effect. The use of the archers, together with the failure to muster the cavalry wings to their expected numbers suggests that these may have been last moment decisions, hastily and rather inadequately arranged. The St-Denys Chronicle suggests that 4000 French crossbowmen had even been sent away and were not at the battle. The French wing positions may have been further cramped by the placing of cannon on the flanks. Although not significant in this battle, we can view here one example of the way that guns were gradually being used more, and one reason why archery would decline. With regard to both the French and English dispositions, it is worth remembering Christine de Pisan's comment that it was customary to place all kind of shooters on the flanks. Monstrelet refers to the cannon on the flanks, and at least one English archer, 'was killed at the Battle of Agincourt by a gun'.[34] There is general agreement that the French lacked in discipline and organisation, and the St-Denys chronicler blames the commander, d'Albret, whom he

[30] Jean Juvenal, p. 520.
[31] Jean Juvenal, p. 519: 'pour rompre leur traict'; compare Jean de Waurin, p. 213.
[32] Titus Livy, p. 19: 'Gallis vero duobus factis cuneis tanquam duobus cornibus.'
[33] See n. 20.
[34] Archers on the flanks: *Chronique du Religieux*, v, p. 558, which comments on the missing 4000 crossbowmen. Compare Jean le Fèvre, i, p. 247. On Christina de Pisan, see Wylie, *Henry V*, i, p. 159; and same page on archer killed by a gun, and see n. 4: 'Occisus fuit apud bellum de Agincourt cum uno gune.'

calls young and presumptuous and accuses of lacking in experience and ability.[35]

The English also formed in the traditional three divisions, but in line abreast. Their numbers were less, and it was the only way to cover the line. This must be the case, as we are told that Henry had not enough men to form a reserve, a dangerous and limiting situation. Henry himself commanded the centre, with the Duke of York on the right, and Lord Camoys on the left. Although there was no reserve, a small force including archers had been left to guard the baggage, and another group of archers had been sent forward on the left secretly, apparently using the wood of Tramecourt to cover the move, and then taking position in a field under cover of hedges and against the French right flank.[36] This was the one unit that gave Henry any possibility of surprise, but at Agincourt he had to rely on the one and only line holding in what must be a bruising defensive battle. In the event, the battle depended upon the way the archers and dismounted men-at-arms were used, but just exactly how were they used? At Agincourt, as elsewhere, the answer cannnot be straightforward. Most historians have believed in triangular wedges of archers placed between the divisions; indeed many talk of *herces* at Agincourt, though no contemporary chronicler uses the term of this battle.[37] The only support for this formation being used, and perhaps the best evidence of any kind for the conventional interpretation of *herce*, comes from a sentence used by the author of the *Deeds of Henry V*. It must be stressed that this author never uses the word *herce*. The author's actual words are: 'intermisisset cuneos sagittariorum suorum cuilibet aciei, et fecisset eos affigere palos coram eis'.[38] The Oxford edition reasonably translates this as: 'he positioned "wedges" of his archers in between each "battle" and had them drive in their stakes in front of them'. This does indeed seem to portray the conventional idea of a *herce*, which we have rejected for the earlier battles in the war. It may be, if we accept the *Deeds of Henry V*, that there were wedges of archers in the middle of the field at Agincourt. There are however problems in accepting this version as it stands, not least that none of the other sources suggests such a scheme. In all of them, without exception, the English archers mentioned in the battle are on the flanks of the army, which as we have come to see was their normal position. The author of *The Deeds of Henry V*, when he himself comes to describe the battle, says: 'the French cavalry stationed on the flanks made charges against our archers on both sides of our army'. The only point in the battle where stakes are involved, is

[35] *Chronique du Religieux*, v, p. 558, blames the impetuousness of youth.
[36] Monstrelet ed. Douët-D'Arcq, iii, p.105: 200 archers sent 'par derrière son ost . . . Et entrerent secretement a Tramecourt, dedens ung pre de l'avantgarde d'iceulx Francois'. Mazas, *Vies*, p. 616, with access to the Tramecourt Chronicle, says 2000 archers were sent to Tramecourt Wood under the command of William Marshal, and were hidden behind hedges, and has 80 men guarding the baggage. Jean Juvenal, pp. 519–20, has an ambush of archers, together with mounted men-at-arms in the woods; compare Jean le Fèvre, i, pp. 243, 249.
[37] For example, Heath, 'Agincourt', pp. 8–9: 'forming a series of wedges, known as a "herse" or harrow'.
[38] *Gesta Henrici Quinti*, p. 82, with translation on p.883.

when the French cavalry wings charge, and some of them come to grief on the stakes. The same author also mentions that the French cavalry rode between the archers and the woods, showing that the archers were on the flanks.[39] Among the chroniclers who speak only of archers on the flanks is the St Albans' writer, who says Henry ordered the archers forward 'to the right and to the left'; St-Rémy, who says that Henry instructed Erpingham to place the archers in the front in two wings, and in the battle has the cavalry attacking the archer wings with the stakes before them; the St-Denys chronicler who has Henry saying 'We must wait on foot, in close ranks without dividing our force', with all the men-at-arms in the centre, and 'on the two sides of the men-at-arms were the archers'; and Waurin, who in the battle has the French cavalry sent to the sides 'to break the two wings of English archers', again with the stakes placed before them.[40] In other words, the weight of evidence at Agincourt is for archers on the wings, and these archers having the stakes before them. What then do we make of *The Deeds of Henry V*, written by a man who was at the battle? Do we simply dismiss it? Perhaps we have simply failed to take his meaning, so engrossed have we become with *herces* and triangles. Two key words in his remark, may be translated in an alternative way. *Intermisisset* can mean 'mixed'; and *cuneos* though literally meaning 'wedges' is frequently used in medieval chronicles to refer to bodies of troops in a very general way without significance for formation, and might be translated as 'troops', or 'groups'. We could then translate this text as saying that Henry 'mixed bodies of archers among the men-at-arms'. When we consider the small size of his army, and the large proportion of archers within it, this would certainly make sense. Whichever translation we prefer, the text suggests stakes either in blocks in the centre, or in a line across the field. This does not match with other accounts.[41] One is inclined to think the author mistaken at this point, but assuming him to be correct, one can only suggest that the stakes had no effect in the centre where there were fewer archers, more thinly distributed. The evidence for Agincourt on archer formation is not easy. It is not possible to offer a categorical solution, but our preference must again be for archers used primarily on the flanks, though on this occasion placing stakes before them for additional protection.

The use of the stakes has always aroused interest. It was not, as has sometimes been thought, a unique occasion in this respect. Stakes were used in other battles, and in the same way. In any case, they were simply fulfilling a function in protecting the

[39] *Gesta Henrici Quinti*, p. 86: 'Gallorum equites ordinati a lateribus irrupciones fecerent in sagittarios nostros ex utraque parte exercitus nostri'; with the cavalry attacking 'inter sagittarios et nemora'.
[40] Archers on the flanks. *St Alban's Chronicle*, p. 95: 'a dextris vero et sinistris fecit sagittarios anteire'; Jean de Waurin, p. 213: 'de rompre les deux hesles des archiers Anglois'; Jean le Fèvre, i, p. 245: 'Aux deux costez des hommes d'armes estoient les archiers'; and i, p. 253: Erpingham 'les mectre au froncq devant, en deux elles'; and *Chronique du Religieux*, v, p. 552 seems to agree, but then also appears on p. 556 to suggest a circle of archers.
[41] If taken to mean groups of archers mixed with the men-at-arms, could explain the *Chronique du Religieux*, v, p. 556 description of archers all round the king; and the Mazas, *Vies* description of the king behind the archers.
[42] Wylie, *Henry V*, ii, p. 186, says York 'had devised the stake'. It is

worth noting that in the Ordinance by the Earl of Shrewsbury, in Nicolas, *Agincourt*, p. 42, every captain is to compel the yeomen to make stakes which were to be eleven feet long.
[43] On the stakes, see Nicolas, *Agincourt*, p. 90; and Wylie, *Henry V*, ii, p. 150. Most of the chroniclers mention the stakes, and there is general agreement on general agreement on their size and shape, about six feet long, and sharpened at both ends. For example, *Gesta Henrici Quinti*, p. 70: 'unum palum vel baculum quadratum seu rotundum, sex pedum longitudinis et grossitudinis competentis, acutum in utroque fine'. Titus Livy, p. 19, has 'palum acutum utriusque pro scuto'; and the *Brut*, ii, p. 555: 'a stake of tre, sharpet at both endyz . . . and pight an end asslope in ye ground before hem'.
[44] *Gesta Henrici Quinti*, p. 70: 'affigeret ante se a fronte palum suum, et alii alios posteriores palos intermedios'; Jean de Waurin, p. 214, has 'hayes de penchons', and the archers come 'hors de leurs penchons'. Keegan, *Face of Battle*, p. 91, comments on the archers fixing their stakes. Jean le Fèvre, pp. 255–6, has the archers 'yssirent hors de leurs penchons'.

archers that was to be noted in most of the battles of this war. Earth banks and fortifications, holes and trenches had all been used on earlier occasions with the same purpose: to protect the archers, especially from a cavalry charge. It has sometimes been claimed that the idea was the Duke of York's, but this is only because we are told that he ordered them to be made. It is unlikely to have been a novel concept. They had been prepared eight days before they were used, when the army was in the woods near Albret, and there had been news of an intended cavalry attack against the archers.[42] One source suggests that they were bow-staves, certainly they were of similar length, but sharpened at both ends. The archers, at least those on the flanks, knocked their own stakes into the ground in front of them, with the upper points leaning towards the enemy.[43] The placing of the stakes raises some questions. We have decided only to view the stakes on the flanks as being significant. The French cavalry were on the wings to attack the archers on the flanks of the English army. The bulk of the French forces, in the centre, were all dismounted. The whole point of dismounting was that cavalry had proved ineffective against well armed and dismounted men-at-arms. There was no point in a cavalry charge against the men-at-arms. All this suggests that the French were aiming against the wings with their cavalry because that is where the English archers were placed. The stakes were also aimed against cavalry; they served no purpose against dismounted men-at-arms. The stakes then were on the flanks. Were they formed as a fence? Our main information is that each archer placed his own stake before him. There were enough archers to make something resembling a fence, and Waurin does refer to 'hedges of stakes', but how literally can we take this? Keegan has made the sensible point that they would have to go on the enemy side to hammer in the stakes at the required angle. How would they then recover their position if they had raised a fence? From references during the battle itself, it seems likely that there were spaces between the stakes. Waurin has the archers coming out from between their stakes, and St-Rémy mentions that the French horses rode between them. The author of *The Deeds of Henry V*, whose comments on the archer formation have posed difficulties, also says that some stakes were put in further back, and again one wonders about the real meaning of his remarks on formation.[44] It seems probable that the stakes were placed at intervals, and staggered, enough to pose a threat to charging horses, but not enough to prevent some movement backwards and forwards by the archers themselves. It is worth adding at this point that one

French chronicler said the English used a new weapon in this battle, lead maces or mallets.[45] It is probable that he meant the mallets the archers had used to hammer in their stakes, and which they later used as weapons when they joined in the advance with the men-at-arms. It argues that in 1415 the French, if they were not familiar with the mallets, were not used to stakes, though it may just be that archers did not often join in charges.

Henry certainly did his best to rouse the feelings of the archers against the French. They were told that if captured, they would have either three fingers, or the whole of the right hand cut off.[46] In fact they would probably be killed anyway! The more racy accounts also have the French dicing in advance over the prisoners they would get, an archer being all one would get for a blank.[47] Both of these comments have the sound of invention about them. Who bothered to take archers prisoner? An English chronicle has Henry making a pre-battle speech, which is probably also invented, but carries more of a ring of truth about it. According to this, Henry called on each soldier in the army to prove himself a good man, presenting himself as a 'true king and knyght', who would never let himself be ransomed, that is who would die rather than allow himself to be captured:

Allso, Archers, to yow I pray, no fote (foot) that ye flee away,
Erste be we alle beten in this felde.

Henry admitted that they were outnumbered by ten to one, but encouraged all to be of good cheer, and at least in the *London Chronicle* so they were: 'lord, knyght, and archere'.[48]

Henry V had initiated action by a diversionary attack behind the French lines. He had also secretly placed archers forward on the Tramecourt side, that is to the left of the English position. Erpingham was instructed to array the archers on the wings in front of the men-at-arms: it could be this mixing of archers and men-at-arms that the author of *The Deeds of Henry V* had in mind. Erpingham later joined Henry in the centre and dismounted to fight alongside. The two armies were not close enough for the archers to strike. There was a frustrating period during which neither side moved against the other. Keegan has ruminated unpleasantly upon the effects of diarrhoea during this period on men forced to remain at their posts, some in full armour![49] Henry had a good defensive position, with stakes fixed. He was not eager to leave it. The French, apparently determined to fight, seem to have been having last minute

[45] *Chronique du Religieux*, v, p. 562, describes the use of a weapon not previously employed, a 'clavam plumbeam'. Titus Livy, p. 43, suggests archers using the stakes as weapons: 'non sagittis tantum, sed acutis pilis utebantur'.
[46] Thomas Basin, p. 42, has Henry telling his men about the hatred of the French. Mazas, *Vies*, p. 615 has the king saying the French will take 'three fingers of the right hand to prevent them from drawing, and as your king, I shall be subject to the same treatment'. Thomas Walsingham, ii, p. 310, also refers to fingers, but Lydgate, in Nicolas, *Agincourt*, p. 318, it has become the 'ryzt hond'.
[47] *Gesta Henrici Quinti*, p. 80, says that they 'cast dice for our king and his nobles', so the story is not entirely a later invention, but the blanks for archers part of it probably is, see Nicolas, Agincourt, pp. 107, 318, and 272: 'and an archir alwey for a blanke of hir mony'. Compare the *Brut*, ii, p. 555: 'every archer for a blank'.
[48] *Chronicles of London*, pp. 119–20, from *BL Cleopatra C IV*: 'Allso, Archers, to yow I pray, no fote pat ze flee away,/ erste be we alle beten in this felde'; 'and so thei dyd at zt word, lord, knyght and archer'.

doubts about the wisdom of attacking an English army in its familiar defensive attitude. In the end the stalemate was broken by Henry giving the order to advance. The English moved to within bowshot range, and then set down in position as before. It was a dangerous move, and a French charge made during the process could have been devastating. No doubt Henry was also grateful that there was no heavy archery against him. Some precautions were taken to protect the advance. The archers moved in stages, and used shouts as signals for volleys, shouts that were also intended for the ears of the hidden flank archers, who made volleys to cover the advance.[50] The English got away with it, and the battle could now begin in earnest.

## The Battle

The English archers were now able to make provocative volleys. Monstrelet says they shot as far as they could, drawing with all their strength.[51] The French cavalry wings prepared to counter this onslaught, but there were fewer men than anticipated. The reason for this remains a mystery, though some may have deserted before the charge rather than during it. No doubt the English flanking archers had also taken their toll. The cavalry attack against the archers on the wings was made, but it did not succeed. A few men and horses were speared on the stakes. William de Saveuses was not supported by his men, and was shot off his horse. According to the *St-Denys Chronicle* the French men-at-arms retreated shamefully, leaving their leaders in the thick of the fighting, and fled as if pursued by lightning and tempest. The archers shot fast and frequently. One French chronicler says the arrows were like hail, and obscured the sky; another says it was as if a snowstorm had obscured the sky, and a thick fog had come suddenly over the sun. Clignet de Brébant himself was killed, and the Count of Vendôme was captured after being trapped under his fallen horse.[52] The retreat of the defeated cavalry caused further confusion in the French army. The second division had probably closed on the first, as had been intended in the Somme plan. There was no space for the cavalry to retreat into, and no room for the dismounted men-at-arms to open up and make spaces for them. They simply retreated into the middle of their own army with an effect seen in modern mass demonstrations.[53]

[49] Keegan, *Face of Battle*, p. 89.
[50] Monstrelet, ed. Douët-D'Arcq, iii, p. 106.
[51] Monstrelet, ed. Douët-D'Arcq, iii, p. 106: 13,000 'archers comencerent atirer a la volée . . . d'aussi loing come ilz povoient tirer, de toute leur puissance'.
[52] *Chronique du Religieux*, v, p. 560, speaks of the shameful retreat, and compares the arrows to hail: 'instar grandinis'; and see p. 562. Thomas Basin, p. 42, has the other meteorogical similes.
[53] Keegan, *Face of Battle*, p. 97.

The failure of the cavalry to break the archers was vital, but it was the defeat of the main French division that decided the battle. Despite the disruption caused by the retreating cavalry, the French van advanced. They were hindered by the very muddy ground into which their legs sank, and were harassed by the flanking archery. Through all this they kept on, and still had enough impact on the one English line to make it recoil, aiming their charge against the three English standards. The English were forced back, but did not break; again it is difficult to envisage fortified bastions of archers in the middle of this. It was the decisive moment in the battle. Had the English line broken, there were no supporting troops, there was no reserve. Not only did the line hold, but it made a counter advance. The English archers, no longer effective now that a mêlée had developed, and short of arrows, threw down their bows and took up whatever weapons they could. They normally carried other weapons, including swords and daggers, but according to *The Deeds of Henry V* they now took up 'axes, stakes, swords, spears — that were lying about'.[54] As we have seen, one French writer said they used lead mallets as well.[55] It was not normal for archers to take part in an action that was properly the role of the men-at-arms, but in Henry's small force their contribution was invaluable. Several chroniclers make it clear that this was the decisive move, and that the English victory depended upon their archers.[56] The French first division began to retreat, and as with the cavalry, had nowhere to go. The French men-at-arms were so crowded together that they were unable to raise their sword arms, and hence were unable to defend themselves against the ferocious English attack. The second division had closed on the first, but did not have a free field of action. Fenin makes the point that once the van was beaten, the French organisation collapsed, because all the main leaders were in the van.[57] The bodies piled in heaps. *The Deeds of Henry V* says they fell in three piles around the English standards, to the height of a man. This is almost certainly an exaggeration, as Keegan has suggested, it is not possible for bodies to reach more than two or three deep in this way. Men with swords and axes fought from the top of the heaps.[58]

The French van had broken, and the English, led by their king, advanced into the French second division. Henry V himself was engaged in some desperate hand to hand fighting. His brother Humphrey was felled, wounded by a dagger in the bowels.[59] The king stood over his brother's body and protected him, saving his life. Eighteen French knights swore to kill Henry

[54] *Gesta Henrici Quinti*, p. 88: 'sagitte consumpte ... arreptis securibus, palis, gladiis et lancearum'; and Monstrelet, ed. Douët-D'Arcq, iii, p. 108: 'espées, haches, mailletz et becs de faulcons et autres bastons de guerre'.

[55] *Chronique du Religieux*, v, p. 562; and see n. 42 above.

[56] Jean de Waurin, p. 214; *Chronique du Religieux*, pp. 558, 562, 564; Jean Juvenal, p. 519; Perceval de Cagny, i, p. 20; and see Wylie, *Henry V*, ii, p. 196.

[57] Pierre de Fenin, p. 382.

[58] *Gesta Henrici Quinti*, p. 90; Keegan, *Face of Battle*, p. 107.

[59] Titus Livy, p. 20.

or die. They did not succeed, but they came very close. Henry's helmet in Westminster Abbey bears the dents which are said to be evidence of the Duke of Alençon's attack on him. The attack was fended off. According to Mazas, who had access to a now lost chronicle, Alençon surrendered to the king, exclaiming: 'I am the Duke of Alençon, I surrrender myself to you'.[60] He handed his gauntlet to the king, but was run through by someone believing himself to be protecting the king. Henry seems to have suffered no ill effects from the blow on his helmet, but his brother the Duke of York was less fortunate, 'his basonet to his brain was bent', and he was killed presumably by the blow rather than by suffocation.[61] With the flight of the second division, the dismounted men-at-arms were beaten, and the battle virtually decided. Henry, however, could not afford to relax. There were still French cavalry forces on the field. A late arrival for the French was Anthony, Duke of Brabant. He was not armed for battle, but with more courage than some of his French allies had shown, he determined to join the fray, which he did with fatal result. Of the remaining French cavalry, the Count of Masle and Fauquenberg collected some 600 mounted men, and threatened a charge.

It was at this point that one of the most controversial incidents of the battle occurred, when Henry V gave orders to kill the French prisoners. This has generally been defended by English historians on the grounds of military necessity. They have suggested that with Henry fearful of a cavalry charge, news came of an attack on the English baggage, and Henry ordered the killing in case the prisoners joined in the fight. French historians on the other hand, have generally expressed horror at an atrocity, the killing of unarmed prisoners of war.[62] Certainly there was an attack on the baggage, led by two local lords, Isambert of Agincourt and Robert de Bournonville. There were a few other men-at-arms, and some 600 peasants. It has generally been thought that this was an unofficial attack for plunder. The leaders were later punished by the Duke of Burgundy, and even French chroniclers have been critical of the act.[63] Our new knowledge from the Somme plan, however, makes it more likely that this was a part of the official battle plan. It is unlikely there were 600 unorganised peasants, and probable that this was an infantry force attached to the army. This might seem to increase the evidence in justification of Henry's act, though his own men defending the baggage, chiefly archers, proved sufficient for their task, and the threatened cavalry attack failed to materialise.[64] If, however, one considers the action in the light of the medieval

[60] Mazas, *Vies*, p. 629.
[61] *Chronicles of London*, p. 120: York would not flee 'Til his basonet to his brayn was bent'. On suffocation, see Nicolas, *Agincourt*, p. 137. John Hardyng, an eye-witness, in chapter 214, says more died of 'presse' than were killed in the fighting; and says Suffolk died of the 'flire', probably meaning in the flight. The suffocation story is a late one, in Leland, and not to be trusted. It seems more likely that York died of the blow just described.
[62] Belleval, *Azincourt*, pp. 88, 120; and Labitte, 'Agincourt', criticise the act as an 'ordre barbare', a hideous crime. Burne, *Agincourt War*, p. 86; Hibbert, *Agincourt*, p. 117, justify Henry's action. Keegan, *Face of Battle*, p. 109, is one of the few English historians to criticise the killing.
[63] Pierre de Fenin, p. 383, says the French leaders of the raid were much to be blamed. Monstrelet, ed. Douët-D'Arcq, iii, p. 109, says there were 'six cens paysans' in the raid.
[64] Monstrelet, ed. Douët-D'Arcq, iii, p. 110, suggests that the charge by the remaining cavalry did occur.

laws and code of war, it is difficult to justify.[65] The fault may have been in taking too many prisoners too quickly, a likely enough development, given the value of ransoms and the greed of the average soldier. Once surrender was accepted though, provided the prisoner kept his side of the agreement, he should be under the protection of his captor. There is no suggestion that the prisoners actually did take up arms again, or make anything but a theoretical threat to Henry, and hence the king had no justification for execution.

This is to assume that Henry did carry out a mass execution, and certainly the chronicles suggest this. An interesting addition to the argument has been made by Keegan, who has queried the logistics of killing so many prisoners in this way.[66] The fact that Henry had to rely on a squire and 200 archers as his execution squad suggests a reluctance on the part of the knights to carry out the act, which would dishonour them as well as the king. Mazas says that the nobles refused to do it.[67] Keegan points out the difficulty, even in modern times, of carrying out mass executions, and it does seem unlikely that thousands of French knights could have been killed unjustifiably and without resistance. Some, it seems, were burned to death in cottages, but this can hardly have been a large number. Keegan is probably right that the scale of the thing has been exaggerated, that some may have been killed as a threat but that it never ran to thousands. Fenin says that those killed were those who had been recently captured, and this may not have been all the prisoners.[68] It is worth noting the large number of prisoners that Henry took on with him to Calais and England. They made their presence felt by protesting that the crossing caused more suffering to them than the battle.[69] The conclusion to all this is probably that Henry did break the military code of his day by executing prisoners of war, but that the extent of his crime has been exaggerated.

The failure of the attack on the baggage brought the battle to a close. The cavalry dispersed. Henry was left in command of the field. According to the author of *The Deeds of Henry V*: the French 'abandoned to us that field of blood together with their wagons and other baggage-carts, many of these loaded with provisions and missiles, spears and bows'.[70]

The archers took part in the general pillaging that followed. Some of them, however, were forced to sell their plunder and their ransom rights in order to buy the food they desperately needed. The dead were buried on the spot, in three large trenches. According to Monstrelet there were 5800 corpses. This

[65] Keen, *Laws of War*, gives an excellent survey of the subject, and shows how seriously the code was taken.
[66] Keegan, *Face of Battle*, p. 111.
[67] Mazas, *Vies*, p. 630.
[68] Pierre de Fenin, p. 383. Wylie, *Henry V*, ii, p. 173: the Duke of Brabant was captured late in the day and taken to a distance where his throat was cut.
[69] Prisoners. See Keegan, Face of Battle, p. 111; Nicolas, *Agincourt*, pp. 143–9; Wylie, *Henry V*, ii, pp. 243, 252; *Gesta Henrici Quinti*, pp. 97, 101; Titus Livy, p. 22, mentions the bad weather. The chroniclers, as is usual where figures occur, vary from 700 to several thousand. Monstrelet, ed. Douët-D'Arcq, iii, p. 120, has 'quinze cens ou environ, tous chevaliers ou escuiers'. Wylie, *Henry V*, ii, p. 244, shows that some were ransomed before the return to England. Nicolas, *Agincourt*, p. 144, says there were also prisoners from Harfleur.
[70] *Gesta Henrici Quinti*, p. 92: 'nobis agrum sanguinis cum quadrigis et vectuariis aliis multis refertis victualibus, ac telis, lanceis et arcubus, reliquerunt'.
[71] Archers pillaging, see Nicolas, *Agincourt*, p. 142. History of the site, see Belleval, *Azincourt*, pp. 88, 120–2; and Labitte, 'Agincourt',

pp. 146–9. Monstrelet, ed. Douët-D'Arcq, iii, p. 122, describes the burials, and gives the figure of 5800. Nicolas, *Agincourt*, p. 139, deals with the boiling.

*A fifteenth century Flemish manuscript showing archers in the front rank.*

area was hedged in, and in the eighteenth century a chapel was built there, only to be destroyed at the time of the French Revolution in 1793. The land was turned to agriculture. In 1816 an English officer bought the right to dig the ground, and it was said that he found bones and weapons, including arrow heads. The corpses of York and Suffolk were boiled, so that the bones could be taken back to England.[71]

There has been some recent denigration of the significance of Agincourt, but to some extent that is only by viewing later events with the benefit of hindsight, and the knowledge that

England's triumph was to be short-lived.[72] It should be remembered that Henry went on from Agincourt to reconquer Normandy, and in the Treaty of Troyes, to obtain the promise of the French crown. That this never came about may have been inevitable, but was certainly made more likely by the premature death of Henry V. Agincourt remained a great victory, and a victory that as a French chronicler said, would not have been won without the archers.[73]

In London Henry was feted; the archers — so far as one can see from the chronicles — forgotten. There was a procession to Westminster, with accompanying pageantry: sparrows were released into the air, there was a mock castle built at Cheapside, virgins in white lined London Bridge and sang a song of victory, while others blew gold leaves on to the king's head.[74] But perhaps a more appropriate last thought on Agincourt, in a history of the archers, is to consider the fate of Thomas Hostell, an archer who survived the battle. He had been wounded both at Harfleur and at Agincourt, but lived on into the reign of Henry VI when he petitioned the king because he had been hit by a 'springolt through the head, losing his one eye, and his cheek bone broken'. By the time of his petition he was 'sore feebled and debruised, now fallen to great age and poverty, greatly indebted, and may not help himself . . . being for his said services never yet recompensed nor rewarded'.[75] Such has often been the fate of heroes from the ranks.

[72] For example, Allmand, *Henry V*, p. 22.

[73] See n. 56 above.

[74] *Gesta Henrici Quinti*, pp. 100–12, gives a detailed account of the celebrations.

[75] Nicolas, *Agincourt*, pp. 172–3. Ellis, *Original Letters*, i, p. 95, has Hostell's letter to the council of Henry VI in 1422, he was wounded by a 'springolt through the hede, lesing his oon ye, and his cheke boon broken . . . sore febeled and debrused; now falle to greet age and poverty; gretly endetted; and may not helpe himself . . . being for his said service never yit recompensed ne rewarded.'

# Chapter 8

# The Last Years
# of Military Archery

## *The Hundred Years' War after Agincourt*

One might imagine from some histories of archery that Agincourt was the last occasion on which the bow was used to any effect in warfare, and that it immediately gave way to guns. In fact, the process of change from bows to guns was a very gradual one, and was not even complete by the end of the medieval period. Cannons had been used in Edward III's Scottish wars, and at Crécy. They were improved during the fifteenth century, especially through the work of Jean Bureau and his brother Gaspard. Jean had for a time been employed by the King of England, but transferred his services to France with some effect.[1] Better forging techniques were introduced, and both large siege cannons and small handguns were made more efficient, though it was many years before they were to replace bows. Guns were expensive to make, not as safe as bows, not necessarily more effective, and slower to use. Most armies of the time maintained a balance of archers and gunners. In effect, military archery remained significant throughout the fifteenth century, just as it had been throughout the middle ages.

The final phases of the Hundred Years' War are less well known in England than the earlier stages, perhaps because England was now less successful, with the war concluding in French triumph. The final French victory was not easily won, and was not easy to foresee in 1415 when Henry surveyed the ruins of the French army at Agincourt, or in 1420 when he

[1] On guns see Hogg, *English Artillery*; and Vale, *War and Chivalry*.

139

obtained from Charles VI the surrender of the future of the French throne to himself and his successors. It took great efforts by such as Charles VII, Joan of Arc and Jean Bureau, by the French armies and the French people, before that conclusion could be reached.

Agincourt was not the last English success, or even the peak of the English advance. Henry V was able to regain more of the old Norman and Angevin territories before his premature death. Even then, his brother, John, Duke of Bedford, who acted as regent for the young Henry VI, made every effort to confirm and extend the gains. There were indeed further triumphs on the battlefield, still owing much to the effect of the longbow. The main French victory, before the emergence of Joan of Arc, was at Baugé in 1421, and it reinforced rather than denied the importance of English archery.[2] Clarence chose to fight the French without waiting for his archers, and it was seen at the time as the reason for his defeat: 'By cause they wolde nott take with hem archers'. Clarence paid for his folly with his life in that battle. Baugé apart, England still seemed to have the upper hand, and there were several victories on the old pattern. At Valmont, in 1416, the archers again used stakes as they did at Agincourt, and as they were to do in most of the battles in this late part of the war. They did so again at Cravant in 1423, where the archers

*Fifteenth century illustration of a siege, showing crossbows, longbows and a cannon.*

[2] On Baugé, see Burne, Agincourt War, p. 148. The quote on archers is from the *Brut*, ii.

140

gave important cover to the Earl of Salisbury when crossing the river, and turned the battle when they 'began to shoot all together'.[3]

At Verneuil in 1424 the archers were responsible for an English victory, in a battle on a large scale. The chronicler Waurin wrote: 'I saw the assembly at Agincourt, and at Cravant, but Verneuil was the most formidable, and the best fought'. The archers again placed stakes before them, as Waurin says: 'in the English fashion'. They set their consciences straight, he says, because the English 'are very devout, especially before drinking'. The archers 'on the two wings' advanced with shouts as they had done at Agincourt. They were met by archery in return, for in this late part of the war the French had learned the need for large numbers of archers, and made efforts to raise ordinary archers as well as crossbowmen, in France and elsewhere. At Verneuil the English archers found themselves faced by a body of Scots employed by their enemy. Waurin says: they 'began to shoot against each other so murderously that it was horrible to watch'. The Scottish kings, like the French, had made efforts to improve and increase their archery, encouraging practice. Froissart had considered that the Scots were 'not skilled in archery', but it seems that a change had been effected. Nevertheless the English archers got the best of the match at Verneuil. Another group of archers had been set to guard the baggage, more strongly than at Agincourt. This force played a significant role in the battle: holding off an attack in which the chronicler Waurin had to

[3] On Valmont and Cravant see Burne, *Agincourt War*, pp. 99, 181. The quote on shooting is from Jean de Waurin, v, p. 44.

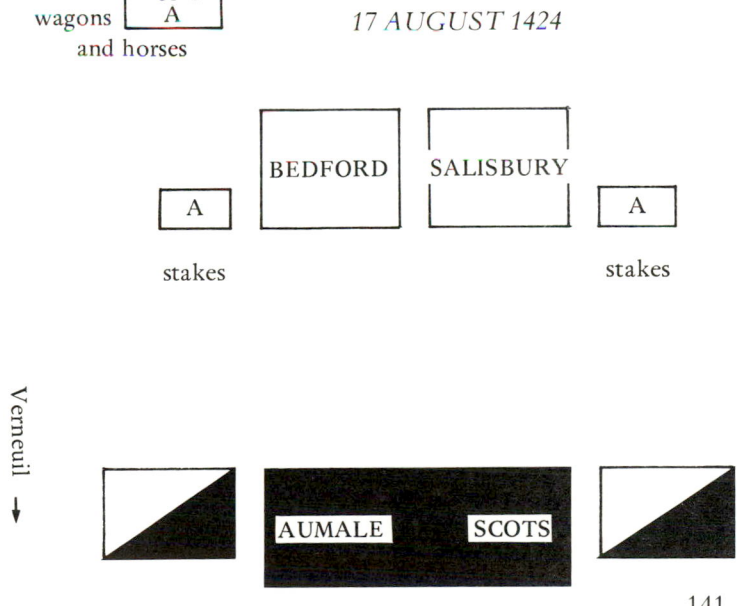

THE BATTLE OF VERNEUIL, 17 AUGUST 1424

defend himself; and then 'fresh and new', they joined in the main fight with a shout, helping to push back the French and being 'a great cause of the victory'.[4]

1429 is generally seen as a turning point in the war. It was the year that saw the emergence of Joan of Arc, the saving of Orleans, and the French victory at Patay. But even in 1429 the English came out on top in the battle of Rouvray, sometimes known as the Battle of the Herrings, because the English army was taking wagons loaded with herrings for Lent to Orleans when it was attacked. Here again the archers held off a French attack, and then joined in the countering charge. Even Patay was far from being the end of the road, and the English archers won a fight at Beauvais in 1430.[5] Although England lost the war, it was not because archery had lost its importance. In these years there were almost annual expeditions to France, always including archers. In 1453 parliament was prepared to grant Henry VI 20,000 archers for six months, though in the end they were not called on.[6]

Guns were used by the French in the last great battles of the war, and this is certainly symbolic of the direction in which warfare was moving, but the fact has been much exaggerated in its significance. The French in these years owed as much to their own improved archery as they did to guns. Patay, like Baugé, really confirms the importance of archery rather than the reverse. The French were able to win this battle by dispersing the English archers before they were set in position on the flanks.

In the battle of Formigny in 1450, which decided the fate of Normandy, there were archers on both sides. The French used guns in the battle, but it was the by-play between the English archers and the French troops in capturing and recapturing the guns that gave them significance in the battle. The battle was decided by the appearance of a second French force under Richemont. Even in defeat the archers fought bravely, five hundred of them standing to the last behind the hedges of a garden.

Castillon in 1453 was the final battle of the Hundred Years' War, and marked the end of the conflict — since there was no concluding peace treaty. Guns certainly were important in this last battle, making it a particularly symbolic fight. The French possessed some seven hundred handgunners, in such numbers it is unlikely they were anything else, though there were also large guns in the French artillery park. The handguns are important to us, for they replaced bows in military functions; just as the large siege and field guns replaced the old engines, catapults, balistae

[4] On Verneuil, see Burne, *Agincourt War*, p. 196. The quotes are from Jean de Waurin, iii, p. 109: of the three battles 'pour certain celle de Verneul fut du tout plus a redoubter et la mieulz combatue'; p. 109: on devotion and drink, 'car de leur propre nature ilz sont tres devotz, devant boire especialement'; p. 110, on stakes: 'penchons aguisies pour mettre devant eulz, selon la mode Angloise'; p. 110, on archers on the wings: 'les archiers sur les deux hesles'; p. 112, on Scots: 'les archers dAngleterre et les Escotz quy avec les Francois estoient encommencerent de traire les ungz a lencontre des autres sy cruelement que horreur estoit a les regarder'; p. 114, fresh and new: 'fres et nouveaulz'; p. 114, Waurin defending himself: 'comme pour moy mesmes deffendre je feusse assez empescie'; and p. 115, archers responsible for the victory: 'furent grant cause de la victore'. And see *Brut*, ii, p. 434.
[5] On Rouvray see Burne, *Agincourt War*, p. 234; Thomas Basin, ii, p. 122. On Patay, Burne, *Agincourt War*, p. 256; Jean de Waurin, pp. 300–3; Jean le Fèvre: 'd'un costé comme d'autre'. On Beauvais, Waurin, p. 350: the French 'reboutez par le

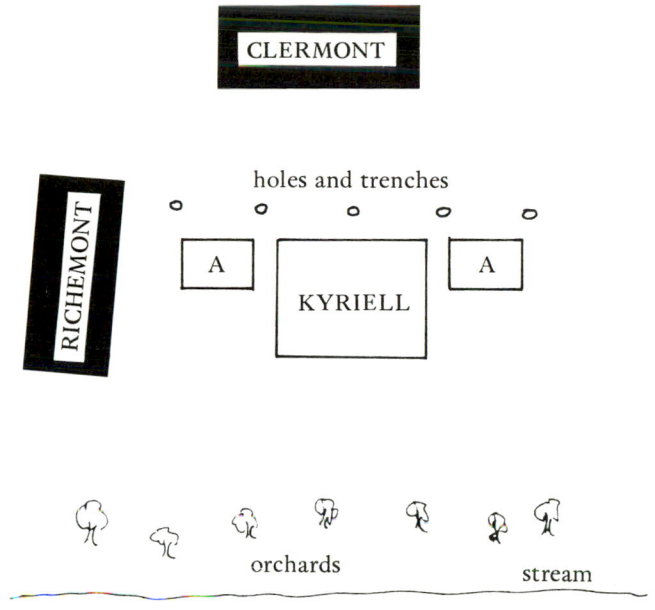

and trebuchets. As with terms like *balista* (which is difficult to interpret as it can mean either a siege engine or a crossbow) so with guns we cannot be sure whether they are large or small unless given additional information: the word *culverin*, for example, can mean either. There is no doubt that handguns were used, and in 1435 there is a clear reference to culverins *ad manum*. Castillon was an important landmark in the increased use of handguns.[8] By the late fifteenth century these had certainly become more effective. A bullet from a handgun could penetrate steel, apparently more effectively than a bow or a crossbow, though some armour was considered proof against either. There is some interesting information in the Statutes of the Gild of Armourers at Angers from 1448, which show that they had two qualities of armour: the best which was proof against a crossbow with a windlass, and the second-class, which was proof against an ordinary bow. Malcolm Vale believes that by the end of the fifteenth century armour could be 'proof against the longbow'. But, even in France, it was not until the sixteenth century that the arquebus clearly replaced the crossbow.[9] The French won the battle of Castillon because the English were not able to capture a position defended by guns, but this does not of itself prove that guns now dominated the battlefield. Talbot, presumably because he was misinformed, chose to attack a strongly defended artillery

trait des archiers
Anglois'.
  [6] Griffiths, *Henry VI*,
pp. 394, 432.
  [7] On Formigny, see
the collection of sources
in Joret, *Formigny*;
Burne, *Agincourt War*,
p.8315.
  [8] On Castillon, see
Burne, *Agincourt War*,
p. 331; Jean de Waurin,
v, pp. 245–7, who refers
to there being 'frans
archiers' present on
p. 246.
  [9] On armour and
statutes see Vale, *War
and Chivalry*, p. 113.

park. It was a suicidal decision. The English, even in 1453, were full of confidence, bearing banners inscribed with medieval graffiti impugning the birth of the French king. The archers fought bravely in the attack, but to no avail. A second French force appeared but the battle was already virtually won. The guns may be said to have won the battle, but only because Talbot made an unwise decision to assault their prepared position. It was a far riskier decision to take than that made by any French commander earlier in the war deciding to attack defended English positions, and much less necessary. When protected archery positions were not attacked, as at Agincourt, the English had sufficient mobility to be able to approach their enemy and provoke battle. It cannot be supposed that the French artillery at Castillon would have been able to take the offensive had Talbot not attacked them.

Nor is the appearance of either siege or handguns the whole story. Continental warfare was altering in other ways. In the 1440s the French had set up their companies of free archers.[10] These were levied by parishes, one man from every 80 hearths. In the mid-fifteenth century there were some 8000 free archers; by the time of Louis XI there were 16,000 in four groups each under a captain. They were recruited by selection of the best men, and were given valuable exemptions in tax. It was part of the development of more professional forces in France, and of the standing national armies which transformed the nature of war. Archery had become a commonplace in European warfare: sometimes English mercenaries were used, but others were trained in the same mould. English archery, though not an English army, was involved at Brouershaven in Holland in 1425, when the archers shot so fast 'that there seemed to be a cloud and a canopy over the field from the denseness of the arrows'. The English were not involved at Montlhéry in 1465, though again there were some English archers present, but now others used their methods.[11] The Count of St Pol had mounted archers whom he dismounted, 'every man with a stake planted before him'. The Burgundian men-at-arms dismounted and fought with their archers, 'which custom they had learned from the English'. The battle began with archery from both sides, now a common-place of European warfare, the King of France's archers 'glittering in their liveries, and very well disciplined'. Commynes, however, still thought that English archers were 'the best in the world'. It is clear that the second half of the fifteenth century, far from seeing the demise of archery, saw its continuation and extension. Other nations had adopted the English system.

[10] On free archers, see Contamine, *Guerre, État*, pp. 304–64, 460–69.

[11] On Brouershaven, see Jean de Waurin, iii, pp. 201–3; on p. 202: 'archiers à tyrer des deux parties'; 'sy onnyement que de lespesseur du trait sambloit estre une nuée et sur le champ une esteullière'. On Montlhéry, see Gillingham, *Wars of the Roses*, p. 42, and Commynes, i, pp. 19–39; p. 22: 'mys a pied hommes d'armes et archiers'; p. 23: 'tous les archiers deshouzez, chascun ung pau plante devant eulx'; p. 23: 'car entre les Bourguynons lors s'estoyent les plus honnorez que ceulx qui descendoyent avecques les archiers . . . et tenoient cela des Angloys'; p. 25: 'toute d'archiers d'un costé et d'autre'; p. 26: 'la souveraine chose du monde pour les batailles sont les archiers, mais qu'ilz soyent par milliers, car en petit nombre ne vallent riens'; p. 26: 'les Angloys qui sont la fleur des archer du monde'.

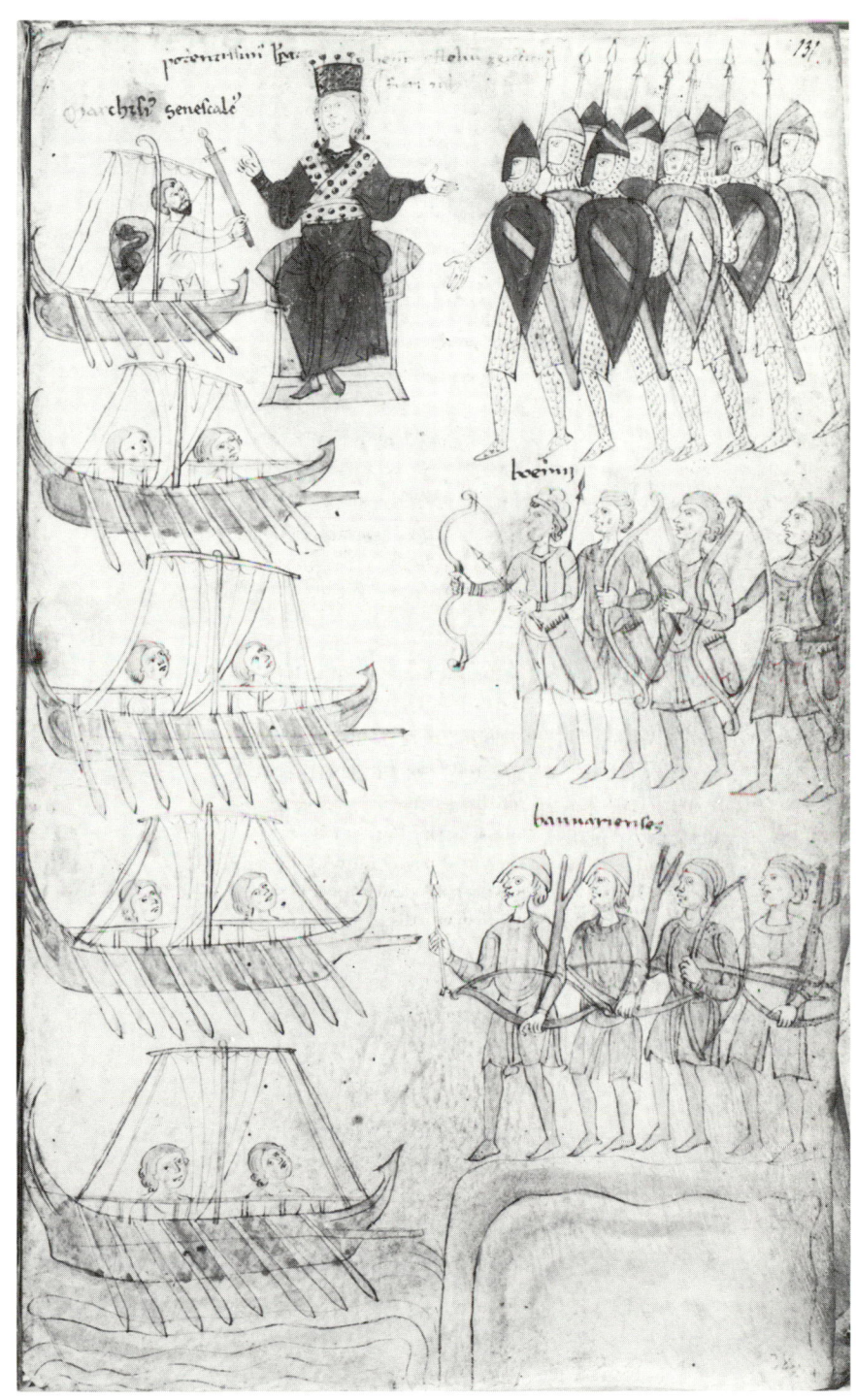

*Twelfth century cross-bowmen in Sicily.*

Charles the Bold of Burgundy's ordinance of 1473 gave detailed instructions for the training of archers: in dismounting, drawing their bows, advancing in co-ordination with pikemen: the pikemen having to kneel while the archers shot over their heads.[12] Burgundy, like France, now possessed a standing army in which archers played an important part. According to Waurin the Burgundians much admired the English archers, thinking more of them than they did of fine clothes. The same chronicler wrote: 'I am of the opinion that the most important thing in the world in battle is the archers, but they must be in thousands, for in small numbers they do not prevail'. By the late fifteenth century archers had become fundamental in the composition of European armies in the west, and Waurin was quite right to see that their effectiveness depended on their mass. The French victory in the Hundred Years' War depended more on their recognition of the need for effective archery, and on successful attempts to produce it, than on the emergence of guns. The outcome of the war suggests that English archery was no longer so dominant, and that was true in so far that guns were increasing in numbers and in effectiveness, and that other nations were developing better archery of their own.

## The Crossbow in the Later Middle Ages

One important factor in the improvement of continental archery was the increased efficiency of the crossbow.[13] The composite crossbow, made of horn, sinew and glue with wood

[12] 1473 Ordinance, Gillingham, *Wars of the Roses*, p. 42.

[13] On crossbows, the outstanding work is Payne-Gallwey, *Crossbow*. A helpful booklet is Wilson, *Treasures of the Tower*. And see Foley, Palmer and Soedel, 'Crossbow', to which my attention was drawn by my colleague, Ted Crawford.

*Carving of a crossbow spanned by hand on a French misericord.*

*Fifteenth century illustration of the siege of Rhodes, showing one crossbow being spanned by one foot, and another by one foot and a cranequin.*

for the shape, was considerably more powerful than the earlier crossbows and was certainly in use by the thirteenth century. Ingenious methods were introduced to make it easier to draw the string of the bow. Most crossbows worked by having a projecting nut at the top of the stock, over which the string was pulled, and which held the string in position until released. There was also normally a trigger arrangement which released the nut and hence the string. The nut was generally made of horn, shaped like a large and thick coin with a groove in the centre of the edge. It fitted into a special socket in the 'box' of the crossbow, so that it would revolve smoothly. When in position in the 'box', the groove round the nut matched exactly against the groove along the top of the stock. The bolt could be placed along this groove and over the nut, and when the string was pulled over the nut it would lay up against the butt of the bolt. There were various ways of drawing the string, or bending the bow. As the bows became stronger, so the crossbowman needed more assistance. In early days, with a wooden bow, it was quite possible to draw the string by hand, sometimes placing both feet inside the bow while pulling the string. The most common aid on a medieval crossbow, was a stirrup at the end of the stock, so that one could place a foot in the stirrup and use the leg power to pull against the hands or the device drawing the string. Either the foot could hold the stirrup on the ground while drawing, or else the string could be held with knee bent, and then by straightening the leg the bow would be pulled away from the string. Several devices were invented to make it easier to pull the string. One was a simple claw which hooked over the string. When this was fixed to the belt, one stooped over and hooked on the claw, then straightened the back, thus drawing the bow. Another idea was to use a small pulley, with a hook on the wheel to hold the string, and a hook on the stock to give the leverage again by straightening up. A popular device, often seen on medieval illustrations of crossbows, was the goat's foot lever, which was introduced in about the middle of the fourteenth century. It was named simply from its similarity to a goat's foot, with a cloven end. It required a specially adapted bow, with a pin projecting from either side of the stock. The lever had claws at one end that fixed under the string. It then rested over the stock, pivoting on the pin. By pressing the handle, the lever pivoted, and the string was drawn.

When the steel bow was developed in the fifteenth century, a tougher bending device was necessary to provide the greater pull. The windlass appeared at the end of the fourteenth century, and could be used on any crossbow. Like the goat's foot lever, it may frequently be seen in illustrations. In essence it was a winding machine, using pulleys. It consisted of strings running from one end that had to be fixed over the butt of the stock, to claws at the other end which pulled the bowstring. The bow was bent by putting a foot in the stirrup and winding the handles of the windlass. The windlass had a pull of something like 1200 lbs, as against say 50 lbs or less required for a longbow.

*A primitive crossbow being spanned by two feet without a stirrup, from the fourteenth century* Luttrell Psalter.

*A bow spanned by one foot in the stirrup and by bending the knee.*

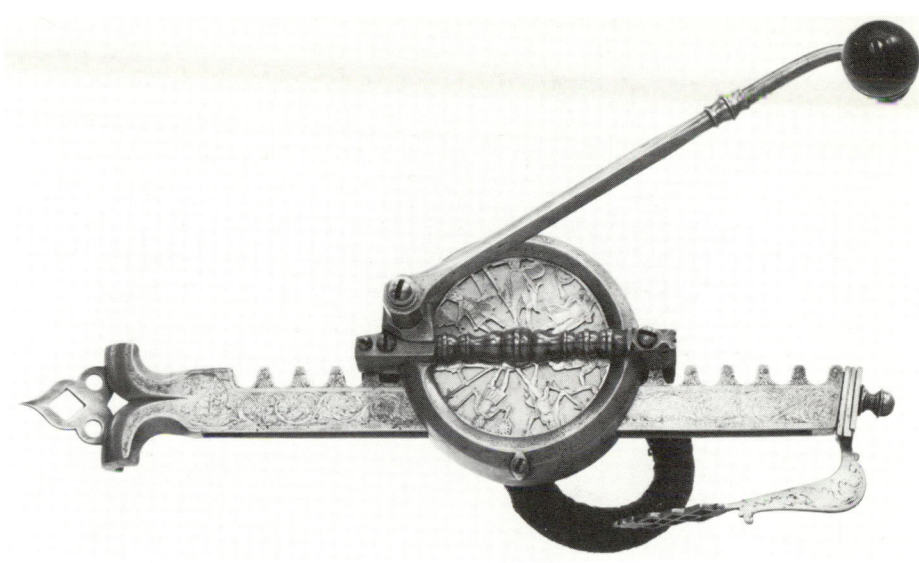

*An eighteenth century cranequin.*

In the last period of the military crossbow, the cranequin was developed, though used more for hunting than for warfare. It was a more sophisticated mechanical device, requiring a metal ratchet bar, and a winder that worked by meshing cogs. Like a goat's foot lever, it needed a pin through the stock to hold it in position. The ratchet bar had claws to fit over the string, and by winding the handle, the ratchet bar was moved away from the bow thus pulling the string with it. This was effective and required very little strength, but it was slow since the handle had to be turned some thirty times. It took about 35 seconds to bend a bow with a cranequin, as against about 12 seconds with a windlass. The cranequin was light and easy and could be used on horseback, and hence its popularity with the huntsman.

Another of the late medieval refinements to the crossbow, was the improvement of the trigger. A trigger from the thirteenth century has been found at Norwich. The normal trigger was shaped rather like a duck. The beak was the tip which locked the nut in position. The edge of the nut had a notch cut into it, and the locked trigger held the nut in place so that it could not revolve. The trigger moved on a pivot, which was placed as the eye of the duck. The long tail was the handle, which projected from under the stock. To shoot the crossbow, this handle was pressed upwards against the stock. This lifted the beak so that the nut could then revolve. The pressure from the drawn string pulled the nut round so that the string was free. The bolt itself might be made of ash or yew, and was about one foot in length, with a flattened and tapered butt. The flight could be made from goose wing feathers. Another useful addition, was a strip of wood with notches in it, which was fixed at the back end, or tiller, of the stock. This was to act as a backsight for aiming. The right thumb fitted into one of the notches, and the crossbowman would look along a line from his thumb to the top of the head of the bolt. If the aim was not correct it could be adjusted by moving the thumb to the next notch.

By the fifteenth century the crossbow with its steel bow was a powerful weapon. It probably had a greater range and a greater impact than earlier bows, even the longbow. The crossbow had advantages in confined positions, and at short range because of its heavier bolt. The steel bow gave it greater range: Payne-Gallwey thought 370 to 390 yards; Malcolm Vale believes up to 500 yards.[14] The crossbowman needed less expertise than the longbowman, less physical strength, and less training. The improved crossbow, together with the longbow ensured the continuing importance of archery in the fifteenth century. English, French and Burgundians used both in their armies, though the English were still recognised as the masters of the longbow, and favoured it more than did the other nations.

## The Wars of the Roses

It is odd, that in an age when English archers were renowned throughout Europe, a civil war could be fought in England and little mention be made of archers.[15] It is sometimes seen as another example of the decline of archery in the fifteenth century, but this is not the case. English warfare was not behind the times, though it had some individual characteristics. Both guns and bows were used in the Wars of the Roses, and as on the continent, the supremacy of guns was far from obvious. One interesting example of a solution to the question of gun or bow is found in the Paston Letters, one of the most fascinating private archives from any age. Sir John Paston sent four men for garrison duty, whom he said could shoot well 'bothe gonnys and crossebowes'. They were named as Peryn Sale, John Chapman, Robert Jackson and William Peny. Of the last-named, Sir John said he was 'as good a man as goeth on the earth, saving a little he will, as I understand, be a little headstrong, but yet he is no brawler'.[16] A letter from Thomas Talbot to William, Lord Berkeley, in 1469, gives a fascinating view of an almost private battle between the two. Talbot wrote: 'I marvel that you come

[14] Payne-Gallwey, *Crossbow*, p. 20; Vale, *War and Chivalry*, p. 113.
[15] On Wars of the Roses, see Gillingham, *Wars of the Roses*; Goodman, *Wars of the Roses*; Ross, *Wars of the Roses*; Cook, *Lancastrians and Yorkists*.
[16] *Paston Letters*, ed. Davis, i, p. 398, no. 238: Sir John Paston to John Paston III, 9 November 1468: 'they kan wele schote bothe gonnys and crossebowes and amende and strynge them'; William Peny 'whyche is as goode a man as gothe on the erthe, sauyng a lytyl he woll, as I understand, be a lytel copschotyn; but yit he is no brawlere'. Gairdner, *Paston Letters*, ii, p. 327, gives 'high-crested' for 'copschotyn'.

not forth with all your carts of guns, bows and other ordnance', and challenged him to meet for battle at Nibley Green at a given time. Berkeley kept the appointment, and in the fighting that ensued Talbot lost his life, but it is interesting that a participant in the war saw guns and bows as central to a battle.[17]

Siege guns figured less in England than in contemporary continental wars, because sieges played little part in the Wars of the Roses. The English war was a mobile war, marked by a surprisingly large number of pitched battles. The heavy artillery of the fifteenth century could not easily be used in a war of this nature. On the other hand, small guns could be useful, and there is evidence of the use of handguns throughout the war. From the Paston evidence it is clear that Englishmen could use guns, but sometimes continental gunners were hired: Warwick used Burgundians for the second battle of St Albans, and Edward IV brought 400 men from Flanders.[18]

The reason that archers do not figure very largely in battle accounts in the Wars of the Roses, is not that they did not participate, but that the chronicles fail to give us details. English chronicles of this period are notoriously few, brief, and lacking in the sort of detail that allows for a close examination of warfare, its tactics, and its weapons. One has to rely on continental accounts, such as those by Waurin and Commynes, for detail. Administrative and local records are on the whole more productive than the chronicles. Such materials can be the basis of excellent works on warfare, but not on tactics, and not on the use of bows. From them we can see something of the organisation of war, for example the production and collection of bows, but not a great deal about their use in battle.[19]

Every type of relevant record makes it abundantly clear that bows were used in considerable numbers in the Wars of the Roses. Many archers were employed, sometimes organised in groups of 20, 100 and 1000.[20] The illustrations of fifteenth century warfare are in a more realistic style than those of the earlier medieval period, and bows figure prominently. Other records show bows being ordered for the royal armoury, for example 3000 in 1459. John Gillingham has recently argued that the proportion of archers to other soldiers in fifteenth century armies increased from about three to one under Henry V, to about seven to one in the Wars of the Roses.[21]

The *Paston Letters* also reflect the common use of bows in the period. When John Paston I was in some danger from local disturbances, Margaret Paston wrote to him suggesting that the windows of the house were such as to make crossbows more

[17] The Talbot letter is in *EHD*, iv, p. 1127, no. 664; from Smyth, *Berkeleys*, ii, p. 109.

[18] Guns, see Payne-Gallwey, *Crossbow*, pp. 38–40. *Historie of the Arrivall*, pp. 18–9; p. 19: 'as well inshotte as in hand-stroks shan they ioyned'. Jean de Waurin, v, p. 661 on Barnet: 'Les deux ostz estoient moult bien garnis de tous engiens a pouldre.' In William Gregory, p. 213: 'the burgeners hadde suche instrumentys that wolde schute bothe pellettys of ledde and arowys of an elle of lengthe with vj fetherys'.

[19] Goodman, *Wars of the Roses*, and Vale, *War and Chivalry* demonstrate what can be done with the available records to illuminate late medieval warfare. On the problems of evidence, see Gillingham, *Wars of the Roses*, p. xii.

[20] Goodman, p. 141.

[21] Gillingham, *Wars of the Roses*, pp. 36–7, on proportion; and p. 102 on 1459.

*Fifteenth century English drawing in realistic style of longbowmen in action.*

effective for defence than longbows.[22] The letter is in English, and she recommended him to get crossbows, windlasses and quarrels, the houses in that part being so long that no man could shoot out with his 'long bowe', and to make special wickets to shoot out from with both bows and handguns. This, incidentally, is an early use of the word 'longbow', the letter being dated about 1448 and hence some years earlier than the earliest reference quoted in the *Oxford English Dictionary*.

There is, in other words, plenty of evidence to show that bows played a major role in the Wars of the Roses, and clearly were significant in the battles even if it is difficult to show how in very much detail. In the first battle of the war, the first Battle of St

[22] *Paston Letters*, ed. Davis, p. 226, no. 130: Margaret Paston to John Paston I, to her 'Ryt wurchipful hwsbond'; she tells him to 'gete som crosse bowis, and wyndacis to bynd hem wyth, and quarell, for zwr hwsis here ben so low hat here may non man schete owt wyth no long bowe how we hadde never so moche nede.'

[23] There is some uncertainty about the nature of Henry VI's wound. Jean de Waurin, v, p. 268: 'fut blechie dune flesche ou bras'; *Dijon Relation*, p. 64: 'et le Roy mesme fut feru en l'espaule d'un trait maiz il ne lui toucha que ung peu la char'.

[24] Ross, *Wars of the Roses*, p. 52, calls Henry a vegetable. For Blore Heath, Jean de Waurin, v, pp. 319–21; p. 320: et devant eulz avoient fichie leurs peux a la fachon dAngleterre'. For Barnet, John Warkworth, p. 13; on Tewkesbury, *Historie of the Arrivall*, p. 22.

Albans, archers were active on both sides. When the Yorkists finally broke into the town, the archers were able to attack the Lancastrian leaders, and Henry VI himself was wounded by an arrow, having to take shelter in a tradesman's house.[23] In the later Battle of Northampton, that same 'useful political vegetable' was captured by an archer. In most of the battles there is some brief mention of archery, but only rarely any detail of its use. One exception is the Battle of Blore Heath, at which, according to Waurin, the archers 'fixed their stakes in the custom of the English'. At both Barnet and Tewkesbury, which were the decisive battles of the war, archers opened proceedings. In the latter, they emerged from their defences on behalf of Edward IV, and gave the Lancastrians a 'right-a-sharpe shwre'.[24] Both John Paston and Sir John Paston were at Barnet, the former being wounded by an arrow, a misfortune that led to a costly reckoning with his doctor.

*The Battle of Barnet from a fifteenth century manuscript.*

*The Battle of Tewkesbury.*

Even if one extends the history of the Wars of the Roses to Bosworth in 1485, or Stoke two years after that, archery is still of importance. Again, an archery exchange opened the Battle of Bosworth, and at Stoke the battle was decided by the royal use of archery, an arm in which the rebels were lacking.

What is notable about the Wars of the Roses is not the replacement of archery by guns, but the almost invariable association of bows with guns. At the first Battle of St Albans Waurin says so great was the shooting and the powder, that 'the sun lost its brightness'. When the Bastard Fauconberg attacked London, he attempted to storm it by a triple attack using guns and bows, but the guns and bows of the City were too much for him. The coming dominance of guns in siege warfare was hinted at here, but it was a rare situation in the English war.[25]

[25] Jean de Waurin, v, p. 268: 'tyrer si onniement que, du trait et de lay pouldriere que faisoient les chevaulz, lair sespessy telement que le solleil en perdy so clarete'. On London, v, p. 674.

## Archery in the Tudor Period

Even into the sixteenth century, it is by no means true that archery had become a military back-number. The relative importance of handguns and bows continued to alter, but it was probably not until the reign of Elizabeth I that the balance finally swung in favour of guns. In the first half of the sixteenth century archery remained vital. The finds from the *Mary Rose* confirm this point. It has produced 138 longbows and 2000 arrows, as well as spacers, bracers and even archers. There is plenty of evidence for the continued use of bows at this time. Henry VIII was himself an archer, and for example, in the first year of his reign, 40,000 yew staves were bought from Venice.[26]

The *Mary Rose* finds also allow us to see the physical nature of longbows, in a way which has not hitherto been possible. There is no reason to believe that these Tudor bows and arrows were in any significant way different from those used in the late medieval period, though Sir John Smythe in 1590 claimed that war bows once had been 'longer than now', and Roger Ascham complained

[26] For the 'Mary Rose', see Rule, *Mary Rose*: statistics on bows, p. 172; three types of bows, p. 180; on arrows, pp. 176, 118.

*Copy of a lost painting of the 1544 siege of Boulogne which includes archers.*

about the quality of contemporary arrows, a point which the *Mary Rose* arrows, made of inferior poplar, do seem to confirm.[27] The bows from the ship are about six feet in length, made of yew, with the heartwood and sapwood used to give the bow spring. The bows have tapered ends, but it is not clear whether or not they had horn nocks. Margaret Rule claims to have distinguished three different types of bows, or at least three varieties of longbow. The first is a large, heavy bow with a carefully made handgrip. She makes the interesting suggestion that this might have been used for shooting fire-arrows. The other two varieties described appear to be simply longbows of ordinary type, but varying in weight and length. The arrows are about 2' 6'' long, made of poplar, with a sliver of horn to protect the nock. The metal heads and the flights have not survived, but it can be shown that the flights were fixed on in a spiral covering

[27] Smythe, *Discourses*, p. 19: 'Warre Bowes being of the wood of Yewgh, were longer than now they use them.' Roger Ascham, p. 112: their bows 'not far differing from the length of our bowes'.

*The Flodden window of St Leonard's, Middleton, showing archers who fought in the battle.*

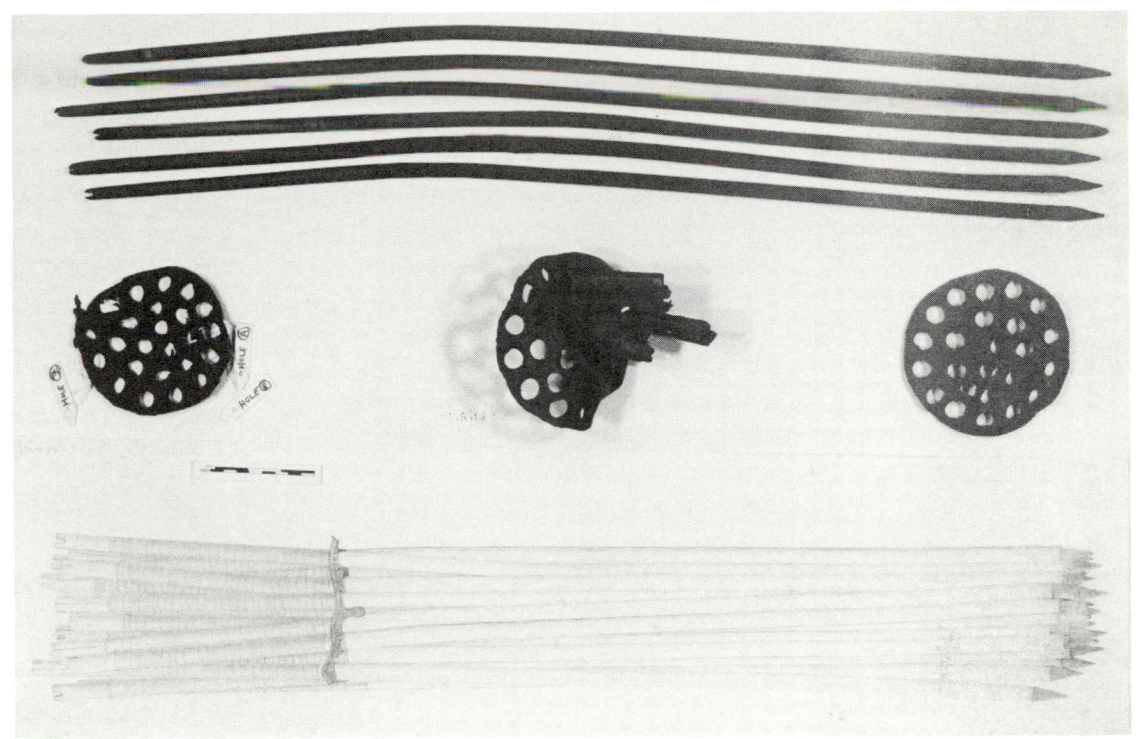

*Arrows and arrow spacers recovered from the 'Mary Rose'.*

about 6 inches, and that the metal heads were of bodkin shape to fit the spacers. These latter objects were circular pieces of leather pierced by a sieve-like pattern of holes. The arrows were fitted through the holes, which kept the shafts apart from each other and prevented damage to the flights. The arrows were mostly in bundles of 24, and stored in rough wooden boxes with rope handles.

Equally informative are the remains of the archers and their personal equipment and clothes. There were 12 bracers: one of horn, and eleven of leather. The leather ones had straps to tie them round the left forearm. Three were embossed with the royal arms, with Tudor roses and castles and pomegranates for Catherine of Aragon, though the queen had been dead some years when the *Mary Rose* sank — perhaps they were old stock. Among the bones of the dead, were those of two men identified by Mrs Rule as archers. They were both in their twenties, but already physically affected by their occupation, which suggests constant training and practice. One had a thickened left fore-arm, from the pressure of drawing his bow; and both had spinal deformations, from the pressure of drawing the bow while the body was twisted sideways. One of the pair was wearing a leather jerkin, and it is possible that the decayed metal near them might have been armour. One of the men seemed to have suffered either illness as a child or malnutrition as an adult.[28]

Archery certainly figures in warfare of the Tudor period: during the Perkin Warbeck rebellion, the Earl of Devon was wounded by an arrow in the arm; and James IV of Scotland was also wounded by an arrow in the battle with the English at Flodden.[29] But by the reign of Elizabeth I, the musket was taking over from the bow, much to the regret of some nostalgically-minded gentlemen. Sir John Smythe complained of efforts to suppress the longbow, which he claimed had 'made our nation famous both in Europe, Affrick and Asia'. He argued that practice with the bow kept men from drinking and other evils, besides providing excellent exercise, and increasing one's strength. He argued that one could shoot five or six arrows, as against one bullet from an arquebus in the same time. He also wanted boys to go on being trained in archery, but except in sporting circles his argument was unavailing. The great days of military archery were over by the end of the sixteenth century. According to Holinshed, the French mocked because 'our strong shooting is decayed'. Similarly on the continent, Cervantes bemoaned the passing from favour of the crossbow, believing that the inventor of firearms must now be in Hell for making it possible that a 'cowardly base hand' could take the life of the bravest gentleman.[30] Gunners had taken the place of archers as the object of scorn, and no doubt fear, for disgruntled military gentlemen.

[28] Rule, *Mary Rose*, p. 173 on bracers; pp. 184–6 on archers; p. 176 on arrows.
[29] For Warbeck, see Goodman, *Wars of the Roses*, p. 190; James IV, see Milliken, *Archery*, p. 41.
[30] Smythe, *Discourses*, p. 27; the quote is in the Proeme. Holinshed is quoted by Milliken, *Archery*, p. 41. The Cervantes quote is in Vale, *War and Chivalry*, p. 129.

# Chapter 9

# The Archer in Society

We have followed the history of the archer from 1066 to the sixteenth century, and it must be clear that, in military terms, the bow was important throughout the whole period without any interval. We have only examined some of the records and given but a fraction of the evidence that would support this conclusion. We have, for example, concentrated on Western Europe, and have done no more than glance at the Crusades. It has not been possible to do more than sample administrative and other governmental records, and indeed there is a good deal of research yet to be done in this area. But even from this restricted evidence, we can be in no doubt that the archer played a prominent role in practically all medieval armies and garrison forces, and that archery was a common part of medieval life: bringing men into law courts, used in sport and hunting, appearing frequently in literature and even in symbolism. Bows and arrows sprang readily to men's minds, and are found often in proverbs and in similes. A vivid example of the latter is found in a poem by the satirical and outspoken troubador, Marcabru, who wrote: 'The whore usually withholds herself from the rich man unless she gets a big reward from him, there where the crossbow stretches'.[1] The symbolism of archery could extend to the most intimate features of everyday life.

It is time to survey the evidence from the point of view of the archer in his world, and give some consideration to his role in everyday life, and in different levels of society. Archery is

[1] Marcabru, poem xliv, l. 65–7: 'Lai on l'arbalesta desten'. Compare Huon de Méry, l. 2570: 'L'arc amoreus'. I am indebted for these references to Ruth Harvey from her research on Marcabru.

159

generally associated with the lower ranks of society, and properly so. The ordinary bow was the weapon of the ordinary man, in civilian and in military life. E. G. Heath has suggested that the medieval archer was the 'Tommy Atkins of the Middle Ages'.[2] Even when military archery was at its height, the aristocrat despised the bow and never adopted it as his own weapon in war, though he was not averse to making use of its advantages for hunting, or sometimes for sniping, when he felt so inclined. In the sixteenth century, when sport rather than war became the province of the bow, the gentry took it to their hearts, but there was a slight air of false nostalgia about this attitude, and for the typical figure of the medieval archer, we should look to the ordinary countryman or citizen.

## Archery Practice

The armies drew their archers from rural levies, city militia, and from men who needed to make a living by fighting as mercenaries. English and other kings recognised the need to encourage the mass of their subjects to practise at archery, lest the supply of trained and skilled men should dry up. On the whole the kings of England had most success in this, probably because archery had taken a stronger hold on the interests of the ordinary Englishman. Archery was a sport for the common man, without any encouragement from above. The habit of Englishmen to go out into the fields and practise target archery is well documented. At Oxford, in 1209, we even find clerical scholars trying their bows, and getting into trouble when they accidentally shot a woman, which led to three of them being hanged. William FitzStephen describes the young men of London going out in summer to practise in the fields around the City in the twelfth century. In 1559 we find the Londoners doing much the same thing in Finsbury Fields, and other nearby open spaces. The famous Moorfields Map of 1559 has delightful drawings of archers shooting at the butts. One London school, Dame Alice Owen's, was founded as the result of a Tudor archery accident, though this time not a fatal one. Alice Owen herself was nearly killed by an arrow, but in gratitude for her Maker preserving her life, she gave money for the founding of the grammar school in Islington.[3]

Such activities gave rise to archery competitions, which are to be found in the medieval period, but which have had a long

[2] Heath, *Grey Goose Wing*, p. 84.

[3] On practising. For 1209 see Tucker, 'Archives', p. 192. William FitzStephen, p. 11: 'In festis tota aestate juvenes ludentes exercentur arcu'. The Moorfields Map is reproduced as the end paper in Holmes, *Moorfields*; with details showing archers in fig. 5, p. 17; fig. 13, p. 27; fig. 14, p. 28. On Alice Owen, see Dare, *Owen's School*, p. 13. The author is one of the many who have benefited from Dame Alice's foundation.

160

FYNNESBVRIE
FIELD.

Fynnesb Cou

*Two scenes of archers practising in the fields outside London, from the 1559 Moorfields map.*

161

*Crossbow competition. As in modern darts, a line is marked for the competitor to stand behind.*

history since the decline of military archery too. The popularity of such competitions in the middle ages must have added to the frequency of practising, and so to the widespread skill with the weapon found in England. The Robin Hood stories are often concerned with such competitions, and indeed give us some details on how they operated. They reflect an interesting variety in the targets that could be used. At Nottingham the butts were 'fair and long', and elsewhere there is reference to a pair of butts. The fourteenth century *Luttrell Psalter* shows a pair of marks, with the familiar 'bullseye' targets. In the Robin Hood tales though, the more common target mentioned is the 'wand' or 'prick', Robin himself of course frequently splitting the wand, as in 'Robin Hood and the Potter' where he 'cleft the prick in three'. In 'Robin Hood and Guy of Gisborne', Guy hit the garland, but Robin hit the wand. Also one finds Robin shooting at the 'brush and broom'. In the tale of Adam Bell, the hero shoots at butts where there are two hazel rods, and Cloudesly with a flight arrow cleft the wand in two. In this latter poem there is also a variation on the William Tell legend, with the hero placing an apple on his son's head, at which he shoots from 120 paces with a broad arrow.[4]

A common target for crossbow shooting was the popinjay. This was a representation of a bird, placed on top of a pole. The word derives from *papegai*, the French for parrot. This target has a long history going back to at least the thirteenth century. In the fifteenth century Bertrand du Guesclin, the great French commander, was the champion at Rennes. In Dresden the target continued in use into modern times, with a bird constructed in

[4] Robin Hood references, Dobson and Taylor, *Rymes*, p. 100: 'The buttes were fayre and longe'; p. 99: 'a pair of fynly buttes'; compare p. 143, where shrubs are cut down and set 'in twinn'; p. 116: 'buske and brome'; p. 130: 'cleffed the preke on thre'; p. 143, the garland; p. 271: 'clave the wand in to'; p. 272: the apple story.

[5] On the popinjay, Payne-Gallwey, *Crossbow*, pp. 223–8, 231–5; *Queen Mary's Psalter*, ed. Lindner, pl. 32.

[6] *EHD*, iv, p. 1182, no. 694. It was repeated,

162

for example as late as 1478. See *Cal. Close Rolls*, 37 Edward III, vol. xi, p. 534; and for the original: Rymer, *Foedera*, iii, II, p. 704: 'artem sagittandi, ante haec tempora, communiter exercebant ... in actibus nostris guerrinis dicta arte quasi totaliter dimissa ad alios ludos inhonestos, et minus utiles, aut valentes, se indulgent de sagittariis, infra breve, deveniet verisimiliter, quod absit, destitutum arcubus et sagittis, vel pilettis aut boltis.'

such a way that it could be destroyed in sections, each piece knocked off being worth a prize, the final piece or the heart calling for the 'king' shot, whoever made it becoming the champion for that year. An illustration from Queen Mary's Psalter clearly shows this kind of target shooting, though it has been incorrectly labelled as 'wild-fowl shooting'.[5]

In the reign of Edward III it was apparently thought that archery practice was in decline: 'whereas the people of our realm, nobles as well as commons, usually practised in their games the art of archery ... now the art is almost totally neglected ... so that the kingdom, in short, becomes truly destitute of archers'. Men in every shire were encouraged to practise on festival days, to 'exercise themselves in the art of archery, and use for his games bows and arrows, or crossbows and bolts'.[6] This kind of measure was to be repeated frequently, and one might therefore think it ineffective. Yet the period after 1363 was the great age of archery in England, so men must have practised. The answer is

*Target shooting with crossbows, an illustration from 1520.*

163

that such measures generally had two aspects: one was to encourage archery; the other was to discourage other sports that were thought to distract men from the useful art of archery, and it was this discouragement from other sports that failed. Thus they were called on not to take part in football, hockey, cock-fighting and other 'dishonest games'. An order of 1467 in Leicester favoured archery rather than the unlawful games like tennis; and in Scotland James II made a similar order against playing golf. Also in Scotland bowmarks were ordered to be placed near parish churches, a practice that was common in England. In Coventry in 1474 it was forbidden to shoot at moving targets rather than standing marks, on penalty of a fine of 6s 8d, presumably because it constituted a greater danger to the public. The nature of the moving target is not revealed.[7]

## Hunting

Although the common folk were thus encouraged to practise at archery, they were very definitely discouraged from hunting with bows. This was a sport reserved for the aristocracy, though poaching could not be stopped. In 1390 artificers, labourers, butchers, shoemakers and tailors 'and other low persons' were ordered not to hunt in parks on holy days when Christians were at church. The reason given in this case was fear of banding together for the purpose of insurrection.[8]

Hunting was a popular sport with the nobility throughout the middle ages. Dominic Mancini visited England in the 1480s, and described people going out into the fields with bows and arrows, even the women. There is good evidence for ladies taking part in

[7] On other prohibitions. For Leicester, see *EHD*, iv, p. 577, no. 372; for James II, Gillingham, *Wars of the Roses*, p. 137; for Coventry, *Coventry Leet Book*, ii, p. 389.

[8] *EHD*, iv, p. 1004, no. 569.

*Fourteenth century manuscript showing a woman hunting a stag.*

hunting, though in one of the poems, said to be by Marie of France, in which a hunt in introduced, she says that the women hung back. Another lady, Isabella d'Este, described a hunting expedition in which she took part in 1492: 'Today we went out hunting in a beautiful valley which seemed to be specially made for the spectacle'. A wolf was killed, making 'fine somersaults in the air, as it ran past us, amusing the whole company'.[9]

Practically every English king hunted; indeed, it was often their favourite leisure activity, and many were skilled at its various facets, including shooting with the bow. We have seen a number of kings using bows, usually crossbows, from William the Conqueror and Richard the Lionheart to Henry VIII, the latter being able to draw the longbow. William Rufus was offered special bolts for the hunt in which he himself was killed by one of the knights in the party.[10] Hunting accidents were common, and if sometimes they were used to cover murder, then they certainly provided good concealment. No doubt in most cases they were genuine accidents, since crossbows were kept ready drawn for use, and sometimes the trigger must have been released unintentionally.

There were many others who hunted legitimately too. As with kings, so with nobles and knights; most hunted, enjoyed hunting, were skilled at it, and sometimes suffered accidents in the course of their sport. Abbots, bishops, and even popes were known to hunt. The inventory taken of the abbot's house at Peterborough in 1460 recorded four bows and six sheaves of arrows in the chamber.[11] As late as 1621 we find an archbishop of Canterbury, Abbott, not only shooting a crossbow, but causing a scandal by his poor shooting, since he killed the servant, Peter Hawkins. No doubt his medieval predecessors were better shots. The king also employed his own huntsmen. The *Constitutio Domus Regis* of the twelfth century refers to men who carried the king's bow, and were paid the relatively high wages of 5d a day. In later times we find king's huntsmen, and yeomen of the bows for the king. Geoffrey Chaucer was a yeoman of the king's chamber, and from the frequent references to archery in his works, and his description of the knight's yeoman with his bow, we may suspect that our great medieval poet was himself an archer.[12]

Our fullest knowledge of medieval hunting comes from the various treatises upon the subject that have survived. They are concerned with all aspects of the sport, but archery has a place in each of them. The earliest surviving English work of this kind is by William Twiti or Twici. He was himself a huntsman of

[9] Ladies hunting: Mancini, p. 98; Marie de France, p. 11; for Isabella, Thomas, *Hounds and Hunting*, p. 7.
[10] Orderic Vitalis, v, p. 288.
[11] Abbot Richard Aston of Peterborough, see *EHD*, iv, p. 1146, no. 678.
[12] For *Constitutio*, see Holt, 'Robin Hood: Some Comments', p. 267; ycoman of the bows, Holt, *Robin Hood*, p. 120; king's huntsmen, for example, William Twiti was huntsman to Edward II, see William Twiti, p. 33. See also Chaucer, i, pp. ix–lxi, for a life of the poet.

Edward II, and it is recorded that in 1322 he was sent to take venison for the king from the forests, chases and parks of the Earl of Lancaster; and in 1326 that he was receiving as wages 9d a day. He retired as a corrodian to Reading Abbey, where he died in 1328. He describes one of the common methods of medieval hunting, with stable, that is with set stables or positions for the archers. Sometimes these were simple shelters, and greyhounds were often used for the chase. The game was driven towards the stables, with such calls on the horn as 'trourourourout', played thrice.

The *Livre du Roy Modus* is a French work from the same century, and contains advice to the son of King John of France on hunting.[13] It begins with an amusing exchange of blows between the falconer and the huntsmen, the one using his lure and the other his horn, before they settle down to a discussion of their respective sports. But deservedly the most famous hunting treatise to come out of France in the medieval period is the *Livre de Chasse* of Gaston de Foix.[14] Gaston is a considerable figure in the history of his day, being the son of the Count of Foix. He married the daughter of the queen of Navarre, and fought against the English at Crécy, even though he was the nephew of the Captal de Buch. His relations with the king of France deteriorated after Crécy, and he was even imprisoned for a time, being released after the king's defeat and capture at Poitiers. Gaston went on crusade against the Slavs in 1358, and played a prominent part in putting down the Jacquerie, the French Peasants Revolt. He had the reputation of being a lady's man, and had bastards by at least four partners. Froissart described his own visit to Gaston at Moncade Castle, Orthez, in 1388.[15] He recounts the tragic story of Gaston's quarrel with his son. The son is said to have tried to poison Gaston, but the powder was given instead to his dog, which 'turned its eyes in its head and died'. The son was locked in a cell. According to Froissart, some days later Gaston visited his son, holding a small knife which he had been using to pare his nails. The knife was in his hand as he drew the curtain, and it accidentally cut a vein in the son's throat, from which he died: a pretty tall story.

At about the time of Froissart's visit to Orthez, Gaston was engaged upon his great work, the *Livre de Chasse*. In the Prologue, Gaston claims: 'All my life I have delighted especially in three things: one is arms, a second is love, and the third is the chase'. He thought that there were many better knights than himself, and many who had had better opportunities in love, but in hunting he acknowledged no master and felt himself perfectly

[13] Madden, *Chapter*, p. 49.
[14] Gaston Phébus, see Madden, *Chapter*; and Gaston Phébus, ed. Tilander.
[15] Froissart, ed. Johnes, ii, p. 94.

*Archers hunting in illustrations from Gaston Phébus' Livre de Chasse.*

qualified to write about it. He was probably right, for his work is a masterpiece.[16]

He argues that hunting was beneficial, not only in providing exercise and fresh air, but also food and medicine. He recommends various bows, including the Turkish shortbow, and the English longbow. He gives measurements for these weapons, which are of particular interest with regard to the longbow at the time of the Hundred Years' War. He describes the longbow as made of yew, and measuring 20 *poignées*, or hands, apparently 5' 8". He says the string should be of silk, and the bow supple, so that it can be drawn easily and quietly. The arrow is 28" long, with a large, barbed head. When drawn, the feathers should be flat against the bow, so that it shoots smoothly. The archers should dress in green for camouflage, and should make defences around themselves. They should put arrow to bow, and be ready when the beast comes, so as not to make unnecessary movement and frighten the beast. Each archer should have dogs. If the beast is not killed, but the arrow found, the amount of damage done can be assessed from the quality of the blood. If it is muddy and fatty, then the wound is mortal; but if the blood is clear, it will not prove fatal. Gaston says, that if you want to know more than

[16] Gaston Phébus, p. 51 on the three things; p. 269, on types of bows; p. 279, on the pleasures of hunting.

167

he can tell you about bows, you must go to England. He recommends that for hunting both bows and crossbows should be green, and that camouflage should be used for people, horses and carts. The *Livre de Chasse* gives one something of the flavour of medieval hunting, and some explanation of its popularity. Gaston enjoyed the fresh air, the birdsong and the dew; he was knowledgeable about weather and the habits of the animals that served him, as well as those he hunted. He described the preparations to be made for an expedition: taking materials for lighting a fire, as well as bread and wine, for, as he says 'one does not know what adventures might result from the chase'. Gaston himself died after a day out hunting in 1391; he was washing his hands before dinner when he suddenly collapsed.

In the fifteenth century an English version of Gaston's work was produced, apparently by Edward the son of Edmund Langley.[17] The author was Master of Game to Henry IV, and dedicated his work to Prince Hal, later Henry V. The author became Duke of York in 1402, and led the right wing of the English army at Agincourt, where he was killed. The work is mostly a translation of parts of the *Livre de Chasse*, with a few modifications and additions. One such addition describes the preparations for a hunt in which the king himself will participate. He describes the king as hunting with a bow, and how the king and his companions must be placed in position. He says that the yeoman of the king's bows should be there to keep and make the king's stand, and stay there without noise until the king comes.

Knowledge of archery, partly gained through hunting, was certainly useful to the nobility, some of whom would have to command archers on campaign, or in garrisons, sometimes in battle. One recalls Erpingham at Agincourt, ordering the English archers. St-Rémy called him 'ung chevalier archier'.[18] In France the position of Master of the Crossbows went to a high-ranking

member of the aristocracy. In the late middle ages it became fashionable for nobles to take part in crossbow competitions. Kings and even queens took part in competitions, and sometimes won them, sometimes even through merit. For sport, for competitions as well as for hunting, the nobility and even royalty needed to practise. A sad example of this is the last record of the sons of Edward IV, the Princes in the Tower, who were seen shooting bows and playing in the Tower before they disappeared from the pages of history.[19] By the sixteenth century, archery for the aristocracy was more of a pleasant pastime than a military activity. A pleasant interlude for Henry VIII, in 1516, was the appearance of a group of nobles, dressed like Robin Hood and his men, who 'captured' the king and forced him to dine with them, saying: 'sir, outlawes breke fastes is venyson'.[20]

## The Bow as a Threat to Society

[17] Edward, Second Duke of York, ed. Baillie-Grohman. Compare Hicks, *George Plantagenet*: the Duke of Clarence was given a shooting glove, a quiver and bowstrings in 1461–2. I am grateful to Nicholas Kingwell for this reference. This work has recently been published.
[18] Jean le Fèvre, p. 253.
[19] Princes in the Tower, see Mancini, p. 127, n. 88; *Great Chronicle of London*, p. 234.
[20] Harris, 'Influence of Robin Hood', p. 13.
[21] Norman, *Medieval Soldier*, p. 142. There were similar attempts in England.
[22] Powicke, *Military Obligation*, p. 89.

On the one hand governments desired men to practise archery and develop skills for the benefit of the national army, but on the other hand all governments and nobles feared the bow as the weapon of the common man, and hence the weapon of outlaw, brigand and rebel. The lower orders were forbidden to train as knights, for example, the Emperor Frederick Barbarossa forbade peasants to use sword or lance; and Louis IX made a similar order in France.[21] The rise of military archery, the development of organised groups of ordinary men capable of posing a threat to even the best trained knights, was a threat to society. Nor was it a groundless fear, for time and again the bow appeared in the hands of those who threatened the safety of medieval society. At times there were attempts to restrict the possession of bows, for example, under Henry II and Henry III, but it was a genuine dilemma for authority: to balance the need for military archery against the fears of popular insurrection.[22]

The examples of archery as a threat to medieval society are manifold. In the twelfth century, we have met Robert Boet, the 'famous archer', who took to bringandage, and was 'as hateful for his acts of villainy as he was skilled in archery'. When it was desired to improve law and order in Flanders, it was specially commanded that bows and arrows be laid aside. Commonly bands of troublemakers included archers, for example those at Lynn in 1266 described as 'a large number of people of the lower orders'; or the band of beggars who appeared in Yorkshire in

1322 and enriched themselves unlawfully 'though when they came into the county, they had nothing but their bows and arrows and the clothes they walked in'. The Robin Hood literature was based on a real world of outlaw bands and violence, of groups of men outside decent society using the bow as their special weapon. In the later middle ages rebels and brigands often took the name of Robin Hood. Robin of Redesdale was one such, the leader of rebels against Edward IV in 1469, described by Waurin as a villein (though he has been widely thought to be a gentleman), and 'captain of all the commons'.[23]

The most frightening episode in medieval English history for the nobility was the Peasants' Revolt of 1381. According to Froissart the peasant leader, Wat Tyler, had been in the wars in France. His peasant followers came 'each with his bow ready to shoot', and when Tyler was killed and fell, 'they began to bend their bows and to shoot'. It was at this point that the young Richard II rode forward and intervened, persuading the rebels to treat him as their king, and finally to disperse, throwing down their bows. Archers appeared again in the Oldcastle rebellion of 1414. After Oldcastle's arrest, a priest named Walter was hanged and drawn for purchasing on behalf of Oldcastle 'as many bows, arrows, and other stuff as cost 9 marks'. There were also archers in the Cade rebellion of 1450. No wonder the nobles viewed archery as a threat.[24]

Archery could also be a threat in the employ of men who lacked legitimate authority. In France, after the making of peace at Brétigny in 1360, the country was plagued by the Companies, acting on their own behalf and not for a prince.[25] They disrupted whole areas of France for a decade: 'seizing, robbing and ransoming the people, burning and destroying buildings, violating and ravishing widows, virgins and other women'. Pope Innocent VI called them 'the enemies of Christianity'.[26] Contamine has described the activities of these Companies, which included archers as a major part of their force, and the way in which the French government gradually won control of them. When similar companies, known as the Écorcheurs, appeared after the Treaty of Arras of 1435, they were far more easily brought to heel by the king. The increase in royal power and wealth, symbolised by the rise of the free archers and a national standing army, was able to harness the threatening elements in society to the national interest.

[23] Archers as a threat. For Boet, see Orderic Vitalis, vi, p. 458: 'qui quanto sagittandi peritia maior; tanto in nequitiis erat detestabilior'. For Flanders, Galbert de Bruges, ed. Pirenne, p. 3; and see ch. 1, n. 1. For Lynn, see Matthew Paris, ed. Giles, iii, p. 361. For Pickering, see Holt, *Robin Hood*, pp. 155–6; this was yet another forest area that produced archers. Jean de Waurin, v, p. 581: 'dun villain nomme Robin Rissedalle, capitaine de tout les commun'.

[24] Rebellions. On 1381, see *Anonimalle Chronicle*, p. 148: 'comencerount a treer lour arkes et a seter'. For Oldcastle, see Kingsford, *Literature*, p. 293: 'a preest that hit syr Water drawen and hanged for treason: the weche preeste, as men seydon, had bought for Cobham as many bowes, arowes and other stuff as cost ix mark.' For Cade see Jean de Waurin, v, p. 261.

[25] Companies. Much work has been done on this subject by Contamine, for example, in *La France*, especially ch. VII; also *La Vie Quotidienne; Guerre, État*; and *War in the Middle Ages*.

[26] Allmand, *Society at War*, p. 92, on activities of the companies; and Contamine, *La France*, p. 382, who also points out that Innocent IV had

# The Social Status of the Military Archer

The archer could be a threatening figure to medieval society, but in general he was used by authority rather than against it. Medieval armies used and needed archers, increasingly as the medieval centuries passed. For that reason, some archers at least gained social status. They were paid more than ordinary infantry, particularly with the demand for mounted archers, and this alone gave them some hope for social improvement. Princes would on occasion make gifts of money or of land. In *Domesday Book*, men described as *balistarii* are in possession of small areas of land, though it is impossible to know if they were men who operated siege engines or crossbowmen. In *Domesday Monachorum* Godfrey *balistarius* is described as *miles*, though probably this should be translated as 'soldier' rather than 'knight'. In 1060 Fulcher the *balistarius* witnessed a charter of William the Conqueror, which suggests that he was a man of at least some standing; and one of Stephen's charters concerning Eye Priory confirms tithes to Walter the *balistarius*. They may not have been crossbowmen, but there is no reason why they should not have been. Crossbowmen were generally recruited as mercenaries, but some individuals were certainly favoured, some remained in royal service for life, so there is nothing improbable in a few receiving small amounts of property.[27]

Comments on the composition of armies, suggests that archers had recognised status, always lower than the knights, but normally higher than the ordinary infantry. Wace referred to a three-fold structure of 'knights with lances, archers with bows, villeins with pikes'. In the eleventh, twelfth and thirteenth centuries, archers were mainly either rural levies, or else they were mercenaries, retainers, even in the king's own household. There was an incident when King John captured Rochester Castle. Several of the crossbowmen in the garrison were hanged for the damage they had done to the royal forces, but one in particular, because, it was said, the king had provided for him from boyhood. In Flanders, Lambert Archei, a skilled archer, is described as a vassal of the Count.[28]

From the fourteenth century, with its increased need of archers, one finds far more examples of the archer as a man of moderate substance. Terms such as sergeant, or yeoman, or valet, give some indication of the slightly improved overall social status of the archer. The rise in the number of mounted archers is a similar indication, since the possession of a horse represents at least modest wealth. A sign of this development is the number of

called a crusade against the companies in 1361.
[27] Crossbowmen. *Domesday Book*, i, pp. 365b–366: the section under the heading 'Terra Odonis Arbalistarij'; for Godfrey, see *Domesday Monachorum*, pp. 83, 105; for Fulcher, Fauroux, *Recueil*, p. 8329, no. 147.
[28] Archer status. See Wace, ed. Taylor, p. 60; on Rochester, Walter of Coventry, ii, p. 226: 'unum solum suspendi jussit, arcubalistarium quem, ut fertur, a puero nutrierat'; on Lambert, see Galbert de Bruges, ed. Ross, p. 78. Compare Sanders, *Military Service*, p. 135, on Ralph de Wyleden in 1245, 'serviens peditus cum arcubus et sagittis', for the fifth part of a knight's fee.

archers in the Black Prince's retinue for the Crécy campaign, in which there were 69 foot archers and 384 mounted archers. Another sign is the increased cost, mounted archers normally being paid more than their brethren on foot. Parliament in 1344 complained at the cost, which they reckoned at a mark or a pound per man, coming to £1000 for each county.[29]

Attempts were made to restrain the social rise of the archer. In 1390 nobles were instructed not to give livery to any varlet 'called a yeoman archer', nor to any one below the estate of squire, unless he was a family servant living in the household. This kind of measure was probably not very effective, and lords obviously did dress their retainers in livery or uniform. Jean le Bel wrote that 'the poorest retainer is now as well and as smartly armed as a noble knight'.[29]

The status of the archer probably rose a little, but in general archers were not admitted to the ranks of the gentry, and were excluded from the benefits of the chivalric code and the medieval laws of war. As a result an archer was far more likely than a knight to be killed in battle, since he had no value in ransom. One recalls the French at Agincourt reckoning an archer as worth a blank on the dice. Paris of Pozzo wrote: 'A man may not torture a prisoner to extort money from him by way of ransom, but it is different in the case of peasants', and for peasants read archers, and any below the status of squires. The archer came within the category of those who might be killed or tortured. As Keen says, there was no common soldier's law; horrific treatment could be handed out to prisoners when the chivalric code was ignored. Henriet Gentian knocked out a prisoner's teeth with a hammer; Jean le Gastelier admitted that his job was to beat up prisoners until they agreed to a large ransom. When such treatment could be handed out to supposedly privileged prisoners what hope was there for the poor archer?[31]

But although not included in the ranks of the privileged, the archer seems normally to have been regarded as some way up the rungs of the ladder of society. The term 'selected' men has generally been ignored as having no real significance. In practice, however, it may well mean exactly what it suggests. When recruitment procedures emerge from the gloom of obscurity in the later medieval period, it can be seen that the general practice was not to call upon every available man, but to review those liable, and 'select' the best. No doubt this did not always work out in practice. We can recall the example of 1315, when John Botetourt complained of the quality of the men he received, 'feeble chaps, not strong enough, not properly dressed, and

[29] Statistics on Crécy campaign, see Wrottesley, *Crécy and Calais*. On 1344, see Prestwich, *Three Edwards*, p. 269.
[30] On 1390, see *EHD*, iv, p. 1116, no. 655. Such statutes were frequent, see, for example, Pickering's *Statutes*, ii, I Richard II, cap. vii, 12 Richard II, cap. vi; 16 Richard II, cap. iv; 20 Richard II, cap. ii, which reads: 'qe vadletz appellez yomen ne null autre de meindre estat qesquier'. For Jean le Bel, see ed. Thompson, p. 38.
[31] Keen, *Laws of War*: p. 243, on Paris; p. 180, on Gentian; p. 181, on Gastelier; and compare p. 191.
[32] Selection. Botetourt in Prestwich, *Three Edwards*; and see ch. 5, n. 22. For Botiller, see *Cal. Patent Rolls*, 1324–7,

p. 27: 7 September; Petworth to 'select 300 foot archers in the forest of Dene, Berkeleyhirnes and elsewhere in the county of Gloucester'. For 1346, see *Catalogue des Rolles Gascons*, p. 60, for example: 'de sagittariis eligendis'. from Oxfordshire, Berkshire and Wiltshire.

[33] Archers as gentlemen. Peter Bridge, in Rowe, 'Contemporary Account', p. 506. For Spain, see Payne-Gallwey, *Crossbow*, p. 48. For free archers, Contamine, *Guerre, État*, pp. 355, 360. *Cal. State Papers, Venice*, pp. 148–9: 'that amongst the said arbalast men there be included four noble youths for each galley'. There is a photograph of the Bollesdun seal in Birch, *Seals*, pl. xxiv, no. 4, facing p. 182, showing an archer with a medium-sized ordinary bow which is drawn. On Decker, Cuyler and Littlejohn, see Papworth and Morant, *Ordinary*, i, pp. 7, 9; and see pp. 340, 347, 348. For Floyer, see Burke, *Armory*. I am indebted to N. Kingwell for the Floyer reference. Compare John Archere, who was on the Council of the Duke of Exeter, in *Letters and Papers*, ii, II, p. 773, though he is only noted because he was executed.

lacking bows and arrows'. But his very comments show that he expected something better, and there is no reason to believe it was not a common and effective method of picking men. From the fourteenth century there are many references to men being selected: for example, in 1324 Thomas le Botiller and William Walsh had to select 300 foot archers from the Forest of Dean and Gloucestershire, and William had to lead them to Portsmouth, for the king's expedition to France. The 1346 Rolls show selected men being taken from Oxfordshire, Berkshire, Wiltshire, and the city of London, the commissioners being instructed to select and array. The same process obviously applied to the free archers in France, who were to be citizens of some standing where possible, possessing their own equipment, able to benefit from tax privileges. Here again, the best men were to be selected. Medieval kings recognised the value of having men in their armies who had character and ability.[32]

There were of course exceptions to the rule, and we do find some archers who rose in rank by their own efforts. Peter Bridge was an archer in the garrison at Tombelaine near Mont-St-Michel in 1420, but nine years later we find him numbered among the men-at-arms in Fastolf's force going to Alençon. In Spain in the late middle ages, it seems that a crossbowman could be ranked as a knight. Some of the free archers of France were of noble rank, and some who began as simple archers, like Peter Bridge, went on to become men-at-arms. In the later medieval period, we find quite a few families who chose archery symbols for their armorials. Some of these were not archers in origin. One of the earliest examples is Thomas Bollesdun, whose thirteenth century seal survives, with an archer upon it. In this case, the symbol is probably a pun upon the name, which is also rendered as Bowsden. Certainly many families were not ashamed to have coats of arms with bows, arrows, and bolts upon them. In many cases there is no obvious pun on the name, and surely, in at least some cases, it is likely that the family owed its landed origin to an archer who had made good. Another explanation in bourgeois families who obtained arms, was that they were associated with one of the archery crafts, and had made their money as bowyers or fletchers. Among the families with archery arms were the Deckers in London, the Cuylers in Hertfordshire, and the Floyers in Devon and several other counties. The arms of the latter were a chevron between three arrows. But even where the arms were a pun, as surely were the three arrows of the Littlejohn family, it is still an interesting social sign of the greater respectability or popularity of archery.[33]

Of course landed and wealthy archers were rare: the typical archer was a relatively humble being. The French at Agincourt could refer to English archers as 'men without worth and without birth'. Many were hired mercenaries, 'stipendiary archers'. The appearance of the free archers in France, denoted an important landmark for the military archer in social terms. Not only were men of standing selected, but they were given a somewhat different social position. To contemporaries they were free not only in the sense of having a franchise regarding taxes, but in terms of personal status, they were men without any lord except the king, and were specifically distinguished from the 'subject archers' who did have a lord. The rise of professional armies gave a new status to the common infantryman.[34]

This new professionalism in the army was to be found in England too, though in a different way. Archers were being raised more on a national basis: the 1453 parliamentary grant of 20,000 archers to the king, demonstrates a move towards the need for national consent for the raising of armed forces. In this case, though it never actually happened, the archers were to be raised from cities, towns, and villages, with a commission of array throughout the realm rather than on a localised basis as previously, and they would be employed through wage contracts. In effect, the indenture system was being generalised. The closest England came in this period to a standing army was the personal bodyguard of the monarch: Richard II's Cheshire archers are famous, even notorious, but they were not exceptional. The royal household commonly included archers, as we can see even from the twelfth century *Constitutio Domus Regis*. In 1334, John Ward, king's archer, entered the royal service with 99 mounted archers from Cheshire as the royal bodyguard for Richard II's grandfather. In 1468 Edward IV had a royal bodyguard of 200 archers, so that Henry VII's formation of the famous Yeomen of the Guard, mainly archers, is not such a novelty as it sometimes is suggested. Other continental princes, such as the Dukes of Burgundy, had similar bodyguards of archers.[35]

This movement towards a national force can also be seen in the way that the county levies were used. More and more they were brought into line with household forces and retinues. An interesting example of this process is in the Perche Orders of the Earl of Salisbury in 1427, when it was ruled that the captains of all archers, whatever the latter's county of origin, if they were under the command of the earl, should join the assembly of

[34] Agincourt: *Chronique du Religieux*, p. 564; on Harfleur, *Gesta Henrici Quinti*, p. 59: 'sagittariis stipendiariis'. Free and subject archers, see Contamine, *Guerre, État*, pp. 304, 339, 466–9.

[35] For 1453, see Griffiths, *Henry VI*, pp. 394, 432. For Ward, see Nicholson, *Edward III*, p. 175. For 1468, see Gillingham, *Wars of the Roses*, p. 29. Compare Vale, *War and Chivalry*, p. 85, on Burgundy.

captains, and they should muster with all the archers as required. In other words, they were not to operate independently as had previously happened.[36]

The importance of archers in citizen militia is another example of the social standing of archers in the later middle ages. Craftsmen concerned with archery played a full role in the towns: bowyers, fletchers and bowstringmakers stood alongside the other craft gilds. At Beverley, for example, in 1467 the fletchers were responsible for presenting the pageant of Envy in the local play cycle. Similarly at Norwich in 1449, the fletchers and bowyers were among those who bore the lights carried around the body of Christ.[37] Citizens of some standing might themselves be archers. In Southampton in the thirteenth century, the citizen Richard of Southwick had a bowstave among his household possessions. Richard Toky was a grocer of London, and the inventory of his possessions included a crossbow with its tackle and four ordinary bows, as well as arrows, bolts and armour.[38] The Kentish list of 1415 shows that citizens who were responsible for the monetary contributions for archers, were also in some cases themselves serving as archers. Towns generally showed some pride in providing good troops to represent them, and equipping them decently. At Bridport in 1457 two-thirds of the citizens were able to provide their own bows, and one man had his own gun and sword as well; some were also marked as being good archers. Coventry in 1455 called out 100 archers under their own captain, though in fact they did not have to fight in that year. Even so, the town council ordered a new banner, together with red and green sashes for the men, and green, violet and red for the captain, clearly a man who meant to be noticed![39]

So the archer's place in society was a humble one, but respectable and increasingly respected. From the time that archers were mounted, they were often numbered among the sergeants. Like many social terms, this one varied in its sense, and may have had shades of meaning that are lost to us. The literal meaning is 'servant', but in its use it normally, in the central middle ages, represents someone of a certain standing, and is perhaps best associated in mind with the serjeanty tenure. This is the social position in which we find archers through the rest of the medieval period, never quite reaching the ranks of the gentry, but sometmes not very far away. The commonest terms linked with archers in the later middle ages are valet or varlet, and yeomen. Neither of the modern meanings of valet or varlet express properly the late medieval social rank, which was perhaps close to the term sergeant, with the sense of serving, as

[36] Keen, *Laws of War*, p. 96.
[37] Gilds. Beverley, in *EHD*, iv, p. 1066, no. 621; Norwich, in *EHD*, iv, p. 1095, no. 643.
[38] Citizens with bows. For Toky, see *Cal. Select Pleas*, 1381–1412, pp. 209–13; p. 209: 'one arblast with the takell, 2s.'; p. 212: '4 bows, 2s.6d., 18 arrows and two bolts, 16d.'. For Southwick, see King, *England*, p. 20.
[39] Hull in *Arch. Cantiana*, pp. 159–166; and see ch. 7, n. 11. For Bridport, see Goodman, *Wars of the Roses*, p. 143. For Coventry, see *Coventry Leet Book*, pp. 282–3.

for example, in the Exchequer Accounts which assigned three archers to each man-at-arms *qui passaient pour leur valets*.[40] The term 'yeoman' is thought to derive from *youngerman*, which makes one think of squires, *iuvenes* and bachelors. The squire in origin served a very similar function, assisting the knight, and in his case entering the ranks of the gentry. 'Yeoman' did not rise quite so high, but certainly came to mean someone of reasonable wealth and status. The social position of the archer cannot be defined any more precisely; individual archers stood in different social levels, but in general, archers in the late middle ages were reasonably respectable countrymen or citizens.

It would be interesting, but beyond the scope of this book, to pursue through the records the social position of individual archers. This certainly might be possible, since in the late middle ages one finds quite considerable numbers of named men in shire lists, retinue lists, garrison lists and elsewhere. The Crécy and Calais lists, for example, name the archers in the king's household, men such as Thomas Forcer and Richard l'Archer. The muster roll for Rouen in 1432 names 43 archers of the garrison, such as Jehan Pute, Guy Colleville, and Robert Cobart (who was sick). Among the archers in the retinue of the duke of Somerset in 1443–4, were James Hobson and Ralph Clerc.[41] Research into the backgrounds of such men might provide us with more certain knowledge about the archer in society, but probably would not alter our general opinion: that they belong in the ranks of the lower classes, but not among the very poorest, and that in the fifteenth century they had rather more hope of rising a little further in society.

The archer might be a poor man, a professional soldier, a looter and brigand, a rebel or a disturber of the peace; or he might be a respectable peasant, a small landowner, a citizen of standing. In national warfare he was the backbone of the army, even a hero. In the *Brut*'s version of Agincourt the enemy were made to stumble by 'God and our archers'.[42] The archer could become a proper figure for literature, in the Robin Hood tales and the *Canterbury Tales*. The countless places named after Robin Hood and his associates reflect not so much the physical context of their lives, as the widespread popularity of the tales in which archery was such a central theme. There is no better picture of a medieval archer, drawn in words, than Chaucer's knight's yeoman: 'in cote and hood of grene', with his sheaf of peacock arrows under his belt, bearing his mighty bow. He wore a bracer, with a sword and buckler at one side, and a dagger at the other. He carried a horn slung on a green baldric, and Chaucer

[40] Wylie, *Henry V*, i, p. 466, and n. 1. On 'yongermen', see Holt, *Robin Hood*, p. 122, suggesting that the word is found in the twelfth century in the *Pseudo-Cnut de Foresta*, where they are equated to under-foresters — again the link between archery and the forest.
[41] Named archers. These examples could be multiplied many times. For 1346, see Wrottesley, *Crécy and Calais*; for Rouen, see Allmand, *Society at War*, p. 61; and p. 82, for the Somerset retinue.
[42] *Brut*, ii, p. 378: 'but God and our archers made hem sone to stumble'.

supposed him to be a forester.[43] If this is discounted as fictional, then let us balance it with the description by the visitor Dominic Mancini, who gave his own view of the English archers. He said their bows were thicker and longer than those used by other nations, just as their arms were stronger for they seemed to have hands and arms of iron, and as a result, their bows had as great a range as crossbows. Almost every man wore a helmet, and each had an iron shield and a sword. Only the wealthy had metal

[43] Chaucer, iv, p. 4: 'A Yeman hadde he . . .'

*The poet John Gower with a longbow.*

177

armour, the ordinary soldiers preferring tunics stuffed with tow, which reached down to their thighs. The more tow there was, the better they were able to withstand blows.[44]

Archery made a great impact on the medieval mind, as both literature and art witness. Numerous carved archers appear over church doorways, or on the capitals of columns.[45] In manuscript illustrations Saint Edmund and Saint Sebastian figure frequently, martyred by arrows. In Orderic Vitalis, the bow was the instrument of divine wrath.[46] No one can understand the middle ages who does not appreciate the significance of archery, for hunting and sport, for warfare and violence. The bow was the most devastating weapon over several centuries of the medieval period, a weapon known and used by men of high and low rank, familiar to every court and in every parish in the land.

# Bibliography

## Abbreviations

| | | | |
|---|---|---|---|
| *ANS* | *Anglo-Norman Studies.* | *JSAA* | *Journal of the Society of Archer Antiquaries.* |
| ANTS | Anglo-Norman Text Society. | | |
| *AJ* | *Antiquaries Journal.* | *Med.Arch.* | *Medieval Archaeology.* |
| BN | Bibliothèque Nationale. | *Med.St.* | *Medieval Studies.* |
| *Bt A* | *British Archer.* | *MGH* | *Monumenta Germaniae Historica.* |
| BL | British Library. | NS | New Series. |
| BM | British Museum. | PR | Pipe Rolls. |
| *BIHR* | *Bulletin of the Institute of Historical Research.* | PRO | Public Record Office. |
| | | *Proc.* | *Proceedings.* |
| *BJRL* | *Bulletin of the John Rylands Library.* | *Rev.Anglo-Fr.* | *Revue Anglo-Francaise.* |
| *CCM* | *Cahiers de Civilisation Médiévale.* | *RIS* | *Rerum Italicarum Scriptores.* |
| Cal. | Calendar. | RHC | Recueil des Historiens des Croisades, 5v, Paris, 1844–95. |
| EETS | Early English Text Society. | | |
| EHD | English Historical Documents. | RHS | Royal Historical Society. |
| *EHR* | *English Historical Review.* | RS | Rolls Series. |
| EHS | English Historical Society. | Ser. | Series. |
| HMSO | Her Majesty's Stationery Office. | SHF | Société de l'Histoire de France. |
| HMC | Historical Manuscripts Commission. | Soc. | Society. |
| *HT* | *History Today.* | Stevenson | *The Church Historians of England,* ed. J. Stevenson, 5 vols, 1853–8. |
| Howlett | *Chronicles of the Reigns of Stephen, Henry II and Richard I,* ed. R. Howlett, 4 vols, RS no. 82, 1889. | | |
| | | *TRHS* | *Transactions of the Royal Historical Society.* |
| *JAAS* | *Journal of the Arms and Armour Society.* | | |

## Primary Sources

Abbo (or Abbon), *Le Siège de Paris par les Normands,* ed. H. Waquet, Paris, 1942.

*Aldhelm: Prose Works,* ed. M. Lapidge & M. Herren, Cambridge, 1979.

*Aldhelm: Opera,* ed. R. Ehwald, *MGH Auctorum Antiquissimorum,* xv, Berlin, 1919.

Alexander, M., *The Earliest English Poems,* Harmondsworth, 1966.

*A Lytell Geste of Robin Hode,* ed. J. M. Gutch, 2 vols, London, 1847.

Anderson, A. O., *Early Sources of Scottish History,* 2 vols, Edinburgh, 1922.

Anglo-Saxon Chronicle: *Two of the Saxon Chronicles Parallel,* ed. C. Plummer, 2 vols, Oxford, 1892–9.

*Annals of Fulda*, ed. G. Pertz, *MGH Scriptorum*, i, Hanover, 1826, Part V, no. xxxv, pp. 337–415.

*Anonimalle Chronicle*, ed. V. H. Galbraith, 2nd edn, Manchester, 1970.

Apulia, William of, *La Geste de Robert Guiscard*, ed. M. Mathieu, Palermo, 1961. (French translation).

Apulia, William of, *Gesta Roberti Wiscardi*, ed. D. R. Wilmans, *MGH Scriptores*, ix, pp. 239–98.

Ascham, Roger, *Toxophilus*, ed. E. Arber, London, 1868.

Avesbury, Robert of, *Historia de Mirabilis*, ed. T. Hearne, Oxford, 1720.

Avesbury, Robert of, *De Gestis Mirabilibus Regis Edwardi Tertii*, in Adam Murimuth ed. E. M. Thompson, RS no. 93, 1889.

Baker, Geoffrey le, *Chronicon*, ed. E. M. Thompson, Oxford, 1889.

Barber, R., *The Life and Campaigns of the Black Prince*, London, 1979.

Barbour, John, *The Bruce*, ed. W. M. Mackenzie, London, 1909.

Barnes, Julians, *Boke of Huntyng*, Cynegetica, xi, Karlshamn, 1964.

Basin, Thomas, *Histoire de Charles VII*, ed. C. Samaran, SHF, 2 vols, Paris, 1933–44.

Bel, Jean le, *Chronique*, ed. J. Viard & E. Deprez, SHF, 2 vols, Paris, 1904–5.

Bourgueil, Baudri de, *Oevres Poétiques*, ed. P. Abrahams, Paris, 1926.

Breton, William the, *Oevres de Rigord et de Guillaume le Breton*, ed. H. F.D elaborde, SHF, 2 vols, Paris, 1882–5.

Bridlington Chronicle, *Chronicles of the Reigns of Edward I and Edward II*, ed. W. Stubbs, RS no. 26, 2 vols, 1882–3.

*BL Cleopatra C VIII.*

*BL Cotton MS Caligula, Dv* 43v–44. (Somme Plan).

Bruges, Galbert of, *Histoire du Meutre de Charles le Bon*, ed. H. Pirenne, Paris, 1891.

Bruges, Galbert of, *The Murder of Charles the Good*, ed. J. B. Ross, 2nd edn, New York, 1967.

*Brut, The*, ed. F. W. D. Brie, EETS, 2 vols, London, 1906–8.

*Brut Y Tywysogyon*, ed. T. Jones, 2nd edn, Cardiff, 1973.

Cagny, Perceval de, *Chronique*, ed. H. Moranville, SHF, Paris, 1902.

*Calendar of the Close Rolls*, xi, 37 Edward III, HMSO, 1909.

*Calendar of Documents of Scotland*, ed. J. Bain, 4 vols, Edinburgh, 1881–8.

*Calendar of Inquisitions Miscellaneous*, i, 1219–1307, HMSO, 1916.

*Calendar of Inquisitions Post Mortem*, i & iii, Edward I, HMSO, 1904, 1912.

*Calendar of Patent Rolls Preserved in the PRO*, Henry III, 1258–66, HMSO, 1910.

*Calendar of Patent Rolls*, v, Edward II, 1324–7, HMSO, 1904.

*Calendar of Select Pleas and Memoranda of the City of London, 1381–1412*, ed. A. H. Thomas, Cambridge, 1932.

*Calendar of State Papers and Manuscripts, Venice*, ed. R. Brown, London, 1864.

*Carmen de Hastingae Proelio*, ed. C. Morton & H. Muntz, Oxford, 1972.

*Catalogue des Rolles Gascons, Normans et Francois*, 2 vols, London, 1743.

Chartres, Fulcher of, *Chronicles of the First Crusade*, ed. H. E. McGinty, Philadelphia, 1941.

Chaucer, Geoffrey, *Compleat Works*, ed. W. W. Skeat, 7 vols, 1894–7.

*Chronicle of Battle Abbey*, ed. E. Searle, Oxford, 1980.

*Chronicle of Bury St Edmunds, 1212–1301*, ed. A. Gransden, London, 1964.

Chronicle of Melrose, *Chronica de Mailros*, ed. J. Stevenson, Bannatyne Club, no. 49, Edinburgh, 1835.

Chronicle of Melrose (translation), in Stevenson, iv, Pt. I, pp. 77–242.

*Chronicles of London*, ed. C. L. Kingsford, Oxford, 1905.

*Chronicles of the Reigns of Edward I and Edward II*, ed. W. Stubbs, RS no. 76, 2 vols, 1882–3.

*Chronicles of the Reigns of Stephen, Henry II and Richard I*, ed. R. Howlett, RS no. 82, 4 vols, 1889.

*Chronicon Abbatiae Rameseiensis*, ed. W. D. Macray, RS no. 83, 1886.

*Chronicon de Lanercost*, ed. J. Stevenson, Bannatyne Club, Edinburgh, 1839.

Chronicon de Lanercost, *The Chronicle of Lanercost*, ed. Sir H. Maxwell, Glasgow, 1913.

*Chronique des Quatre Premiers Valois*, ed. S. Luce, SHF, Paris, 1862.

*Chronique du Religieux de St-Denys*, ed. M. L. Bellaguet, 6 vols, Paris, 1839–52.

*Chronique Normande de XIVe Siècle*, ed. A. & E. Molinier, SHF, Paris, 1882.

*Chroniques des Comtes d'Anjou*, ed. P. Marchegay & A. Salmon, Paris, 1856–71.

*Chroniques des Comtes d'Anjou et des Seigneurs d'Amboise*, ed. L. Halphen & R. Poupardin, Paris, 1913.

Coggeshall, Ralph of, *Chronicon*, ed. J. Stevenson, RS no. 66, 1875.

Commynes, Philippe de, *Mémoires*, ed. J. Calmette, SHF, 3 vols, 1924.

Commynes, Philippe de, *The Memoirs of Philip de Commines*, ed. A. R. Scoble, 2 vols, London, 1855.

Comnena, Anna, *The Alexiad*, ed. E. R. A. Sewter, Harmondsworth, 1969.

Coventry, Walter of, *Historical Collections*, ed. W. Stubbs, RS no. 58, 2 vols, 1872–3.

*Coventry Leet Book*, ed. M. D. Harris, EETS, 4 vols in 2, 1907–13.

Cynan, Gruffydd ap, *History*, ed. A. Jones, Manchester, 1910.

*De Expugnatione Lyxbonensis*, ed. C. W. David, New York, 1976.

Dickinson, W. C., Donaldson, G., & Milne, I. A., *A Source Book of Scottish History*, Edinburgh, 1952.

*Dijon Relation*, ed. C. A. J. Armstrong, 'Politics and the Battle of St Alban's, 1455', *BIHR*, xxxiii, 1960, App.I, pp. 63–5.

Dobson, R. B. & Taylor, J., *Rymes of Robyn Hood, Introduction to the English Outlaw*, London 1976.

*Domesday Book*, ed. Sir H. Ellis, 2 vols, London, 1833.

*Domesday Monachorum*, ed. D. C. Douglas, London 1944.

Durham, Symeon of, *Historia Regum*, ed. T. Arnold, RS no. 75, 2 vols, 1882–5.

Durham, Symeon of, *The Historical Works of Simeon of Durham and Continuation*, Stevenson, iii, Pt. II, pp. 423–756.

Eadmer, *Historia Novorum in Anglia*, ed. M. Rule, RS no. 81, 1884.

Edward, Second Duke of York, *The Master of Game*, ed. W. A. & F. Baillie-Grohman, London 1904.

Ellis, H., *Original Letters Illustrative of English History*, 11 vols, London, 1824–46.

*English Historical Documents*, ed. D. C. Douglas; ii, 1042–1189, ed. D. C. Douglas; iii, 1189–1327, ed. H. Rothwell, 1975; iv, 1327–1485, ed. A. R. Myers, 1969.

*Enseignements de Théodore Paléologue, Les*, ed. C. Knowles, Modern Humanities Research Association: Texts & Dissertations, xix, London, 1983.

*Eulogium (Historiarum Sive Temporis)*, ed. F. S. Haydon, RS no. 9, 3 vols, 1858–63.

Eustace the Monk, *Le Romans de Wistasse li Moine*, ed. D. J. Conlon, N. Carolina, 1972.

*Exchequer Rolls of Scotland*, ed. G. Burnett, RS no. 104, 23 vols, 1878–1908.

*Exeter Book*, ed. I. Gollancz, 2 vols, London, 1895–1934.

Fantosme, Jordan, *Chronicle*, ed. R. C. Johnston, Oxford, 1981.

Fauroux, M., *Recueil des Actes des Ducs de Normandie, 911–1066*, Caen, 1961.

Fenin, Pierre de, *Mémoires*, ed. G. de Tievlaine, Collection Universelle des Mémoires Particuliers Relatifs à l'Histoire de France, Paris, 1785, v, pp. 305–384.

Févre, Jean le, Seigneur de St-Remy, *Chronique*, ed. F. Morand, SHF, 2 vols, Paris, 1876–1881.

FitzStephen, William, 'Life of St Thomas, Archbishop of Canterbury and Martyr', *Materials for the History of Thomas Becket*, iii, RS no. 67, 7 vols, 1875–85.

FitzWarin, Fulk, *Fouke le Fitz Waryn*, ed. E. J. Hathaway, ANTS, 1975.

FitzWarin, Fulk, *Gesta Fulconis Filii Warini*, ed. J. Stevenson, RS no. 66, 1875.

Fordun, John, *Scotichronicon*, ed. T. Hearne, Oxford, 1722.

Fordun, John, *Chronica Gentis Scotorum*, ed. W. F. Skene, 2 vols, Edinburgh, 1871. (With translation).

*France, Marie de, Lais*, ed. A. Ewert, Oxford, 1944.

Froissart, Jean, *Chroniques*, ed. S. Luce, 15 vols, Paris, 1869–1975.

Froissart, Jean, *Oevres de Froissart: Chroniques*, ed. M. le Baron Kervyn de Lettenhove, 29 vols, Brussels, 1867–77.

Froissart, Jean, *Chronicles*, ed. J. Jolliffe, London, 1967. (Translation).

Gabrieli, F., *Arab Historians of the Crusades*, London, 1969.

Gaimar, Geoffrey, *L'Estoire des Engles*, ed. T. D. Hardy & C. T. Martin, RS no. 91, 2 vols, London, 1888–9.

Gaimar, Geoffrey, 'The History of the English', Stevenson, ii, Pt. II, pp. 727–809.

*Gesta Francorum*, ed. R. Hill, Oxford, 1962.

*Gesta Henrici Quinti*, ed. F. Taylor & J. S. Roskell, Oxford, 1975.

*Gesta Stephani*, ed. K. R. Potter & H. R. C. Davis, Oxford, 1976.

Gough, H., *Scotland in 1298, Documents Relating to the Campaign of King Edward I in that Year, and especially to the Battle of Falkirk*, London, 1888.

*Great Chronicle of London*, ed. A. H. Thomas & I. D. Thornley, London, 1834.

Gregory, William, 'Chronicle of London', *Historical Collections of a Citizen of London*, ed. J. Gairdner, Camden Soc., NS, xvii, 1876, pp. 55–239.

Guisborough, Walter of, *Chronicle*, ed. H. Rothwell, Camden Soc., lxxxix, 1957. (Walter of Hemingford or Hemingburgh is the same chronicler).

Hardyng, John, *The Chronicles of the Firste Begynnyng of England, London, 1543*, Amsterdam & Norwood, New Jersey, 1976. (Facsimile).

Hefele, C. J. & LeClercq, H., *Histoire des Conciles*, 11 vols in 21 vols, 1907–52, v, Pt. I, Paris, 1912.

Heworth, P. L., *Jack Upland, Friar Daw's Reply and Upland's Rejoinder*, Oxford, 1968.

Hexham, John of, 'Continuation of Symeon of Durham', Symeon of Durham, RS, ii, pp. 284–332.

Hexham, John of, 'The Chronicle of John, Prior of Hexham', Stevenson, iv, Pt. I, pp. 1–32.

Hexham, Richard of, 'Chronicle', Howlett, iii, pp. 139–178.

Hexham, Richard of, 'The Acts of King Stephen and the Battle of the Standard by Richard Prior of Hexham', Stevenson, iv, Pt. I, pp. 33–58.

*Historiens Occidentaux*, in *Recueil des Historiens des Croisades*, i, Pt. II, Paris, 1884.

*Historie of the Arrivall of Edward IV in England*, ed. J. Bruce, Camden Soc., i, 1838.

Huntingdon, Henry of, *Historia Anglorum, BL Arundel MS, 48*.

Huntingdon, Henry of, *Historia Anglorum*, ed. T. Arnold, RS no. 74, 1879.

Hyde, Book of, see *Liber Monasterii de Hyda*.

*Jesus College Oxford MS, li*.

Jumièges, William of, *Gesta Normannorum Ducum*, ed. J. Marx, Rouen, 1914.

Juvenal des Ursins, Jean, *Histoire de Charles VI Roy de France*, ed. J. F. Michaud & J. J. F. Poujoulat, Paris, 1836.

*King Henry IV Pt. I*, ed. A. R. Humphrey, London, 1966.

Langtoft, Peter de, *Chronicle*, ed. T. Wright, RS no. 47, 2 vols, 1866–8.

Langtoft, Peter de, *Chronicle*, ed. T. Hearne, 2 vols, Oxford, 1725.

Langland, William, *The Vision of William concerning Piers the Plowman*, ed. W. W. Skeat, EETS, London, 1869.

Langland, William, *Piers Plowman*, ed. G. Kane & E. Talbot, London, 1975.

*Letters and Papers Illustrative of the Wars of the English in France*, RS no. 22, 1864.

*Liber Monasterii de Hyda*, ed. E. Edwards, RS no. 45, 1866.

*Liber Monasterii de Hyda, The Book of Hyde*, Stevenson, ii, Pt. II, pp. 481–520.

*Livre des Seyntz Medicines*, ed. E. J. Arnold, Oxford, 1940.

Livy, Titus, *Vita Henrici Quinti*, ed. T. Hearne, Oxford, 1716.

*Luttrell Psalter*, ed. E. G. Millar, London, 1932.

Major, John, *Historia Majoris Britanniae*, Edinburgh, 1740

Major, John, *A History of Greater Britain, 1521*, ed. A. Constable, Scottish Hist. Soc., x, Edinburgh, 1892.

Malmesbury, William of, *De Gestis Regum Anglorum*, ed. W. Stubbs, RS no. 90, 2 vols, 1887–9.

Malmesbury, William of, *Historia Novella*, ed. K. R. Potter, Edinburgh, 1955.

Mancini, Dominic, *The Usurpation of Richard III*, ed. C. A. J. Armstrong, 2nd edn, Oxford, 1969.

Marcabru, *Poésies complètes*, ed. J. M. L. Dejeaune, Toulouse, 1909.

*Memorials of Henry V*, ed. C. A. Cole, RS no. 11, 1858.

Méry, Huon de, *Li Tornoiement Antecrit*, ed. G. Wimmer, Marburg, 1888.

Minot, Laurence, *Poems*, ed. J. Hall, Oxford, 1914.

Monmouth, Geoffrey of, *Historia Regum Britanniae*, ed. A. Griscom, London, 1929.

Monmouth, Geoffrey of, *History of the Kings of Britain*, ed. L. Thorpe, London, 1969.

Monstrelet, Enguerrand de, *Chronique*, ed. L. Douët-D'Arcq, SHF, 6 vols, Paris, 1857–62.

Monstrelet, Enguerrand de, *Chronicles*, ed. T. Johnes, 13 vols, London, 1810.

Monte, Robert de, see Robert of Torigny.

Muratori, L. A., see *Rerum Italicarum Scriptores*.

Murimuth, Adam, *Chronica Sui Temporis, 1303–1346*, with continuation to 1380, ed. T. Hog, 1846.

Murimuth, Adam, *Continuatio Chronicarum*, ed. E. M. Thompson, RS no. 93, 1889, pp. 3–276.

*Pageant of the Birth, Life and Death of Richard Beauchamp Earl of Warwick*, ed. Viscount Dillon & W. H. St. J. Hope, London, 1914.

Paris, Matthew, *Chronica Majora*, ed. H. R. Luard, RS no. 57, 7 vols, 1872–83.

Paris, Matthew, *Drawings*, ed. M. R. James, Walpole Soc. Publication, xiv, Oxford, 1926.

Paris, Matthew, *English History*, ed. J. A. Giles, 3 vols, London, 1852.

*Paston Letters and Papers of the Fifteenth Century*, ed. N. Davis, 2 vols, Oxford, 1971–6.

*Paston Letters*, ed. J. Gairdner, 2 vols, Edinburgh, 1910.

Paston Letters, R. Barber, *The Pastons, a Family in the Wars of the Roses*, London, 1981. (Modern English version).

Phébus, Gaston, *Livre de Chasse*, ed. G. Tilander, Cynegetica xviii, Karlshamn, 1971.

Pickering, D., *The Statutes at Large*, 28 vols, Cambridge, 1762–9.

*Pipe Rolls*, Pipe Roll Society: 31 Henry I, ed. J. Hunter, 1833; 2, 3, 4 Henry II, ed. J. Hunter, 1844.

Poitiers, William of, *Histoire de Guillaume le Conquérant*, ed. R. Foreville, Paris, 1952.

*Prince Noir, Le*, ed. F. Michel, Paris, 1883. (With English translation).

Prüm, Regino of, *Chronicon, MGH Scriptorum*, l, pp. 1–906.

*Queen Mary's Psalter*, ed. K. Lindner, Hamburg & Berlin, 1966.

*Queen Mary's Psalter*, ed. Sir G. Warner, London, 1912.

Rastell, John, *The Pastime of People, 1529*, ed. T. F. Dibdin, London, 1811.

*Regesta Regum Anglo-Normannorum, 1066–1154*, ed. C. Johnson & others, 4 vols, Oxford, 1913–69

*Rerum Italicarum Scriptores*, ed. L. A. Muratori, 25 vols in 28, 1723–51.

Rievaulx, Ailred of, *Relatio de Standardo*, Howlett, iii, pp. 181–99.

Rishanger, William of, *Chronicle of the Monastery of St Alban's*, ed. H. T. Riley, RS no. 28, 2 vols, 1865.

*Rotuli Parliamentorum*.

*Rotulorum Originalium in Curia Scaccarii Abbrevatio*, for Henry III, Edward I, Edward II, HMC, 1805.

Rouen, Etienne de, *Draco Normannicus*, Howlett, ii, pp. 589–781.

Rymer, T., *Foedera*, London, 1816–69.

*St Alban's Chronicle*, ed. V. H. Galbraith, Oxford, 1937.

Saxo Grammaticus, *Danorum Regum Heroumque Historia*, ed. E. Christiansen, 3 vols, Oxford, 1980–1.

*Select Cases in the Court of the King's Bench*, Edward III, v, Selden Soc., lxxvi, 1957.

Smythe, Sir J., *Certain Discourses*, London, 1590.

Stenton, F. M., *The Bayeux Tapestry*, 2nd edn, London, 1965.

Strecche, John, 'Chronicle', ed. F. Taylor, *BJRL*, xvi, I, 1932.

Sturluson, Snorri, *Snorre Sturlason: Heimskringla*, ed. E. Monsen, Cambridge, 1932.

Sturluson, Snorri, Heimskringla: *King Harald's Saga*, ed. M. Magnusson & H. Palsson, Harmondsworth, 1966.

Suger, *Vie de Louis VI, Le Gros*, ed. H. Waquet, Paris, 1929.

Thompson, P. E., *Contemporary Chronicles of the Hundred Years' War*, London, 1966.

Torigny, Robert of, *Chronicle*, Howlett, iv, pp. 3–315.

Torigny, Robert of, Interpolations, see William of Jumièges.

Torigny, Robert of, *The Chronicles of Robert de Monte*, Stevenson, iv, Pt. II, pp. 673–813.

Torigny, Robert of, *The History of King Henry I by Robert de Monte*, Stevenson, v, Pt. I, pp. 1–39.

*Très Riches Heures de Jean Duc de Berry, Les*, ed. P. Durrieu, Paris, 1904.

*Très Riches Heures du Duc de Berry, Les*, ed. J. Longnon, London, 1969.

Trivet, Nicholas, *Annales*, ed. T. Hog, EHS, 1845.

Twiti, William, *The Art of Hunting, 1327*, ed. B. Danielsson, Cynegetica Anglica I, Stockholm, 1977.

Tyre, William of, *Historia Rerum in Partibus*, RHC, Historiens Occidentaux, i, Pt. II.

Venette, Jean de, *Chronicle*, ed. R. A. Newhall, New York, 1953.

Villani, Giovanni, *Istorie Fiorentine, RIS*, xiv.

*Vinland Sagas*, ed. M. Magnusson & H. Palsson, Harmondsworth, 1966.

*Vita Edwardi Secundi*, ed. N. Denholm-Young, London, 1957.

Vitalis Orderic, *The Ecclesiastical History*, ed. M. Chibnall, 6 vols, Oxford, 1969–81.

Wace, *Roman de Rou*, ed. A. J. Holden, 3 vols, Paris, 1970–3.

Wace, *Master Wace his Chronicle of the Conquest*, ed. E. Taylor, London, 1837. (Translates part of *Roman de Rou* relating to the Conquest).

Wales, Gerald of, *Opera*, ed. J. F. Dimock, RS no. 21, 8 vols, 1861–91.

Wales, Gerald of, *The Journey Through Wales and the Description of Wales*, ed. L. Thorpe, Harmondsworth, 1978.

Walsingham, Thomas, *Historia Anglicana*, ed. H. T. Riley, RS no. 28, 2 vols, London, 1863–4.

Walsingham, Thomas, see *St Alban's Chronicle*.

Warkworth, John, *A Chronicle of the First Thirteen Years of King Edward IV*, ed. J. O. Halliwell, Camden Soc., 1839.

Waurin, Jean de, *Jehan de Wavrin: Chronicles and Ancient Histories of Great Britain now called England*, ed. E. L. C. P. Hardy, RS no. 39 (French) and no. 40 (English translation), 8 vols, 1864–91.

Wendover, Roger of, *Flowers of History*, ed. H. G. Hewlett, RS no. 84, 3 vols, 1886–9.

Worcester, Florence of, *Chronicon*, ed. B. Thorpe, EHS, 2 vols, London, 1848–9.

Worcester, Florence of, 'The Chronicle and Continuation', Stevenson, ii, Pt. I, pp. 169–372.

Wright, T., *The Political Songs of England*, Camden Soc., vi, 1839.

Wrottesley, G., *Crécy and Calais from the Original Records*, London, 1898.

Wyntoun, Andrew de, *The Orygynale Cronykil of Scotland*, ed. D. Laing, 3 vols, Edinburgh, 1872.

## Secondary Sources

Allmand, C. T., *Henry V*, Historical Association, 1968.

Almand, C. T., *Society at War*, Edinburgh, 1973.

Anstee, J. W. & Biek, L., 'A Study in Pattern-Welding', *Med.Arch*, v, 1961, pp. 71–93.

Bachrach, B. S., 'Military Organization in Aquitaine under the Early Carolingians', *Speculum*, xlix, 1974, pp. 1–33.

Bachrach, B. S., 'The Feigned Retreat at Hastings', *Med.St.*, xxxiii, 1971, pp. 344–7

Barber, R., *Edward, Prince of Wales and Aquitaine*, Woodbridge, 1978.

Baring, F. H., *Domesday Tables*, London, 1909.

Barrington, Hon. D., 'Observations on the Practice of Archery in England', *Archaelogia*, vii, 1785, pp. 46–48.

Barrow, G. W. S., *Robert Bruce and the Community of the Realm of Scotland*, London 1965.

Beaupré de Calais, Pigault de, 'Agincourt', *Rev.Anglo-Fr.*, iii, 1835, pp. 148–9.

Bellamy, J., *Robin Hood, an Historical Enquiry*, Beckenham, 1985.

Bellamy, J. G., 'The Coterel Gang: An Anatomy of a Band of Fourteenth Century Criminals', *EHR*, lxxix, 1964, pp. 698–717.

Belleval, R. de, *Azincourt*, Paris, 1865.

Bernstein, D., 'The Blinding of Harold and the Meaning of the Bayeux Tapestry', *ANS*, v, 1982, pp. 40–64.

Bilson, F. L., *Modern Archery*, London, 1949.

Birch, W. de Grey, *Seals*, London, 1907.

Boase, T. S. R., *Kingdoms and Strongholds of the Crusaders*, London, 1971.

Bolland, W. C., *A Manual of Year Book Studies*, Cambridge, 1925.

Brooks, N. P. & Walker, H. E., 'The Authority and Interpretation of the Bayeux Tapestry', *ANS*, i, 1978, pp. 1–34.

Brown, R. A., 'The Battle of Hastings', *ANS*, iii, 1980, pp. 1–21.

Brown, R. C., 'Observations on the Berkhamstead Bow', *JSAA*, x, 1967, pp. 12–15.

Burke, Sir B., *The General Armory*, London, 1884.

Burke, E., *The History of Archery*, London, 1958.

Burne, A. H., *The Agincourt War*, London, 1956.

Burne, A. H., *The Crécy War*, London, 1955.

Burne, A. H., 'The Battle of Poitiers', *EHR*, liii, 1938, pp. 21–52.

Campbell, J., *The Anglo-Saxons*, London, 1982.

Cange, C. du F., Sieur du, *Glossarium*, 7 vols, Paris 1840.

Carus-Wilson, E., 'Haberget: a Medieval Textile Conundrum', *Med.Arch.*, xiii, 1969, pp. 148–66.

Chambers, Sir E. K., *English Literature at the Close of the Middle Ages*, Oxford, 1945.

Chew, H. M., *The English Ecclesiastical Tenants-in-Chief and Knight Service, Especially in the Thirteenth and Fourteenth Centuries*, Oxford, 1932.

Christison, Sir P., 'Bannockburn: a Study in Military History', *Proc. Soc. Antiquaries of Scotland*, xc, 1956–7, p. 170.

Clark, J. G. D., 'Neolithic Bows', *Proc. Prehistoric Soc.*, xxix, 1963, p. 87.

Contamine, P., *Agincourt*, Paris, 1964.

Contamine, P., Guerre, État et Société à la Fin du Moyen Age, Études sur les Armées des Rois de France, 1337–1494, Paris, 1972.

Contamine, P., *La France au XIVe et XVe Siècles, Hommes, Mentalités, Guerre et Paix*, London, 1981.

Contamine, P., *La Vie Quotidienne pendant la Guerre de Cent Ans*, Paris, 1976.

Contamine, P., *War in the Middle Ages*, Oxford, 1984.

Cook, D. R., *Lancastrians and Yorkists: The Wars of the Roses*, Harlow, 1984.

Cottrill, F., 'A Medieval Description of a Bow and Arrow', *AJ*, xxiii, 1943, pp. 54–5.

Dare, R. A., *A History of Owen's School*, Wallington, 1963.

David, C. W., *Robert Curthose*, Cambridge, Massachussetts, 1920.

Davis, H. W. C., 'A Contemporary Account of the Battle of Tinchebrai', *EHR*, xxiv, 1909, pp. 728–32.

Davis, R. H. C., 'The Carmen de Hastingae Proelio', *EHR*, xciii, 1978, pp. 241–61.

Davis, R. H. C. & others, 'The *Carmen de Hastingae Proelio*: a Discussion', *ANS*, ii, 1979, pp. 1–20.

Dodwell, C. R., 'The Bayeux Tapestry and the French Secular Epic', *Burlington Magazine*, cviii, 1966, pp. 549–60.

Earle, P., *The Life and Times of Henry V*, London, 1972.

Edwards, J. G., 'The Battle of Maes Madog and the Welsh Campaign of 1294–5', *EHR*, xxxix, 1924, pp. 1–12.

Engelhardt, H. C. C., *Nydam Mosefund, 1859–63*, Copenhagen, 1865.

Farnham, G. F. & Skillington, S. H., 'The Skeffingtons of Skeffington', *Leicester Arch. Soc. Transactions*, xvi, 1929–31, pp. 74–128.

Favier, J., *La Guerre de Cent Ans*, Paris, 1980.

Foley, V., Palmer, G., & Soedel, W., 'The Crossbow', *Scientific American*, cclii, 1985.

Fowler, K., *The Age of Plantagenet and Valois*, London, 1967.

Fowler, K., *The Hundred Years' War*, London, 1971.

Franklin, J. A., 'The Romanesque Cloister Sculpture at Norwich Cathedral Priory', *Studies in Medieval Sculpture*, ed. F. H. Thompson, *Soc. of Antiquaries of London*, 1983, pp. 56–70.

Fraser, A., *King James VI of Scotland and I of England*, London, 1974.

Freeman, E. A., *The History of the Norman Conquest of England*, 6 vols, Oxford, 1867–79.

Fryde, N. M., 'Welsh Troops in the Scottish Campaign of 1322', *Bulletin of the Board of Celtic Studies*, xxvi, 1976, pp. 82–6.

Galbraith, V. H., 'The Battle of Poitiers', *EHR*, liv, 1939, pp. 473–5.

Gautier, J. J., *Histoire d'Alençon*, 2 vols, Alençon, 1805–21.

Glover, R., 'English Warfare in 1066', *EHR*, lxvii, 1952, pp. 1–18.

George, H. B., 'The Archers at Crécy', *EHR*, x, 1895, pp. 733–8.

Gillingham, J., *Richard the Lionheart*, London, 1978.

Gillingham, J., *The Wars of the Roses*, London, 1981.

Goodman, A., *The Wars of the Roses*, London 1981.

Gordon, H. & Webb, A., 'The Hedgeley Moor Bow at Alnwick Castle', *JSAA*, xv, 1972, pp. 8–9.

Griffiths, R. A., *The Reign of Henry VI*, London, 1981.

Hardy, R., *Longbow*, Cambridge, 1976.

Harris, P. V., *The Truth about Robin Hood*, Mansfield, 1973.

Harris, P. V., 'Archery in the First Half of the Fourteenth Century', *JSAA*, xiii, 1970, pp. 19–21.

Harris, P. V., 'The Influence of Robin Hood on Archery', *JSAA*, xv, 1972, pp. 10–14.

Harris, P. V., 'The Longbow in Battle', *Bt A*, iv, 1953, pp. 183–4.

Hatto, A. J., 'Archery and Chivalry: a Noble Prejudice', *Modern Language Review*, xxxv, 1940, pp. 40–54.

Heath, E. G., *The Grey Goose Wing*, Reading, 1971.

Heath, E. G., 'Agincourt', *JSAA*, ix, 1966, pp. 7–9.

Heath, E. G., 'The English Medieval War Arrow', *JSAA*, iii, 1960, pp. 17–9.

Hewitt, H. J., *The Black Prince's Expedition of 1355–7*, Manchester, 1958.

Hewitt, H. J., *The Organization of War under Edward III*, Manchester, 1966.

Hewitt, H. J., 'The Organization of War', in Fowler, *Hundred Years' War*, pp. 75–95.

Hibbert, C., *Agincourt*, 2nd edn, London, 1978.

Hicks, M. A., *The Career of George Plantagenet, Duke of Clarence, 1449–78*, unpublished D.Phil thesis, Oxford, 1974.

Hicks, M. A., *False, Fleeting, Perjur'd Clarence*, Gloucester, 1980.

Hill, J. W. F., *Medieval Lincoln*, Cambridge, 1948.

Hilton, R. H., *Peasants, Knights and Heretics*, Cambridge, 1976.

Hogg, O. F. G., *English Artillery, 1326–1716*, London, 1963.

Hollister, C. W., *The Military Organization of Norman England*, Oxford, 1965.

Hollister, C. W., 'The Strange Death of William Rufus', *Speculum*, xlviii, 1973, pp. 637–53.

Holmes, M. R., *Moorfields in 1559*, HMSO, London, 1963.

Holt, J. C., *Robin Hood*, London, 1982.

Holt, J. C., 'Robin Hood: Some Comments', in Hilton, *Peasants, Knights*, pp. 267–9.

Holt, J. C., 'The Origins and Audience of the Ballads of Robin Hood', in Hilton, *Peasants, Knights*, pp. 236–57.

Houghton, B., *St Edmund — King and Martyr*, Lavenham, 1970.

Hull, F., 'An Early Kentish Militia Roll', *Archaeologia Cantiana*, lxviii, 1954, pp. 8159–66.

Hull, F., 'An Early Kentish Militia Roll', *JSAA*, vi, 1963, p. 12.

Hunter, J., *The Great Hero of the Ancient Minstrelsy of England: Robin Hood*, London, 1852.

Jenks, E., *Edward Plantagenet*, 2nd edn, London, 1923.

Joret, C., *La Bataille de Formigny*, Paris, 1903.

Keegan, J., *The Face of Battle*, London, 1976.

Keen, M. H., *The Laws of War in the Late Middle Ages*, London, 1965.

Keen, M., *The Outlaws of Medieval Legend*, 2nd edn, London, 1977.

King, E., *England, 1175–1425*, London, 1979.

Kingsford, C. L., *English Historical Literature in the Fifteenth Century*, Oxford, 1913.

Labitte, C., 'Azincourt', *Rev. Anglo-Fr.*, iii, Poitiers, 1835, pp. 133–47.

Lake, F. H. & Wright, M. F., *A Bibliography of Archery*, Manchester, 1974.

Leadman, A. D. H., 'The Battle of the Standard', *Yorkshire Arch. & Topographical Journal*, x, 1889, pp. 377–86.

Legge, M. D., 'The Unerring Bow', *Medium Aevum*, xxv, 1956, pp. 79–83.

Leroux, M., *La Bataille de Tinchebray*, Tinchebray, 1972.

Lethbridge, T. C., 'Excavations at Burwell Castle', *Cambridge Antiquarian Soc. Proceedings*, xxxvi, 1934–5, pp. 121–33.

Lloyd, E. M., 'The "Herse" of Archers at Crécy', *EHR*, x, 1895, pp. 538–41.

Longman, C. J., & Walrond, H., *Archery*, Badminton Library of Sports and Pastimes ed. Duke of Beaufort, London, 1894.

Louandre, F.-C., 'The Battle of Crécy', *Rev. Anglo-Fr.*, iii, 1835, pp. 245–70.

Madden, Rt Hon D. H., *A Chapter of Medieval History*, London, 1924.

Maddicott, J. R., 'The Birth and Setting of the Ballads of Robin Hood', *EHR*, xciii, 1978, pp. 276–99.

Mazas, A., *Vies des Grands Capitaines Français du Moyen Age*, 6 vols, Paris, 1828.

McGuffie, T. H., 'The Long-bow as a Decisive Weapon', *HT*, v, 1955, pp. 737–41.

McLeod, W., 'An Ancient Treatise of Military Archery', *JSAA*, v, 1962, pp. 10–11.

Meiss, M., *French Painting in the Time of Jean de Berry, The Boucicaut Master*, London, 1968.

Milliken, E. K., *Archery in the Middle Ages*, London, 1967.

Morice, Dom P.-H., *Histoire Ecclésiastique et Civile de Bretagne*, 2 vols, Paris, 1750.

Morris, J. E., *Bannockburn*, Cambridge, 1914.

Morris, J. E., *The Welsh Wars of Edward I*, Oxford, 1901.

Morris, J. E., 'Mounted Infantry in Medieval Warfare', *TRHS*, 3rd ser., viii, 1914, pp. 77–102.

Morris, J. E., 'The Archers at Crécy', *EHR*, xii, 1897, pp. 427–36.

Munz, P., *Life in the Age of Charlemagne*, London, 1969.

Neufville, M. le Neuf de, 'Combats d'Alençon', *Bulletin Soc. Hist. & Arch. de l'Orne*, ii, 1883, pp. 200–19.

Nicholson, R., *Edward III and the Scots, the Formative Years of a Military Career, 1327–35*, Oxford, 1965.

Nicolas, Sir H., *History of the Battle of Agincourt and of the Expedition of Henry V into France*, 2nd edn, London, 1832.

Norman, V., *The Medieval Soldier*, London, 1971.

Odolant-Desnos, P. J., *Mémoires Historiques sur la Ville d'Alençon, et Ses Seigneurs*, 2 vols, Alençon, 2nd edn, 1858–64.

Oman, C. W. C., *A History of the Art of War in the Middle Ages*, 2 vols, 2nd edn, London, 1924.

Oman, C. W. C., *The Art of War in the Middle Ages*, revised edn, Ithaca, 1953.

Oman, C. W. C., 'Review of G. Kohler', *Academy*, xxxix, 1891, pp. 229–30.

Owen, L. D. V., 'Robin Hood in the Light of Research', *Times Trade and Engineering Supplement*, 1936.

*Oxford English Dictionary*, vi, L–M, Oxford, 1933.

Oxley, J. E., *The Fletchers and Longbowstringmakers of London*, London, 1968.

Palmer, J. J. N., *Froissart Historian*, Woodbridge, 1981.

Palmer, J., 'The War Aims of the Protagonists and

Negotiations for Peace', in Fowler, *Hundred Years' War*, pp. 51–74.

Papworth, J. W. & Morant, A. W., *Ordinary of British Armorials*, London, 1874.

Patourel, J. le, 'The Origins of the War', in Fowler, *Hundred Years' War*, pp. 28–50.

Payne-Gallwey, Sir R., *The Crossbow*, London, 1958.

Perroy, E., *The Hundred Years' War*, London, 1965.

Philpotts, C., 'The French Plan of Battle During the Agincourt Campaign', *EHR*, xcix, 1984, pp. 59–66.

Poole, R. L., 'The Battle of Tinchebrai: a Correction', *EHR*, xxv, 1910, pp. 295–6.

Powicke, M., *Military Obligation in Medieval England*, Oxford, 1962.

Powicke, M., 'The English Aristocracy and the War', in Fowler, *Hundred Years' War*, pp. 122–34.

Prestwich, M., *The Three Edwards*, London, 1980.

Prestwich, M., *War, Politics and Finance under Edward I*, London, 1972.

Prince, A. E., 'The Importance of the Campaign of 1327', *EHR*, l, 1935, pp. 299–302.

Prince, A. E., 'The Strength of the English Armies in the Reign of Edward III', *EHR*, xlvi, 1931, pp. 353–71.

Richmond, C., 'The War at Sea', in Fowler, *Hundred Years' War*, pp. 96–121.

Roberts, T., *The English Bowman, Tracts on Archery*, London, 1801.

Ross, C., *The Wars of the Roses*, London, 1976.

Ross, D. J. A., 'L'originalité de "Turoldus": le maniement de la lance', *CCM*, v, 1963, pp. 127–38.

Round, J. H., *Feudal England*, London, 1895.

Rowe, B. J. H., 'A Contemporary Account of the Hundred Years' War from 1415 to 1429', *EHR*, xli, 1926, pp. 504–13.

Rudorff, R., *The Knights and their World*, London, 1974.

Rule, M., *The Mary Rose*, 2nd edn, London 1983.

Runciman, S., *The First Crusade*, Cambridge, 1980.

Sanders, I. J., *Feudal Military Service in England*, Oxford, 1956.

Smyth, J., *The Lives of the Berkeleys*, ed. Sir J. Maclean, 3 vols, 1883–5.

Scoffern, J., *Projectile Weapons of War and Explosive Compounds*, 3rd edn, London, 1858.

Seward, D., *The Hundred Years' War*, London, 1978.

Sherborne, J. W., 'The Cost of English Warfare with France in the Later Fourteenth Century',

*BIHR*, l, 1977, pp. 135–50.

Stones, E. L. G., 'The Folvilles of Ashby-Folville, Leicestershire and their Associates in Crime', *TRHS*, 5th ser., vii, 1957, pp. 117–36.

Switsur, R., 'The Prehistoric Longbow from Danny, Scotland', *Antiquity*, xlviii, 1974, pp. 56–8.

Thomas, J. B., *Hounds and Hunting through the Ages*, 2nd edn, London, 1934.

Tourneur-Aumont, J. M., *La Bataille de Poitiers, 1356, et la Construction de la France*, Paris, 1940.

Tout, T. F., *Collected Papers*, 3 vols, Manchester, 1934.

Tout, T. F., 'Some neglected Fights between Crécy and Poitiers', *EHR*, xx, 1905, pp. 726–30.

Tout, T. F., 'The Tactics of the Battles of Boroughbridge and Morlaix', *EHR*, xix, 1904, pp. 711–5.

Tselos, D., *The Sources of the Utrecht Psalter Miniatures*, 2nd edn, Minneapolis, 1960.

'Tuck', 'Norman Doodle Depicts Ancient Archer', *Bt A*, vi, 1954, p. 175.

Tucker, W. E., 'Bows of the Nydam Galleys', *JSAA*, i, 1958, pp. 7–9.

Vale, M., *War and Chivalry, Warfare and Aristocratic Culture in England, France and Burgundy at the end of the Middle Ages*, London, 1981.

Vaughan, R., *John the Fearless*, London, 1966.

Verbruggen, J. F., 'La Tactique militaire des Armées des Chevaliers', *Revue de Nord*, xxix, 1947, pp. 161–80.

Verbruggen, J. F., 'Un Plan de Bataille du Duc de Burgogne (14 Septembre 1417) et la tactique de l'époque', *Revue Internationale d'Histoire Militaire*, xx, 1959, pp. 443–51.

Viard, J., *La Campagne de Juillet-Août 1346 et la Bataille de Crécy*, Paris, 1926.

Walker, J. W., *The True History of Robin Hood*, Wakefield, 1952.

Warner, P., *Fontana British Battlefields: The South*, London, 1972.

Wells, H. Bartlett, 'A Problem in the Techniques of the Medieval European Swordsmith', *JAAS*, iv, 1962–4, pp. 217–229.

Wells, H. Bartlett, 'Contributions to the History of the Heat Treatment of Steel', *JAAS*, vi, 1968–70, pp. 217–30.

White, G. H., 'Henry's Illegitimate Children', in G. E. Cokayne, *The Complete Peerage*, xi, London, 1949, App. D, pp. 105–21.

Wilson, G. M., *Treasures of the Tower*, Crossbows, HMSO, 1976.

# Index